Show–Me Kings

To order additional copies, please contact us.
BookSurge, LLC
www.booksurge.com
1-866-308-6235
orders@booksurge.com

MIKE
MITCHELL

SHOW–ME KINGS

Bootheel Ball, The Cookson Clan, & A Run and Gun All-Star Show

2005

Show—Me Kings

CONTENTS

ACKNOWLEDGEMENTS

T his book was born out of a desire and a dream: a desire to taken on a new challenge in life and a dream to write a book about a region of the country I called home for 18 years. For several years, I kicked around the idea of writing a book about my hometown, but could never come up with what I thought would be an interesting way to tell the story. Then one day, the light bulb came on. Instead of focusing on a single community, why not expand the idea to tell the story of Missouri's Bootheel region through the lens of some of its greatest sports teams and coaches? With that established, the focus became easy, or so I thought. No program in the history of Missouri high school basketball has won more state championships than Ronnie Cookson and his Scott County Central Braves. What started with a letter to coach Cookson has resulted in the pages that follow this one.

One thing I quickly realized on this journey; to tell the story of Ronnie Cookson one also has to explore the biography of his brother Carroll, and for both men, the story begins in Puxico, Missouri. The story that unfolds is part history and part biography, but one hundred percent Bootheel ball. The Bootheel region of Missouri is unique in the state for many reasons: its geography, its culture, its heritage. That too is a necessary part of the saga.

Near the end of these pages is a complete list of all people I interviewed for this endeavor. To them I extend my heartfelt thanks. Without their words and memories, these pages would be nothing but a robotic resuscitation of dates, facts, and figures. They have provided the soul. History is not just a book on a shelf or a class on a college campus; it lives and breathes in all of us.

Many people deserve a special thanks. Betty Mirly at the Chaffee Historical Society and Karen Whitaker at the Chaffee High School Library graciously volunteered time and access to key information. Ronnie Whitaker and Charlie Vickery allowed me to borrow books and data compiled by others. Mike Jensen provided historical context on the

Bootheel region, John Merk offered perspective on Slater basketball, and Chris Abernathy gave insight to the early history of Chaffee and the Frisco Railroad. A few authors who have gone down this road before need to be singled out. In his book, *My Name is Mr. Ryan*, author Matt Chaney has written the seminal text on Puxico basketball. In many ways, where his story ends, this one begins. For anyone who cares about the history of high school basketball in Missouri, *From The Beginning....The History of Missouri High School Championships* is an invaluable resource. Seemingly anytime I had a question about Missouri high school hoops, George Wilson and Robert Vestal's text had an answer.

Ronnie, Carroll and the entire Cookson family were especially generous with their time, information, and their insights, so too was the Sanders family. Family and friends offered encouragement along the way while Steve Bennett, Caroline Pfefferkorn, and April Wagner provided invaluable feedback on the manuscript.

My wish is that you had as much fun reading this as I had while writing it. The experience was a sheer joy.

Cheers!

Mike Mitchell

December 2004

CAST OF CHARACTERS

Teams, Eras, Coaches and Players of Primary Programs
mentioned
(Graduation year of players in parenthesis)

Puxico Indians 1945-1952
- Coach Arnold Ryan
- Ancel Cookson (1949)
- Leon Cookson (1951)
- Frank Hoggard (1951)
- Winfred Wilfong (1951)
- Forest Arnold (1952)
- Carroll Cookson (1952)
- Grady Smith (1952)
- Gene Wilfong (1952)

Advance Hornets 1966-1979
- Coach Carroll Cookson (1966-1978)
- Coach Jim Keeling (1978-79)
- Richard Hitt (1972)
- Richie Walker (1972)
- Darrell Croy (1973)
- Kenny Emerson (1973)
- John Rhodes (1973)
- Terry Wills (1973)
- Ron Oller (1975)
- David Tropf (1975)
- Steve Cookson (1976)
- Joe Bradshaw (1979)
- Eddie Dunivan (1979)

Scott County Central Braves 1970-1995

- Coach Ronnie Cookson
- Denny Alcorn (1971)
- Otto Porter (1976)
- Ricky Thomas (1976)
- James "Frog" Williams (1976)
- Anthony Jones (1980)
- Jeff Limbaugh (1980)
- Donnie McClinton (1980)
- Mike Montgomery (1980)
- Melvin Porter (1980)
- Mayfield Timmons (1980)
- Melvin Johnson (1981)
- Anthony "Moon" Timmons (1983)
- Doug Blissett (1985)
- David "Bullnose" Harris (1985)
- Tim Ware (1985)
- Stanley Blissett (1986)
- Jay Cookson (1986)
- Ricky Sims (1986)
- Terry Bell (1987)
- Terry Blissett (1988)
- Jerry Porter (1989)
- Marcus Timmons (1991)
- Mark Mosley (1991)
- Brad Cookson (1995)
- David Heeb (1996)

Chaffee Red Devils 1977-1983

- Coach Nick Walls
- Coach Mick Wessel
- Coach Terry Glenzy
- Tony Dalton (1979)
- Charles Felker (1979)
- Jim Fowler (1979)
- Monty Montgomery (1979)
- Steven Whitaker (1979)

- Anthony "Moose" Austin (1980)
- Wade Sanders (1980)
- Doug Sanders (1982)
- Chris Payne (1984)
- Kevin Uhrhan (1984)
- Eric Glastetter (1985)
- Gary McLard (1985)

Charleston Bluejays 1975-1993
- Coach Mitch Haskins (1975-1977)
- Coach Lennies McFerren (1977-1993)
- Ricky Frazier (1977)
- Jewell Crawford (1980)
- Lamont Frazier (1990)

Other Programs (Names) Frequently Mentioned
- Cape Girardeau Central Tigers (Ronnie Jones, 1980)
- Cape Girardeau Notre Dame Bulldogs (Coach Ed Arnzen 1970-1979)
- Clopton Hawks (Coach Dale Miller 1976-1991)
- Glasgow Yellowjackets (Lawrence Butler, 1975)
- Kelly High Hawks (Coach Nick Lanpher)
- Oran Eagles (Fred Johnson, 1969)
- Sikeston Bulldogs (Football Coach Charlie Vickery 1978-2003)
- Slater Wildcats (Joe Kleine,1980)
- Wellsville Tigers (Coach Fred Norman 1978-1986, Fred Johnson, 1986)

PROLOGUE

On Saturday, February 24, 1979, *The New York Times* headline blared "New Surge In Prices Threatening Plans to Fight Inflation." That same weekend, in the middle of the country, the *St. Louis Post-Dispatch*, the largest paper in the state of Missouri, had a front-page story detailing the city's unionized teachers strike. The two-week old walkout had shutdown classes for more than 70,000 students.[1] About two hours south of St. Louis in the town of Morley, Scott County Central coach Ronnie Cookson was thinking about basketball. This wasn't news. Cookson always thought about basketball. But the coach's thoughts were especially focused this time of year as his team had once again entered state tournament play as regional champions. Only four games separated the Scott County Central (a.k.a. Scott Central) Braves from a state championship, one that would be their second in the past four years. The Braves would begin state play on Monday night against the Chaffee Red Devils, a conference rival that Cookson's team had already beaten three previous times that season. Still, Cookson wasn't taking anything for granted. He never did.

Just the night before, his team had narrowly survived in a three-point victory over Puxico, the town where Cookson grew up and the school where he played his high school basketball. On this Saturday night, less than forty-eight hours before a big game, Cookson would also be thinking about, worrying about, and checking up on his players. Curfew for basketball players was 10 p.m., every night of the week. The players knew their coach could show up at their house a few minutes before the appointed hour, just to make sure they were obeying his rules. He had done it before. When Cookson's head finally hit the pillow, rain had begun falling outside. The forecast was for one to two inches of snow by morning.

Fifteen miles away in the northern part of the county, Chaffee's players enjoyed their Saturday night. Weekend curfews were set by parents, not by the coach, if they were set at all. Not that the team and its coach took its tasks lightly. The 1978-79 season represented a breakthrough for coach Nick Wall's program. Monday night would be the first ever appearance for the school in a state basketball tournament. Just a few months earlier, most of the Chaffee squad was not shooting baskets, but tackling and blocking. In small schools, the best athletes played multiple sports and Chaffee was no exception. The football team made the state playoffs, won its first game in convincing fashion, and was a favorite at home in the second round. They were upset by the eventual state champions.

Basketball practice at Chaffee did not begin until the football season was over. Given the compressed practice schedule, Walls thought it a miracle they had performed so well. Like Scott Central, the Red Devils clinched their regional championship in an exciting contest, beating Advance, the school where Cookson first coached and where his brother Carroll had guided two state championship squads. Advance had done something that season Chaffee had failed to do – beat Scott Central. Now after defeating Advance, Nick Walls' team had to hope the fourth time against Ronnie Cookson's team could be different. Still, the players and coach had to think it would take an act of God for them to beat Scott County, widely considered the best small town team in the area and perhaps the state. That act of God would soon fall in the form of ever larger white flakes.

Residents in Southeast Missouri awoke Sunday morning to the worst blizzard of their lives. A forecast of a few inches had turned into two feet of snow. The region was paralyzed. Interstate 55 was shut down. A state of emergency was declared. In Chaffee, part of the roof of a local shoe factory collapsed. Police ordered all automobile traffic off the road. Walls walked to the grocery store that weekend to get food for him and his wife. One of his players, Jim Fowler, almost didn't make it home. The snow that would soon begin to come down started out as a thunderstorm. Out on a date Saturday, he was nearly convinced by the girl's parents into staying overnight rather than drive several miles through the rain. He decided to go home instead. When his dad woke him up Sunday morning and told him it was snowing, he didn't believe him. Then he heard an unusual sound and looked outside. The noise was that of a local farmer going up the road on his tractor. It was the only thing moving. He knew it wasn't an average snowstorm when he opened the door and the drifts hit the 6'5" center at waist level.

The blizzard meant something else. Scott Central and Chaffee would have to wait to play for the fourth time that season. Monday's night game was postponed. The furious snowfall and fifty mile an hour winds finally stopped Sunday. The weather improved the next day and crews began making headway in clearing area roads. It wasn't an easy task. A National Guard truck sent to Chaffee became stuck in a snow drift. It was pulled out by an area farmer with a four wheel drive tractor.[2] Doctors were airlifted in to treat patients at the local hospital. The Governor declared the region a disaster area. But with warmer temperatures and passable roads, the decision was made to reschedule the game for Tuesday afternoon.

While conditions on the highways had greatly improved by Tuesday, conditions on county roads and residential areas were still treacherous. But the push was on to get the game completed that day. Quarterfinals games were scheduled for Wednesday with the final four teams going to Columbia for the weekend to play the last two rounds. Given the compressed schedule, everyone had to improvise. One of Scott Central's players, Melvin Porter, was stranded at his house in Haywood City until a teammate arrived on a snowmobile. With the help of tractors, plows and four-wheel drive trucks, the two teams managed to arrive at their destination, but another weather related issue soon surfaced.

When players and coaches arrived in the Stoddard County town of Bloomfield for the game, they confronted a new problem. The heat in the gym wasn't working. They would start the game with the temperature inside not much warmer than outside. When the game did start, the Chaffee players adjusted immediately to their unusually cool surroundings. Scott Central did not. Their players felt like they were moving in slow motion, unable to get loose and comfortable. During one timeout, Melvin Porter looked around at his teammates. Everyone's nose was running. The results showed on the scoreboard. By the end of the first quarter, Chaffee led by eight points.

Watching from the sidelines, Ronnie Cookson couldn't believe his eyes. This didn't look like the same teams on the floor that he had watched all season. Then he had a thought; *maybe it was football.* Almost all of the players on Chaffee had grown comfortable playing sports out in the elements. They frequently played football games in conditions not dissimilar to what they encountered in Bloomfield that afternoon.

It was also a sport they didn't play at Scott Central. Football, the game that always came first at Chaffee, was paying dividends in an unlikely place. Maybe a basketball game played in football-like conditions was exactly what Chaffee needed to upset its rival. Midway through the second quarter, that looked to be the case. The Red Devils had stretched the lead to 12 points. Then the Chaffee coach made a decision to start stalling the basketball, a decision akin to a prevent defense in football. The move backfired.

Cookson's Braves played basketball one way. Their style was fast-paced, fast break, and full-court. The coach had learned to play that way growing up in his hometown, where his older brother played for Arnold Ryan's legendary Puxico teams of the early 1950's. His Braves were quick, explosive and in phenomenally good shape. It was only a matter of time.

A 16-2 run near the end of the second quarter put the Braves in the lead by one point at halftime. In the second half, the lead gradually widened, and with five minutes to go in the game, it looked to be all but over. Chaffee trailed by 10 points. Then Walls made another move. The slower but taller Red Devils always played a one-three-one zone defense. He decided to go man-to-man. It worked. Chaffee started chipping away at the lead. In their three previous games, the Red Devils never led in the fourth quarter. But after back to back three point plays, Chaffee had a one point lead. The seesaw action continued till the very end. With less than a minute to go, Scott Central made a bucket to put them back into the lead. Chaffee failed to score at its end and was forced to foul. The Braves converted one shot from the free throw stripe and with less than twenty seconds to go, led by two points.

Chaffee had one last chance. The last moments of that ballgame are frozen in time in the mind of their coach. The Red Devils broke the Scott Central press. A pass sent to the ball to forward Charlie Felker. Standing somewhere between the wing and the baseline, about 15 feet from the goal, Felker let it fly. The ball hit the rim. It bounced straight up in the air and came back down. It went through the net. With seven seconds to go, Chaffee had tied the game. Just then, the whistle blew. Nick Walls couldn't believe what happened next. In the few remaining seconds, it wouldn't be the last unbelievable play of the game.

INTRODUCTION

I f you drive Interstate 55 south from Saint Louis toward Memphis, you'll pass through Cape Girardeau about two hours into your journey. Cape is the largest town you'll pass on your way to Graceland, and is known to outsiders today (if it's known at all) as the hometown of talk show host Rush Limbaugh. About thirty minutes south of Cape is Sikeston, the second largest town you'll pass on your way to Beale Street, and is known to outsiders today (if it's known at all) as the home of Lambert's Café and its legendary "throwed rolls." Sikeston received some national press coverage in passing starting in 1992 when biographies and stories began to appear on then Arkansas Governor Bill Clinton and his bid for the presidency. Clinton never knew his biological father. While his mother was pregnant with him, William Jefferson Blythe II died in a car wreck outside of Sikeston in May of 1946.[3]

About halfway between Sikeston and Cape, a traveler would see the exit for Chaffee. No one famous has ever lived here, or died here for that matter. A right at the stoplight, eight miles, rows of corn and one train track later, you would arrive in the "City with a Smile," as a sign informs you. You would see three thousand forty-four sets of teeth should everyone in town decide to flash a grin in your direction. From the spring of 1969 to the fall of 1984, or from the time I was three years old to the time I was eighteen, one of those smiles would have belonged to me. My father, mother, brother, sister and I moved to Chaffee in April of 1969 from Oran, another small town just eight miles to the south. We came to Chaffee because my father started working at the bank in town a year earlier.

Life in small town Missouri in the 1970's was far from perfect; it was no Lake Woebegone ("where all the children are above average"). Many residents in Chaffee, Scott County, indeed throughout much of Southeast Missouri lived at or near the poverty line. When we were issued textbooks at the beginning of every year in the public schools, there was a place for a signature. It was always interesting to see who had the book before you.

More than once, I came across my sister's name (nine years older) or my brother's (eleven years older). Never do I remember being issued a new textbook. The main High School building was built in the 1920's, with all wooden floors and no air conditioning. When I graduated, the school had one computer. I was fortunate. My parents had good jobs and being the youngest of the family, I was rarely denied anything I truly wanted. Life was peaceful, pleasant, not to mention insulated from much of the world around it (with all the positive and negative implications). When I was eight years old, we moved across town to a new subdivision. From there, I walked the 100 yards or so every day to grade school. In the early grades, I remember reciting the Pledge of Allegiance daily and even praying in the public schools ("God is good, God is great, thank you for our daily food, Amen.")

Tuesdays meant new comic books had arrived at Lankford's drug store. I remember riding my bike downtown faithfully every week to buy the latest Superman or Batman comic book or catch up on the adventures of Sgt. Rock. Lankford's was also one of the few, if not the only place in town, where you could buy *Playboy* magazine. It resided at the back of the magazine rack, just behind the comic book stand. My friend and next-door neighbor, Doug Sanders, mastered the art of tucking a *Playboy* inside a *Sporting News* or *Sports Illustrated* and quickly flipping through the pages. Yes, it's true- the articles were great. When we got really adventurous, we ripped out a few, selected pages from the magazine and discreetly slipped them into our pockets. At least once, we sold some pictures to another friend of ours. Hedonism and capitalism mixed well in Chaffee.

By 1978 or around the time I became a teenager, cable television had just arrived in town with all of seven channels, no one had a personal computer and the Internet was only something academics and the government used. Before cable, most residents received only two to three channels. The television market around Chaffee is the only one in the country where three network affiliates are in three different states. CBS (Cape Girardeau) is the real local station, just fifteen minutes away. NBC (Paducah) serves the residents of western Kentucky, and ABC (Harrisburg) resides in Southern Illinois. Reasons of proximity and a bad television antenna left me watching a lot of CBS growing up. The NBC station came in reasonably well, but ABC was often fuzzy. You had to be patient to endure the bad reception. Monday Night Football was one of the few events on ABC that got my attention.

Cardinal baseball was, and probably still is, the most popular professional sport to people of Southeast Missouri. In the late 70's, the only times we ever caught them on TV was the game of the week (rare in those days because the Cardinal teams of the late 70's were really bad) or road games on Sunday. That was it. If you wanted to catch any live action, you either drove to Busch Stadium (120 miles away) or listened to them on the radio.

Sometime around the age of ten or eleven, my parents bought me a ten-band radio from Montgomery Ward. Every night, I would tune in KMOX radio and listen to a game or a sports talk show. Baseball Hall of Fame Broadcaster Jack Buck called the Cardinal games, Hockey Hall of Fame Announcer Dan Kelly did the Blues broadcasts, St. Louis football tackle and future NFL Hall of Fame Inductee Dan Dierdorf was on a call-in show with teammate and quarterback Jim Hart, and a young Bob Costas did the play by play for University of Missouri basketball. It was quite a lineup on KMOX back then. I listened avidly and intently. There were probably years in which I listened to or watched every Cardinal baseball game. Not just part of the game – *the entire game.* One summer night with the Cardinals on the West Coast, San Francisco Giant catcher Milt May beat the Redbirds with a bottom of the ninth home run off reliever Mark Littell. Listening in my bedroom, I became so upset I started yelling and pounding the bed with my pillow. My dad, previously asleep in the bedroom next door, walked into my room, turned off the radio and turned off the light as he walked back out. I don't think he ever said a word. I guess he was used to it.

But professional sports, for all the enjoyment they provided, were remote. Only three to four times a year would we make the trip to Saint Louis, and then only to see one game and drive back home. I never remember spending the night in the city and catching an entire weekend of action. Big time college sports were even farther away. The University of Missouri was a four-hour drive. The teams and athletes we watched in person week-to-week, year-to-year all played high school sports. Growing up, local high school athletes were every bit the heroes to us as professional sports stars. We watched them closely, imitating them, idolizing them, wanting to be like them. In those days before the Web, before ESPN, before 24-hour news channels, we had our bats, balls, and a lot of time on our hands.

***

The 1970's were an awful time in so many ways. Gas lines at home, hostages overseas, a miserable economy in a country struck by malaise, Americans turned on the TV or opened their newspapers everyday to see a country disappointed, disheartened or distraught over any number of events. But not everyone saw it that way. In November of '79, Ronald Reagan officially declared his Presidential candidacy for the 1980 election in a speech in New York City. He directly challenged the conventional wisdom of the day:

> *"There are those in our land today…who would have us believe that the United States, like other great civilizations of the past, has reached the zenith of its power; that we are weak and fearful, reduced to bickering with each other and no longer possessed of the will to cope with our problems.*
> *…They tell us we must learn to live with less, and teach our children that their lives will be less full and prosperous than ours has been; that the America of the coming years will be a place where – because of our past excesses – it will be impossible to dream and make those dreams come true. I don't believe that. And, I don't believe you do either."*

The same month that Reagan announced his candidacy, Whitey Herzog was fired from his manager position with the Kansas City Royals. Like Reagan, who failed in his presidential election bid of 1976, Herzog never quite made it to the summit with the Royals. Each year, the Yankees would dash the hopes of Kansas City and its fans in the playoffs. But the fortunes of both men would soon change dramatically.

A year later, both Reagan and Herzog would be in new positions in new cities. Herzog was hired by the St. Louis Cardinals in June of 1980. Cardinal baseball would be transformed by "Whitey Ball," an aggressive base running style that helped the Cardinals to one World Series title and three National League pennants during the 80's. Along with the rest of the Cardinal Nation, fans in Southeast Missouri, as diehard Cardinal

Country as anywhere in the Midwest, would flock to Busch Stadium in numbers not seen since the 1960's.

Five months after Herzog took the reigns in Saint Louis, Reagan defeated Jimmy Carter in the Presidential election of 1980. Much of Southeast Missouri would be considered quintessential Reagan Country. Reagan Democrats helped propel him to a landslide reelection four years later. Both men survived crises in the middle of their reigns. In 1985, one pre-season publication predicted Herzog to be the first major league manager fired. A few years later, the Iran-Contra scandal had official Washington whispering and wondering if Reagan could survive. Not only would both men survive but would ultimately prosper as incredibly popular leaders.

By October of 1987, Cardinal fans celebrated their team's third World Series appearance in six years. One thing was constant during this run – manager Whitey Herzog. That same month, the Dow Jones Industrial Average stood at roughly 2,700 up more than 200% since Business Week magazine had famously proclaimed "the death of equities" in 1979. The 80's saw a dramatic decline in inflation, the end of gas lines, and a renewed confidence in America. Conservatives, Republicans and indeed much of the country gave one man a lion's share of the credit: Ronald Reagan. All future Cardinal managers and GOP presidential aspirants would be judged by how they measured up to these two men.

But this was the 1970's. The 80's boom belonged to another time, one that seemed remote and almost impossible to imagine for people living through the era. In 1979, Whitey Herzog was a fired ex-manager from the other side of the state and Ronald Reagan just an ex-governor from the other side of the country.

***

At the time, I was completely oblivious to the national politics and international crises. Life revolved around the sports calendar. When we didn't play, we watched. When we didn't watch, we talked or read about it. Football season rolled into basketball, which melted away in the spring to track and baseball season. Summertime meant more baseball, and the cycle started over again by Labor Day. Life was stable, disciplined and sheltered. Friday nights meant a high school football game. Saturday afternoons were for mowing the yard, and Sunday mornings meant Sunday School at the First Baptist Church. I never saw an illegal drug until I went to college. I never heard anyone scathingly criticize the U.S. government until a freshman year U.S. history class at the University of Missouri. And everyone I called a friend was white, middle class and either Catholic or Protestant. My experience with black people was limited to sporting events, typically basketball or football. I didn't grow up with any hatred for people of color. I'm sure I looked at many of them as poor and uneducated, but also regarded quite a few as supremely talented and athletic. Those athletic impressions were greatly formed by another tiny school 15 miles south of town – Scott County Central. They were the best team I ever saw, and for anyone reading this outside of Missouri, probably the greatest team you never heard of.

The Scott County Central Braves were led back then by coach Ronnie Cookson. Cookson's coaching career is full of wonderful juxtapositions and symmetry. In his first coaching job out of college, his eighth grade club didn't win a game. His seventh grade team didn't lose one. He spent his entire college career playing basketball and attending class – every single credit hour – with his older brother Carroll. After graduation, they took jobs at the same school: Ronnie as the junior high coach, Carroll as the head coach of the high school team. After four years of coaching junior high, Ronnie finally got his opportunity at the high school level. His big brother was his first opponent. Carroll's teams won two high school championships and Ronnie contributed to both. His undefeated seventh grade team was the nucleus of Carroll's first state champion squad in 1972. The core of Carroll's last state champion team in 1975 was the last seventh grade team Ronnie coached at Advance, Missouri.

When Ronnie took over the high school coaching job at Scott County Central in the fall of 1970, the team had never called itself state champions. Since he retired from coaching in 1995, the team has yet to claim another title. But in the quarter century in between, Cookson's Scott Central teams dominated like few others ever have. In racking up 12 state titles, his teams won nearly 83% of their games. Winning the game was an understatement. Dismantling the opponent was more like it. They ran relentlessly. They pressed constantly. Exhorted on to victory by their screaming and prodding head coach, they intimidated and demoralized their opponents, defying them to stop their fast break attack. They were a hell of a lot of fun to watch.

While I enjoyed seeing the Braves whenever possible, they were not my team. I rooted for the hometown Chaffee Red Devils. The focus and energy at the schools could not have been more different. Scott Central only offered basketball and baseball for its male athletes, and basketball consumed nearly all the time of both athletes and coaches. At Chaffee, football was the marquee program, but male athletes could also play basketball, baseball, track, and tennis. At Scott Central, basketball was a year round affair. At Chaffee, basketball was practiced and played in the winter months only after the football season ended. Nevertheless, when the temperature dropped and the days got shorter, the Red Devils would suit up and meet other small town schools on the basketball court –most of them like Scott Central - without a football program to compete for the attention of its athletes. Some of the games described in these pages I remember vividly. Not just the game itself but the entire ambiance. You could walk into one of these gyms and hear the clapping of the cheerleaders, the blowing of a referee's whistle, the sound of Converse sneakers on hardwood floors, and the most vivid of all, the smell of popcorn at the concession stand.

But this story is not about me. It's about my heroes growing up: small town athletes who pursued excellence not for a paycheck or even a college scholarship in many cases, but for the love of their sport, a tale of communities and teams in one small corner of our country. It is also a celebration of basketball in the Bootheel, the rural counties tucked into the southeastern corner of Missouri. College basketball coaches Norm Stewart and Charlie Spoonhour, former NBA player Joe Kleine and former NFL referee Gene Barth all have something in common; a brief brush with the history of Bootheel ball.

The history of the Bootheel region plays an important part of the story as well. It's where the American South begins. For many of the athletes, geography was destiny. Their families settled in southern Missouri to farm the land: more specifically, to pick the cotton crop. Cotton fever and an earthquake craze were two manias that swept the region in different parts of the 20th century. The Cookson Clan represents the opposite extreme – consistent success measured over decades. They, and so many others whom you'll meet on the pages to come, are basketball ambassadors from Missouri, the "Show-Me" state. They are the true Show-Me Kings.

CHAPTER ONE
It's Our Fault
1811-1990

"We produce more murders per unit of population than any other part of the U.S.A., whether urban or rural. In my own small county we aim to produce one murder per month. If a month passes without its killing, we feel that we are slipping. But usually we come back with a double killing next month. I have heard our No. 1 pioneer, philosopher and great gentleman, Mr. A.J. Matthews, comment on our high murder percentage. He said, 'It is not to our discredit, because, as anyone can see, we have so many more people that need killing.'"

Bootheel farmer and author Thad Snow. *From Missouri.*

It was right there in black and white. On the pages of *The New Yorker* magazine, no less. When its well-heeled, upscale readers opened their February 11, 1991 edition, they saw a lengthy article featuring a place most of them had never heard of, in a part of the country they had never visited. The magazine regularly printed a column entitled "Our Far Flung Correspondent," in which writers would regale the readership with tales from "exotic" locations – exotic, that is, if your pied-à-terre faces Central Park. In other issues, the column had taken its readers to such locales as Colin, Michigan (magic capital of the world) and Plymouth Rock, Massachusetts, where the Pilgrims landed in 1620. In one column, a reporter traveled to El Paso, Texas to investigate the whereabouts of Pancho Villa's skull. What part of "fly over country" had the editors chosen for its readers this week? Before we get that answer, it's necessary to travel back in time a bit further and venture 3,000 miles across the country to the West Coast.

In October of 1989, the baseball World Series featured a Bay Area rivalry, the San Francisco Giants vs. the Oakland A's. Oakland was making its second of three consecutive World Series appearances. Tony La Russa's club had the "Bash Brothers" Mark McGwire and Jose Canseco and probably the greatest leadoff hitter in baseball history, Rickey Henderson. Across the Bay, the San Francisco Giants hadn't played in the Fall Classic since the Kennedy Administration. But twenty-seven years after Willie McCovey lined out to Tony Richardson to end the 1962 series, the Giants were back, led National League MVP Kevin Mitchell and their hard-hitting first baseman Will Clark. The A's had taken the first two games of the series in Oakland, and game three was set to begin on a Friday night in San Francisco. The fans filed into Candlestick Park. The players warmed up. Then the earth opened up. As millions of baseball fans tuned into the action on television, they heard announcer Al Michaels say at exactly 5:04 p.m. Pacific Daylight Time, "I'll tell you what, we're having an earth--!"[4] The picture went dead. The most devastating earthquake since 1906 had struck California. Registering 7.1 on the Richter Scale, the Loma Prieta quake would be blamed for the deaths of more than 60 people and caused billions of dollars in damages. No one at the ballpark was killed that night, but the World Series would be delayed for ten days, with the A's eventually sweeping the Giants in four games. Down in Albuquerque, New Mexico, a self-proclaimed "vulcanologist" was taking credit for predicting the whole thing.

Iben Browning was 72 years old before he received his 15 minutes of fame. Born in Texas, he received his first college degree at the age of 19 from Southwest State Teachers College.[5] During World War II, he was a test pilot and "spent his off hours reading the 'Encyclopedia Britannica.'"[6] He later went to the University of Texas, acquiring degrees in zoology, genetics and bacteriology[7] (perhaps just as significant, no degrees in geology). Before anyone took notice of his earthquake predictions, Browning drew his biggest crowds at investment conferences. He was convinced the earth was getting cooler, and advocated agricultural futures as a way for investors to make money. But Browning's biggest bull market was to come. Because of the speech he gave a few months after the San Francisco quake, he would soon enjoy a gold rush of media attention.

Browning's alleged forecast of the San Francisco earthquake made its way to Missouri, where the state agricultural department was convening an annual conference. Organizers were looking for a speaker and someone suggested Browning. Officials were skeptical at first, but relented, and Browning was invited to address the conference. The words Browning spoke hit the region like a thunderbolt. His speech in December of '89 caused all hell to break loose one year later. What was Browning talking about? Where was he talking about? It was all there in *The New Yorker*. Page 2. Table of Contents. "**Our Far Flung Correspondent – New Madrid, MO.**"

***

New Madrid, Missouri sits on the Mississippi River, about 160 miles south of St. Louis. It's the name of a town, a county, and outside of California, the highest risk earthquake fault zone in the United States. The New Madrid Fault stretches from eastern Arkansas to southern Illinois. In 1811 and 1812, a series of earthquakes thought to be among the most powerful in the nation's history rocked the region, causing a portion of the Mississippi River to flow backwards for a period of time, creating Reelfoot Lake in Tennessee, and causing the town of New Madrid to relocate to its present location. The old location is no longer dry land.

Since the earthquakes in the early 19th century, rumblings along the seismic zone, although frequent, had been relatively small and without major damage. One in 1895 registered an estimated 6.4 on the Richter scale, but that was before much of the area was settled. It did claim one fatality when a barn collapsed, killing a mule.[8]

Earthquakes can be measured in two ways; intensity and magnitude. The Richter scale measures magnitude and uses a logarithmic scale. A quake with a magnitude of 7 is ten times as large as a magnitude 6 quake and releases 30 times more energy.[9] A magnitude 7 is considered a major earthquake and releases enough energy to heat New York City for an entire year. While the Richter scale wasn't developed at the time, it's believed the New Madrid earthquakes in the early 19th century were in the range of 7.0 or even higher. A major quake in the near future was Browning's message when he spoke in Missouri at the December '89 conference.

Browning based his prediction on tidal forces. According to him, the sun and moon would be in line with the earth the following year, creating high tidal forces, which in turn, would trigger volcanoes and earthquakes. Browning told conference attendees, "We are back in the same triggering-force configuration as of December 3rd next year as we were when the great New Madrid earthquake went off."[10] Given his alleged reputation at the time, Browning's words alone were a cause of concern, certainly something that merited additional attention. But like nearly all manias and panics, Browning was aided by a series of fortuitous events and enablers along the way. Perhaps his biggest advocate was working at a university in Cape Girardeau, Missouri.

David Stewart had a Ph.D. in geophysics and was a member of the faculty at Southeast Missouri State University. Prior to joining the faculty in 1988, he became director of the Central United States Earthquake Consortium, a group of quake preparedness officials. He later became director of the University's Center for Earthquake Studies. It was this role that gave him credibility in the media and consequently gave Browning a certain legitimacy. Stewart believed in Browning's predictions. Commenting on Browning, he once said "He is, perhaps, the most intelligent man I've ever met."[11] Months after Browning had given his speech to the agriculture conference, Stewart paid him a visit in New Mexico. Upon returning to Missouri, Stewart wrote a memo, widely circulated among federal and state emergency management officials, praising the scientist and noting that Browning was concerned about possible earthquakes in three areas; California, Tokyo and the New Madrid Fault. That concern had a date range; December 3, 1990 "plus or minus two days." Iben Browning started the fire in December of the previous year. Now David Stewart was pouring on the fuel.

Stewart himself had been making predictions before Missouri residents had ever heard the name of Iben Browning. In September of 1989, the *St. Louis Post-Dispatch* reported there was a one in ten chance of a 7.6 quake in the region in the next decade. Stewart noted in the article that such an event would cause $6 billion in damage in Missouri alone.[12] A month later, after the San Francisco quake struck, he upped the ante. This time, he told the paper that the odds of a similar earthquake along the New Madrid Fault were "one in three by the year 2000."[13] By June of 1990, Stewart had been to New Mexico to meet with Browning and had written the widely circulated memo. The story line that had now developed was that the probability of a major earthquake was 50% - a one in two chance of heavy damage along the New Madrid fault. On July

21st, Stewart told the *Post-Dispatch*, "What Dr. Browning is doing cannot be explained merely by chance."

Browning's forecasting resume was also growing. In addition to the San Francisco Bay area quake of the previous year, the paper said the scientist had also predicted the eruption of Mt. Saint Helens in 1980, a 1985 earthquake in Mexico City, a volcano eruption in Columbia that same year, as well as a 1971 earthquake in San Fernando, California. Four days later, the paper editorialized under the headline, "It can happen here" by noting that Browning "has a good record of accurate predictions – good enough to be taken with a great deal of caution. That means he should be heeded; if it takes a prophet to wake Missourians up, so be it."[14]

By late summer, Missourians were wide-awake. In August, an earthquake registering 3.4 was felt in Tennessee and Arkansas. A month later, a temblor measuring 4.6 struck the Missouri Bootheel, the six county area in the southeastern corner of the state.[15] To increasingly worried residents, the quakes were getting stronger and closer to home. What once would have been minor news articles became front page headlines and lead stories on the six o'clock news. Just when it looked like it was all gloom, doom, and despair, a couple of events occurred that attempted to quell the unrest and make people take a second look at the "prophet" and his biggest enabler.

In October, the National Earthquake Evaluation Council released a report after convening a team of 11 earthquake experts. The panel raised several questions about Browning, his predictions and methodology. Its findings should have dismantled any claims to legitimacy by the New Mexico climatologist. The unanimous consensus was that Browning's prediction was not scientifically valid. Browning's forecast was based on tidal forces that he thought would trigger earthquakes. While some studies in the past had found positive correlations between the two, others found no relationship at all. Only one of five major earthquakes along the New Madrid Fault in 1811-1812 occurred during a period of high tidal forces. Using Browning's own methodology, the panel examined 182 earthquakes during a three-year period. Only fourteen of them occurred in the window of time that Browning would have predicted.[16] As one panel member explained, the scientist could have done just as well "by throwing darts at a calendar."[17] Browning claimed a fifty-percent probability of a quake in early December. The actual odds of an earthquake during any two-day period were more like one in sixty thousand. The panel also said it could find no evidence that Browning had accurately predicted any of the volcanoes or earthquakes as claimed by him and his supporters.

In the same month the scientific community rallied to put sanity back into scientific forecasting, the *St. Louis Post-Dispatch* was digging into David Stewart's background. What they discovered would prove worthy of a tabloid headline. In fact, it all started with a story from National Enquirer magazine many years before. It turned out that this wasn't the first earthquake scare in which Stewart had been involved.[18] Earlier in his career, he was on the faculty of the University of North Carolina. In 1975 while standing in line at the grocery store, he saw a story in the National Enquirer about a psychic who claimed to have successfully predicted earthquakes in the past. One of Clarissa Bernhardt's many other predictions was that tennis star John McEnroe would retire and begin to play baseball for the San Francisco Giants. Stewart claimed to have data supporting a possible earthquake in the region and decided to invite her to North Carolina. They toured the state by airplane to assess the landscape. Soon afterwards, she issued a new prediction; an 8.0 earthquake would strike the Wilmington area within a year, most likely within a few days of January 17, 1976. It never happened. Stewart was later denied tenure and left the University.

Stewart also admitted to the paper that he was a believer in psychic phenomena and stood by his previous statements on the matter. "The psychic and the intuitive approach to scientific endeavor is both valid and valuable. Psychic phenomena is a fact." He also insisted that the Browning prediction was completely different. "He is going beyond the scientific method. I just call it judgment." After leaving the University of North Carolina, Stewart became an author and publisher for a period of time. In 1988, he resurfaced as an academic by joining the faculty at Southeast Missouri State and within two years had become embroiled in another earthquake prediction fiasco.

Denunciations of Browning and the discrediting of Stewart came too late. Browning's prediction had reached the tipping point; enough people believed him, others were perhaps looking for a reason to believe him. There was this acknowledgement by a schoolteacher in southern

Missouri who told *The New Yorker's* Sue Hubbell that "I listen to my kids and parents. They want an earthquake. They remember all that TV coverage of the one in San Francisco and it's almost as if they are saying, 'Hey, we could have one of those. Just like the big city. We could be on TV and all.'" In November, while Stewart announced he would no longer talk to the media, Browning had moved on to his next prediction; the United States would be in the middle of a depression by 1993.[19]

As the date grew closer, urban legends began to spread: A St. Louis utility had ordered six thousand body bags; someone was offering school children magic markers and plastic bags so they could help out (soon to be) overwhelmed funeral homes; all flights out of the region prior to December 3rd had been booked; black birds were flying backward across the Mississippi River. But fictional stories almost pale in comparison to what actually transpired: The Red Cross distributed whistles to the children of New Madrid; schools all over Southeast Missouri canceled classes; one store manager reported that "if it cooks, heats, or gives off light, we're out of it." The United States Figure Skating Association postponed its event in St. Louis. The originally scheduled date? December 3rd.

In fairness, many people regarded Browning as a quack and didn't take him seriously. Typical was a comment by Peter Kinder on the pages of the *Southeast Missourian* the week of Browning's prediction, "Do you suppose that just perhaps, by Wednesday (December 5), we might all resume our daily lives?"[20] But while Kinder was making those comments on the paper's opinion pages, the front page featured an article on four local county court houses shutting down on December 3rd. Officials weren't taking any chances.

What started with a speech the year before was now spinning out of control. Hype had turned into hysteria and an all out media blitz. A small town in Southeast Missouri had become the center of the media universe, or as it was being called at the time, "shake central." A Washington Post reporter described the scene on December 2nd. "People who live atop the New Madrid fault zone have gone a bit bonkers. Grandmothers are setting up tents in cotton fields. Mothers and children are being shipped out of state ...A circus atmosphere is taking over the little town of New Madrid (pronounced New MAD-rid). A preacher is prowling the streets in his van, broadcasting 'The End Is Near' over a pair of loudspeakers. The governor plans to arrive Monday to eat lunch. They're buying earthquake insurance. They're buying batteries, flashlights, kerosene, charcoal and T-Shirts that say: "Visit New Madrid While It's Still Here."[21]

On December 3rd, New Madrid was still there. Governor John Ashcroft came and had lunch. Down at Hap's Bar and Grill, the "Shake, Rattle and Roll Party" lasted all day, complete with beers and bottomless gumbo. For the people who did stay, it was probably hard to figure out the higher number – residents who decided to stick it out or members of the media. *The New Yorker* reporter counted fifty vehicles with satellite dishes and news logos, then "got tired and quit." The rest of the day passed without incident. So did the 4th and 5th. Browning's window of time on his prediction had run out.

Schools reopened, vacations ended, and life returned to normal in Southeast Missouri. One week after the final media blitz, David Stewart would resign as the director of the Center for Earthquake Studies.[22] He would eventually leave Southeast Missouri State University as well. Iben Browning was steadfast and unapologetic to the end. The following May, he told the Albuquerque Rotary Club, "It wasn't a prediction. It was a probability. I am a business consultant. Business people know how to deal with probability – the public doesn't." Browning died two months later, the victim of a heart attack. There would be no major seismic activity along the New Madrid fault line the entire decade of the '90's.

In hindsight, the Iben Browning earthquake predictions developed into the sort of panic or mania that any student of stock market history would recognize. Be it the frenzy for tulips in 17th century Holland or 20th century investors craving dot.com companies, even the words to describe it would have an eerie echo. Just a few years after the New Madrid scare, Federal Reserve Chairman Alan Greenspan, worried that prices were too high, made headlines and rattled investors around the world when he warned of "irrational exuberance" in the stock market. In 1990, George Kennedy at the University of Missouri School of Journalism described the earthquake hysteria this way. "There was a kind of momentum and a level of fascination that is irrational."[23]

The state's largest newspaper was embarrassed. Just six months after calling Browning a "prophet," *The Post-Dispatch* editorialized, "Missouri's reputation as the hard-nosed, skeptical Show-Me state is ruined. Destroyed. Left scattered about in little pieces. Iben Browning and media hype did it, and now Missourians look to all the world like they were left holding the bag in one of the biggest snipe hunts in American history."[24]

Not everyone felt that way. Closer to the Bootheel, others had a more sanguine outlook. Reflecting on the Iben Browning saga ten years after the fact, Cape Girardeau writer Christopher Morrill summed it up this way. "*We* were the center of the world. That's what was so appealing about the earthquake hysteria was that it was so localized; it was only Southeast Missouri, really. *We* were all in it together. Under a national microscope, we got to show our asses to the nation. For all the wrong reasons, as it turned out. But wasn't it kind of fun while it lasted?"[25]

***

The real New Madrid earthquakes happened without predictions or media hype. From December of 1811 through February of 1812, a series of quakes devoured the land, ruptured the Mississippi River and rang church bells on the East Coast. Under Spanish control at the end of the Revolutionary War, the European power began to lay out a road that would lead to St. Louis. The Spanish colony had its headquarters in New Orleans and the government wanted a way to deliver the King's messages from Louisiana to the Missouri city. Messengers would navigate up the river, stopping at what became New Madrid, and then going by land to St. Louis.

It was Revolutionary War soldier George Morgan who coined the name. After the war, Morgan laid out plans to set up a trading outpost along the Mississippi. Hoping to gain favor with Spanish authorities, he named the town New Madrid. He lured settlers with the promise of cheap land, sold at 12.5 cents per acre. Spanish officials ultimately rejected Morgan's request to colonize the region, but they did set up a fort along the river and levy duties on river traffic. France took control of the land in 1800 and when President Thomas Jefferson made the Louisiana Purchase in 1803, New Madrid became a part of the United States. By the time of the earthquakes, around three thousand people lived in the county.[26]

The earthquakes that would change the history of the Bootheel began on December 16, 1811. By some estimates, five earthquakes registering at least 8.0 on the Richter Scale affected more than one million square miles of land over the next three months.[27] The quakes produced 2,000 aftershocks. Earthquakes were felt in twenty-eight states and the District of Columbia. It would take decades for the Bootheel to recover. The region developed a reputation for being "sickly and visited by earthquakes."[28] Over the next decade, New Madrid County lost thirty percent of its population. George Morgan's dream of a booming trading post along the Mississippi River never came to fruition. A commercial hub for the Missouri Bootheel did develop, but it would take place years later and in a town twenty-five miles to the north. When New Madrid County was divided by state officials a decade after the quakes, the northern portion became Scott County. Sikeston would become its largest city.

When John Sikes named the town after himself, the United States was preparing to go to war with itself. The Civil War started the following spring, and like the nation as a whole, Missouri was divided. While the state didn't secede from the Union, it had strong Southern sympathizers. The results can be seen from presidential elections. In 1860, Abraham Lincoln received all of six votes in Scott County (and zero in neighboring Stoddard County). The other 650 white men who went to the polls that day split their vote among three other candidates.[29] Lincoln's poor showing was a reflection of how he did statewide. But four years later, Missouri voted for Lincoln by a more than a two-to-one margin, but he still couldn't carry Scott County. He improved his vote total to 155, but received 31 less votes than his Democrat rival, former General George B. McCellan.[30]

The same year Sikeston was founded the railroad arrived. The first trains into Southeast Missouri belonged to the Cairo & Fulton Railroad. Starting in Cairo, Illinois and crossing the Mississippi River into the Bootheel region, the tracks reached Charleston by 1859 and Sikeston a year later. Construction continued on the lines westward toward Poplar Bluff, but the Civil War stopped all activity. It would be many years before it would resume.[31]

By the late 19th century, railroad tracks dotted the regional landscape with increasing frequency. In 1873, the Iron Mountain Railroad started running regular trains from St. Louis to Little Rock.[32] By the 1880's, Sikeston boasted that it shipped more grain than any other town of its size in the state.[33] Around this time, businessmen and entrepreneurs began paying increasing attention to the area's first great source of wealth: its timber. "Some of the most valuable timber in all the United States was found in Southeast Missouri; great forests of cotton wood, of white oak, of gum, of cypress and poplar existed."[34] Early settlers saw the timber as a nuisance, believing the land was more valuable without it and did everything they could to destroy the trees.[35] The valuable lumber stood worthless for many years due to a lack of transportation and manufacturing facilities. The widespread development of the railroads, though, changed the equation, and workers began harvesting timber in abundance.

Even in its heyday, people recognized the timber boom would not last forever. The land upon which the trees sprouted contained rich soil, suitable for growing a variety of crops. "As the timber fails, and this source of wealth disappears, its place will be taken by the products of the soil, for practically all the land which is being deforested is valuable for agricultural purposes."[36] But just as the timber industry needed the railroads to provide access to the land, farmers needed modern machinery and engineering to ensure the value of their crops. Much of Southeast Missouri was nothing more than swampland.

With the Mississippi and Ohio Rivers to the east, and the Ozark Mountains and smaller rivers to the west, the Bootheel region served as a vast flood plain. One estimate placed as much as ninety percent of the land underwater during some portion of the year.[37] Recognizing the problem and the vast agricultural potential of the region, people began to build ditches and levees. One of the largest formal efforts was undertaken by the Little River Drainage District. Formed in 1907, the district stretches more than 90 miles from Cape Girardeau to the Missouri-Arkansas border. In a fourteen-year period, workers built more than 900 miles of ditches and constructed more than 300 miles of levees.[38] By the 1920's, their efforts had transformed the landscape. The value of the land skyrocketed. Farmland that once sold for sixty cents an acre was now fetching two hundred dollars an acre.[39] The timing of the enterprise was fortuitous. In the cotton fields of the South, a bug was chewing its way through the crop, and devastated farmers sought relief. They focused their gaze on the increasingly attractive farmlands of Southeast Missouri. Their arrival would change the region forever.

The boll weevil is native to Mexico and Central America. It was first detected in the United States in the 1890's when it advanced into Texas.

In thirty years time, it chewed its way to the Atlantic Ocean, wreaking havoc on the Cotton South in the process. In the state of Georgia, cotton production was cut in half by 1923 because of the insect.[40] The tiny bug lays its eggs inside unripe cotton bolls and the young weevils proceed to eat their way out. Lacking modern eradication methods, many cotton farmers solution to the problem was to find new fields for the crop. When farmers set their sights on the Missouri Bootheel, they discovered a potential "Goldilocks" climate – warm enough to grow the crops but also cold enough for a winter freeze to kill the boll weevil. Flat fertile soil, much of it bordering the Mississippi River, also helped make it just right.

The dateline for this transformation can be targeted with some precision. On December 8, 1922, the *Sikeston Standard* foretold the changes that would soon occur at the northern end of the Bootheel. Under the headline, "Southern Negroes Coming To Missouri," the paper noted a ten million dollar cotton crop produced that year in Dunklin and Pemiscot Counties (the two southern most counties in Missouri). Citing the Memphis Commercial Appeal as its source, the paper went on to say that the bumper crop would soon bring change to the entire Bootheel. "With suitable weather conditions next summer, a wonderful change will be seen in that territory, according to reports. Cotton will be planted next summer as far as Oran, Mo., a town in the foothills of the Ozarks."[41] Oran was north of Sikeston, in the middle of Scott County. The summer of 1923 would be a first for the region. "It is the farthest north cotton has been grown, but farmers in that territory say they can make it and next year will bring about the change."[42]

By the following month, northern Bootheel farmers began projecting a cotton crop in 1923 twenty-five times larger than the previous year, with 15,000 acres of the crop planted in Scott County alone.[43] A farm bureau official commented, "Scott County must make hay while the sun shines" and plant as much cotton as possible. Cotton had become Bootheel gold. Stories, most likely apocryphal, began to appear of the riches that awaited those who dared make the transformation from wheat and corn. One Scott County farmer had planted three hundred acres of wheat. His wife told him to plant cotton. When he refused, she planted three acres herself. When it came time to sell, the three acres of cotton made more money than the three hundred acres of wheat.[44]

With the promise of riches, people soon followed. A post card arrived in Charleston from a Mississippi farmer, asking if there was land available to rent. When the local farm agent replied in the affirmative, thirty-one families packed up their belongings and headed north.[45] The mad dash to the new cotton capital was captured in this letter from a New Madrid County farmer:[46]

> *"It is a sight here in Lilbourn (town in New Madrid County) to see the cotton growers come from the South. Last Friday, I counted 52 wagons and three trucks all right close together and about one and one –half miles to the north were six more wagons. Every freight train has from one to three cars and the local always has a few. All this immigration is scattered from Morley and Vanduser (in Scott County) south. Yesterday a total of 52 persons including children moved to Lilbourn. Last Saturday the main street of Lilbourn looked like Broadway at Cape."*

In Sikeston, three new cotton gins were constructed, 250 houses were built on area farms and Scott County's population swelled by 600 people in just a few months. They came from Arkansas, Tennessee and Mississippi.[47] Almost overnight, Sikeston went from a mercantile center for the region with small scale farming to the agricultural and commercial hub for large-scale cotton production. Southern cotton farmers moved in, not only buying land, but also bringing their own labor. Many of those experienced sharecroppers were black. "They are the class of Negroes who believe in growing cotton; those who know nothing else and have no inclination to try out any of the so-called 'northern generosity.'"[48] The county's black population more than quadrupled from 1920 to 1930.

News of the Bootheel cotton boom made its way to Como, Mississippi. That's where Edwin Pope (E.P.) Coleman, Junior was born and raised on the family's cotton plantation. When he arrived in Sikeston in 1923, he didn't come alone. He brought with him $50,000 and "a handful of Mississippi sharecroppers, most of who (sic) were black."[49] By the time of the Second World War, Coleman had accumulated 16,000 acres of area farmland. His business and philanthropic activities would leave a permanent mark on the Bootheel. More than any other farmer, it is Coleman who is credited with bringing large- scale cotton production to Southeast Missouri.

Wealthy landowners, poor sharecroppers and an expanding cotton crop influenced more than just the agriculture. It changed the culture of the Bootheel. The timber industry brought the first wave of migration; cotton brought a vastly different second wave. Thad Snow was a Bootheel farmer who witnessed it all first hand. "So now we have both the white timber people and the Negro cotton croppers to give our lowland section its distinctive cultures. We are therefore different socially from other farming areas in Missouri."[50] In an amazingly brief period, the region was transformed. "We moved south, or rather the Cotton south moved and absorbed us in two months time."[51]

This southern influence was demonstrated in this description from a new arrival to the Bootheel a few years later. "People were extremely friendly, kissed each other a lot, said 'Honey' and 'Darlin,' called their fathers, 'Papa,' spoke of fur pieces as 'Fuhh pieces,' and never wore white shoes before Easter or after Labor Day. The women who had high, lilting voices made conversations downright musical."[52]

Helen Reuber took a job as a Sikeston schoolteacher in 1929, moving to Missouri from Kansas. She arrived in downtown on a Saturday night, and was surprised not to see a white face in the crowd. It was later explained to her this way; "Oh, this is Saturday night and most of 'Sunset,' our colored section, and the niggers in the country come to town that night. You won't have any of their children in school, though, they have their Lincoln School out in the addition."[53]

The Sunset Addition was on the west side of town and where Sikeston's black population lived and went to school. Race wasn't the only distinction that Reuber noticed after arriving in town. Even at the all-white school she taught, fault lines were drawn. "Social class distinction was something I had never known in Kansas, so one student's refusal to work with another because she lived on the wrong side of the Missouri Pacific tracks took me by surprise."[54]

Wealthier whites lived north of the tracks; those not as well off lived south of them. North-South. Black and White. The carefully cordoned off sections of Sikeston society would reside together in relative calm for many years. But one day, those boundaries were crossed. It all started with an encounter between a west side black man and an east side white woman. The result and its aftermath would also expose yet another fault line; between the cotton filled flatlands of southern Scott County and its neighbors to the north in the hilly section of the county where the cotton didn't grow.

****

As a lifelong resident and publisher of the local paper, Mike Jensen knows Sikeston and its history well. Growing up, he remembers two stories about the town that became the stuff of urban legend. One of the things often repeated to him (and is still said by people in the community today) is that Sikeston has the most millionaires per capita than any other city in the United States. It's a claim made by a lot of other places as well.[55] "It's not based in any fact," says Jensen who has researched the matter. "It is true that Sikeston, not only now, but then as well, had an abundance of millionaires, of very wealthy families, but also had an abundance of extremely low-income (people), of farm laborers, and so there was this dichotomy, of differences, of stark differences between the wealthy north end and the impoverished west end of Sikeston."

The second story that Jensen remembers hearing about as a child was something that wasn't said as loudly nor as often as the first claim. It concerned one of the town's former residents on the west end. Locals said that a black man (Cleo Wright was his name) had raped a white woman. This resulted in the last lynching to take place in the United States. This too was not exactly true. But it's also a case where fact trumps fiction. The real story of the encounter between Wright and Grace Sturgeon and the resulting aftermath is one of horrific violence and vigilante justice. It all took place on a Sunday morning in early 1942.

Just a month before, the *Southeast Missourian* reminded its readers, "It is time to button up the lip and buckle down to work." That same month on December 10th, at the northern end of Scott County, Chaffee mayor L.D. Lankford called a meeting of its citizens to discuss civilian defense. It was three days after the Japanese attack on Pearl Harbor. War had come to the heartland.

Back in November of 1941, the men of Company K of the 140th Infantry took part in an Armistice Day celebration in Springfield, Missouri. The soldiers had departed from Camp Robinson, Arkansas at 4:30 a.m. and arrived in Springfield eleven and a half hours later. The *Sikeston Standard* noted, "There is a promise of a ten-day furlough for every man in the Second Army for the Christmas holidays." That furlough never came. After the bombing of Pearl Harbor on December 7th, Company K soon departed for the west coast. Supply Sgt. J.D. Sturgeon sent a letter to a friend back home shortly before leaving Camp Robinson.

"Our trip delayed 24 hours. We don't know for sure as yet where we are going and don't care. This company is like a fighter on a fine edge. We are just waiting for the bell. And we will deal out plenty too when we get started. Everyone is smiling here. Nearly every regiment has gone now except us. And we'll be on our way when you get this."[56]

"Sarge" Sturgeon had family back in Sikeston. His wife Grace and their young son Jimmy lived on the east side of town that now totaled nearly 8,000 residents. Sturgeon's brother John was also in the military and his wife Laverne, had moved in with her sister-in-law at their Kathleen Avenue residence in early January, 1942.

The weather during this period mirrored the national outlook in the wake of the surprise attack: depressing and bleak. The temperature dropped to twelve below near the middle of the month as Sikeston experienced its coldest weather in at least a decade.[57] That's what made Saturday, January 24th such a welcome relief. Sunny skies and unusually warm temperatures brought people out that day. Sikeston had always been a destination point on Saturdays for farmers and people in surrounding, rural communities. Now everyone had a chance to visit and socialize after being cooped up for days on end. Grace Sturgeon spent the morning working at the shoe factory. She later visited with family and remembered her last chore of the day as scrubbing her porch, taking advantage of the pleasant weather. Grace, Jimmy and Laverne had a quiet evening at home. By 10:30 p.m., everyone was "sound asleep."[58] Peaceful dreams wouldn't last long. In just a few hours, Grace Sturgeon would come face to face with Cleo Wright. It would be the fight of her life.

***

Born Ricelor Cleodas Watson in 1916, Cleo Wright grew up just outside Pine Bluff, Arkansas. His mother Alonzo taught school while his father Albert farmed the land – "cotton for cash, corn and hay for livestock, and vegetables for food."[59] Cleo completed the eighth grade, but would quit school soon thereafter. At the age of 19, he entered the Navy. He signed up for a four-year enlistment in September of 1935. He was out of the service and back in Arkansas six months later. Cleo received an undesirable discharge in March of 1936 (less serious than a dishonorable one) for a series of offenses, the last one coming just a few days prior for disregarding orders and serving time in solitary confinement.[60]

Back in Pine Bluff, Cleo took a job as a truck driver but it didn't last long. Out of work the following year, he and three other men – including his older half-brother Wiley – robbed a grocery store and took $80. They did so without masks during business hours. Wiley was arrested within days and named Cleo as an accomplice. Cleo ran. He started going by the name Cleo Wright. He wound up in Sikeston, Missouri.

By January of 1942, Cleo had a job, a wife and a child on the way. But the move to Sikeston didn't mean his troubles were behind him. Shortly after arriving in town in the spring of 1937, he tried to break into a state police car and steal a pistol. He served sixty days in the county jail. He married Ardella Gay in February of 1940 and three months later, burglarized a store for less than $16.[61] He was caught and sentenced to two years in the state penitentiary. He served seven months in Jefferson City and was released on parole. Parole ended on January 3rd. Cleo Wright had been a free man for three weeks.

It was now Saturday in late January. Cleo had to be at work at 10 o'clock that night at the Cotton Oil Mill on the east side of town. Cleo started working there while on parole. He left home in the afternoon, many hours before the start of his shift. He stopped by the Farmer's Market at around nine o'clock that night and reported to work on time. Upon arrival, he was told that his shift had been canceled. So late on a Saturday night, Cleo found himself with an unexpected free evening and no expectation of being home until morning. Instead of heading west back to the Sunset Addition (where he and Ardella lived), Cleo would make his way south toward Kathleen Avenue. It would prove to be a fateful decision. Cleo Wright had less than twelve hours to live.

It began around one a.m. Grace thought she heard someone at the back door. A half hour later, her sister Laverne rose up out of bed only to see Grace awake and a man standing in their room. He had entered through a bedroom window. Spotting the two sisters, Wright seemed surprised. "There are two of you son-of-a-bitches," he said, adding that he would kill them if they screamed.[62] Laverne took off running to the telephone, called the police and then ran outside to a neighbor for help. Grace also tried to escape. She didn't make it. Wright grabbed her from behind. He had a knife. He attempted to slash her throat. Grace blocked his efforts with her hand. The knife slashed three of her fingers. He then cut her across her stomach. With Grace's intestines spilling out, Wright then quickly ran out through the rear window by which he entered. Grace waited outside the house for the ambulance. In a few minutes, the brutal encounter had ended.

The ambulance and police arrived a few minutes later. Seeing the trail of blood out of the house, policeman Hess Perrigan and Jesse Whitley, a neighbor of the Sturgeons, hopped into a squad car and began to follow it. They started heading east along the Missouri Pacific railroad tracks. After a few miles, they turned the car around and started heading back into town. That's when they spotted a black man in front of a grocery store with blood covering his clothes. Perrigan asked him where he had been. Wright told him he had "been in a fight with two Negroes."[63] When the police officer searched him, he discovered a long and bloody knife. Wright got into the police car in the back with Perrigan. Whitley drove the car. What the officer didn't know was that Wright had another knife, this one hidden in his shoe. He reached down, pulled it out and stabbed Perrigan in his upper lip, the knife piercing his tongue and coming out underneath his right jaw. Like Grace Sturgeon just moments before, Perrigan was fighting for his life. The police officer took out his pistol and fired four times. The wounded Wright collapsed and gave up the struggle. At the Dunn Hotel, the men met police officer Roy Beck. According to Beck, Perrigan said, "I got the son-of-a-bitch and he almost got me."[64] Perrigan went to the hospital. Beck and Whitley took Wright to the police headquarters located at city hall.

Back on Kathleen Avenue, Grace was rushed to the hospital with her wounds. The knife attack had produced a seven-inch gash on her side. She received three blood transfusions.[65] While receiving treatment Sturgeon heard a voice she recognized instantly. Someone in the emergency room basement of the hospital screamed out, "Oh God!" The voice belonged to Cleo Wright. A few hours after the attack Sturgeon and Wright were in the hospital at the same time being treated for their wounds. Policeman Beck didn't realize Wright had been shot until after they arrived at the police station. He only saw the wounds after Wright complained that he was getting sick.

After a doctor treated Wright, police took him to his home in Sunset. His family, already beginning to hear stories of what happened and rumors of what may come next, wanted no part of him. They told the officers they were afraid of what might happen if Wright died at home. After spending just a few hours with his family, police returned to the Wright residence, and found Cleo "in a dying condition."[66] The officers took Wright back to city hall where he was placed in a detention room of the women's center on the main floor.

With two people stabbed and one person shot overnight in Sikeston, telephone lines lit up all over town in the early morning hours of Sunday, Between 1:30 and 7:00 A.M. an estimated 666 phone calls were placed.[67] News of the attack spread rapidly. By the early morning hours, a crowd began to mingle outside the detention center. In a few hours, that crowd would become a mob.

Highway Patrol Officer Melvin Dace was on his way to Sunset to interview Wright's wife on Sunday morning when he noticed an unusually large crowd gathering outside city hall. His immediate assumption was that Wright had died and people were looking for him. Entering the building through its front doors, Dace discovered a group of about 75 people trying to break into the women's detention center. Wright was still alive and the mob wanted him. When Dace ordered the crowd out of the building, they told him, "Let's go get our guns and burn nigger town."[68] Escorting the crowd out of the building, Dace also discovered something else. He could find no police officers on duty at city hall. Concerned by the lack of protection for Wright, Dace began calling for backup. He called the Prosecuting Attorney, other Highway Patrol officers and the Sheriff's department. He requested reinforcements as soon as possible.

By 11:00 a.m. Sunday morning, a crowd estimated anywhere from 300 to 800 stirred outside. Their intentions were clear. "Let's go get the black S.O.B.," they shouted. By this time, a few reinforcements had arrived. One of the people attempting to calm the crowd was Prosecuting Attorney David Blanton. Blanton had been hunting that morning when his wife received a call from Dace for him to come to city hall as quickly as he could. After conferring with Dace, Blanton decided to address the increasingly restless crowd. Standing on the steps of the building as shouts for Wright's scalp grew increasingly louder, the Harvard Law School educated attorney sought to calm the crowd and warned them that if anything happened to Wright, the men could be prosecuted for murder. "Why don't you go home where you belong," they shouted back.

Sometime around 11:30 A.M., the mob would not be denied. They rushed the courthouse door. One of the men pushed Blanton's arm up and another man punched him, breaking his rib. They flooded the courthouse entrance and went in search of Wright. It didn't take long for them to bust down the door to his cell and pull him out. They dragged him down the courthouse steps and slung his knees over the bumper of a car. With a badly wounded Wright in tow, the men took off for Sunset – the black area of Sikeston. Arriving at the intersection of Lincoln and Fair streets, the caravan came to a halt. They unhitched Wright from the car and the mob gathered around. Someone had a can full of gasoline and poured it on Wright. A second person lit a match. Then, they set the body of Cleo Wright ablaze. His badly charred remains would remain there for several hours, until a city dump truck came along and scooped him up. During those Sunday afternoon hours, hundreds of curious onlookers came to visit the site. No funeral home in Sikeston would prepare his body for burial. He was eventually buried in a small cemetery north of town. A few weeks later, his family exhumed the grave and returned it to Arkansas.[69]

News of the incident and reaction to it were swift. Editors at the St. Louis Post-Dispatch wanted to know, with hundreds of people outside of city hall, why more witnesses did not come forward. "Is Scott County going to add to the mob crimes of lawlessness and brutality the community crime of tacit approval?"[70] It also wasn't lost on either side of the debate that the racial violence in Sikeston took place at the time of a World War against totalitarianism. The New York Times noted, "How sadly do such events tarnish the cause of democracy! There are few happenings in the United States that afford more comfort to the Nazis than evidence of lawlessness. Lynchings are their prize exhibit in proof of the alleged hypocrisy of the free societies."[71] A few days later, the Times received a letter of support from a Sikeston resident.

"I have before me the editorial of January 27ᵗʰ relating to the recent tragedy in our little city. I wish to commend you for your clear-cut and correct statement and for your sympathetic understanding of our sorrow and shame. One wild Negro on the loose and 300 white hoodlums do not represent either the whites or Negroes in our community."[72]

It was signed E.P. Coleman, Jr., the Mississippi land baron who came to Sikeston during the Bootheel cotton craze of the 1920's. Coleman's opinion was not necessarily the majority view in Southeast Missouri. Closer to the scene of the vigilante justice, mob support was strong. From Mississippi County, twenty miles to the east of Sikeston, the *Charleston Enterprise-Courier* put it this way: "We live on the northern boundary of the Cotton South. We have our problems and they are peculiar to the South. Let those who know nothing of this problem, and they are many, confine their activities to their part of the country and let us handle our troubles in our own way. "[73] The *Sikeston Standard* was even more blunt. "The mobbing of the negro, Cleo Wright, Sunday forenoon, was an unfortunate incident, but was deserved." Publisher and editor C.L.Blanton also added, "It was the feeling of those near City Hall Sunday where the mob formed, that it was their duty to protect the wives of the soldier boys, and that was the thing that influenced the men. This should be a warning for all bad negroes to stay out of Sikeston."[74]

In the immediate aftermath of the lynching, authorities in the Bootheel took measures to ensure the violence didn't spread. On Sunday and Monday nights, state highway patrolmen guarded the entrances to Sunset. The city of Sikeston hired five temporary police officers Sunday afternoon. Grace Sturgeon, although "seriously wounded," gradually improved. Because she lost so much blood, officials worried she may die. Her improving health condition, along with the news that Hess Perrigan would survive his attack was good news, not just for them, but perhaps for many others as well. In twelve hours time, both a woman and a police officer were stabbed, and the accused assailant dragged through town and set on fire. As violent as Sunday morning there has ever been in Sikeston, things could have been even worse. Had Sturgeon and Perrigan died, one is left to speculate that perhaps all of Sunset, and not just Cleo Wright, would have been set ablaze on that day. Many black residents left town, some for a brief period of time, others permanently. With additional law enforcement patrolling the streets, order was restored. Survival, exodus, and reinforcements separated Sikeston between a single lynching and potentially an all-out race war.

With situations stabilizing on all fronts across the town, investigations and finger pointing began. One area under scrutiny was the lack of police at the courthouse Sunday morning. Why weren't more authorities there to help turn back the mob? Could their arrival have made a difference? One of the groups under fire was the Scott County Sheriff's Department.

This part of the story leads to the northern part of the county where the culture and history stood in stark contrast to Sikeston. This portion of Scott County was largely unfazed by the crush to plant cotton in the 1920's. There were no population spikes or vast demographic changes during this period. The largest towns in this area; Chaffee, Illmo, and Oran, owed their existence to no crop, but rather to the railroads. If one were to divide Scott County in two, the line would be drawn right around the town of Morley, just south of Benton and Oran. It is here the soil becomes sandy, the accents become thicker and the rolling hills give way to the delta flatlands. Focusing on Sheriff John Hobbs, a Chaffee resident, Author Dominic Capeci zeroed in on the cultural differences between north and south.

"He (Hobbs) served as Chaffee chief of police for fourteen years before becoming deputy sheriff in 1938 and sheriff in 1940. He and his wife, Nona Mae Heeb, making their home in Chaffee, raised two daughters and a foster son. At the time of the lynching, Hobbs was nearing his fifty-third birthday and understood the northern, self-sufficient farming part of the county, with its close knit, all white, mostly German and Dutch families; like them, he was suspicious of outsiders. He related less well to the southern, plantation economy of the delta region that boasted equally tight though less ethnic families, relied on large numbers of black sharecroppers, and contained the commercial center of Sikeston, which marked the southernmost tip of the county and, in effect, the

northernmost point of the delta. In short, Hobb's loyalties lay
above the county seat in Benton. For all practical purposes, he
and Sikeston police officials protected separate turf and rarely
cooperated with one another. "[75]

This lack of cooperation between the Sheriff's department and
Sikeston Police was corroborated by the Prosecuting Attorney. David
Blanton told the FBI there was "definite friction" between the two
organizations. Hobbs was tending to the county jail on that Sunday
morning when the call came from Sikeston for help. When the Sheriff
received the request, it was 11:00 a.m. Hobbs was working the jail by
himself and later told the FBI he couldn't leave the prisoners without
someone in charge. He called two deputies, one to relieve him, and a
second to go with him to Sikeston. By the time he arrived at City Hall,
the mob had already left with Wright. Departing City Hall and heading
toward Sunset, "he could see a heavy smoke rising."[76] Cleo Wright was
already dead.

Whether or not additional police protection could have stopped the
mob is a question with no definitive answer. But with up to 800 people
in the crowd, would local law enforcement have opened fire on their
neighbors and friends? Hobbs defended his actions by noting that prior
to the 11:00 a.m. Sunday morning call (which came from State Highway
Patrolman Melvin Dace), no one had notified him or his office of any
trouble in Sikeston. He told the FBI the Sikeston Police Department
should have notified his office immediately after Cleo Wright was picked
up so he could be taken to the Scott County Jail.

Prosecuting attorney Blanton pursued the case through a grand jury
investigation. Twelve grand jurors debated the evidence put in front of
them at the county courthouse in Benton. Sheriff Hobbs selected the
panel that included three members from Chaffee. Mayor L.D. Lankford
was among them. The grand jury convened on a Monday in March less
than two months after the lynching. By Tuesday, the panel was dismissed.
No one was indicted in the death of Cleo Wright. One eyewitness to their
announcement described it this way:

"Less than 50 persons were in the circuit court room when
R.H. Mackley, Blodgett merchant-farmer read the report

23

from the jury box to Judge McDowell seated on the bench.
Two Negro farmers had been seated at the rear of the room
shortly before the report was read but they left shortly before.
No other members of their race were in the court room."[77]

A second grand jury investigation, this one at the federal level, also failed to produce any indictments. But the federal grand jury in St. Louis harshly criticized the Sikeston Police Department, censuring it for "failing completely to cope with the situation." It also exonerated Sheriff Hobbs. "The sheriff is located miles away at the county seat and his deputies are scattered," said the grand jury's report. "Although the evidence shows he got one deputy and started promptly when called by the highway patrol sergeant, the mob had achieved its purpose before he reached Sikeston."[78]

While the lynching of Cleo Wright went unpunished, the actions of that day live on in the memories and stories of Sikeston residents. As of 2004, people still live in the town who witnessed the events of that morning. Sikeston resident Mike Jensen knows one of them. "We have a fellow in town, he is now in his mid-eighties who was at that time a 15 or 16 year-old boy," recalls the newspaper publisher. "This gentleman later came to a level of great prominence in our community. I have visited with him formally and informally about this particular Sunday morning. Even having known this gentlemen for fifty years and after calling him a friend for thirty years of my adult life – to this day, if you'll ask him about – he'll smile and he'll wink and he'll say 'I was rabbit hunting that morning.' He wasn't rabbit hunting that morning; he was on Center Street (at City Hall) that morning. He knows it and I know it, and I certainly don't mean to implicate him in any part of the mob. Just simply to say that he was there and he witnessed what went on."

Sikeston native, author, and columnist Terry Teachout wasn't yet born when the incident occurred. He heard whispers of the tale growing up. Writing about his hometown and Cleo Wright a few years ago in the pages of *The New York Times*, he summed it up this way.

"Of course his murders should have been brought to trial,
though it is hard to imagine that they would have been
convicted, not least because there was no serious question as

to Wright's own guilt. (Presumably this is why his name is no longer widely remembered.) But since they were never even indicted, might it be for the best that they were forgotten, their ultimate punishment left to the all-knowing disposition of a higher court? I know only one thing for sure; I feel no temptation to further disturb their unquiet sleep."[79]

With the grand jury investigations concluded, Sikeston and the rest of the nation moved on. News from World War II consumed the thoughts and actions of people for the next three years. The FBI files from the event were buried in the vaults of the federal government for more than three decades until Mike Jensen filed a Freedom of Information request in the 1970's. Southwest Missouri State Professor Dominic Capeci walked into his office in the early 1980's and told Jensen he was investigating the lynching. The two men began collaborating. The result was Capeci's book, *The Lynching of Cleo Wright*, the seminal text on the event.

"It's a legacy of our community that continues to this very day," said the newspaper publisher. "It's felt today in some areas and I suspect it will never go away." While the lynching was never repeated, divisions do remain in Scott County, one of them being the rift between Sikeston and its neighbors to the north, particularly when it comes to local politics. "If one could go back and redraw county lines, Scott County obviously would be divided," points out Sikeston native Jensen. "We have a lot more commonality with New Madrid than we do with Chaffee, (New) Hamburg, Kelso, Benton, Scott City or Cape and beyond." To this day, the county government continues to be divided between Sikeston and northern Scott County. "This split is not recent, not current, and it's certainly not going to change."

One of those caught in the crossfire of that division was Scott County Sheriff John Hobbs. Leaving the Sheriff's office in Benton in 1944, John Hobbs returned to the private sector in his hometown. He ran a bar in Chaffee. One afternoon in March of 1951, Hobbs refused to serve a patron. According to a Frisco Railroad special agent, Hobbs thought O.T. Turner "had had enough." The two men started arguing and Hobbs began to escort Turner out of the bar. Turner, described as an elderly man between 60 and 70, pulled out a knife and stabbed Hobbs twice, once in the abdomen and a second time in the chest. Just as Grace

Sturgeon and Hess Perrigan did nine years earlier, Hobbs survived his knife attack but the chest wound did require several stitches to close. After first hiding in the warehouse of a nearby downtown store, Turner was caught an hour and a half later in a field north of town by the Police Chief and the Deputy Sheriff.[80]

The stabbing of a former Sheriff was big news in a place where violent crime had become rare. Almost a half century after its founding, the town had reached a crossroad of sorts. The days of passenger train service and a thriving downtown business district would soon be no more. From its beginnings Chaffee linked its destiny to the trains; a true railroad town if there ever was one. But trouble loomed on the horizon for both the railroads and for Chaffee almost from the start. Seven years after the town was founded, Henry Ford rolled his first mass produced vehicle off the assembly lines of Detroit.

CHAPTER TWO
City With a Smile
1905-1951

"Chaffee, just three years old, is in Scott County, Missouri - the Gateway to Southeast Missouri, the richest agricultural section in the world – and ten miles west of the great Thebes Bridge across the Mississippi River."

Map of Chaffee - 1905[81]

"Chaffee is destined to become the leading city of Southeast Missouri, Cape Girardeau and Sikeston, NOT excepted."

Chaffee Signal, March 17, 1911

Adna Romanza Chaffee was born in the small Ohio village of Orwell in 1842. At the age of 19, he joined the Army. He would be in the military for the next forty-five years of his life. Encountering Chaffee near the end of his military career, an Australian soldier wrote that the soldier reminded him of a famous Missourian. "He had the same clear-cut jaw, heavy eyebrows, and grizzled moustache, and he spoke, as Mark Twain always did, like a man rehearsing a lecture."

When Chaffee joined the Sixth Cavalry in 1861, the Civil War was underway. The young Union soldier saw action on several battlefields, including Gettysburg, where he was wounded. By early 1865, near the war's conclusion, Chaffee had risen to the ranks of first lieutenant. With the Civil War over, Chaffee transferred to Texas, where he spent several years chasing hostile Indians and outlaws. Promoted to a Captain during this time period, he and his men gained the name Chaffee's Guerillas. In a later Indian battle, he exhorted his troops with the line, "Forward; if any man is killed, I will make him a corporal!"[82]

Promoted to Brigadier-General in May 1898, Chaffee achieved

fame during the Spanish-American war with the capture of El Caney. He later commanded a United States contingent in the Boxer Rebellion in China, served as military governor and commander of U.S. forces in the Philippines and a year before he retired, served as grand marshal for President Theodore Roosevelt's inaugural parade. Chaffee had a fort in Arkansas named for him, later a World War II tank and in the year he left the military, a small town in Southeast Missouri officially incorporated, taking his last name.

Chaffee (pronounced with a short a) was founded in 1906. Like many small towns with little recorded history, there are often multiple versions of events. Even the origins of the name of the town are in dispute. While for decades people have attributed the name to the former Army general, others believe the name came from a real estate transaction. It was this transaction that turned sparsely populated farmland into a bustling community within a decade.

The Chaffee Real Estate Company came to Southeast Missouri in the early 20th century looking for land. In the northwest section of Scott County, they found willing sellers. Whether it was a business partner or a subsidiary of the St. Louis – San Francisco Railway (the relationship is not clear), the companies worked in tandem. Shortly after purchasing 1,800 acres of land for $140,000, the real estate company announced plans to give 150 acres to the railroad. The "Frisco" would be coming here to establish a terminal point for its river division. The railroad started work in the later summer months of 1905. By August of 1906, the town of Chaffee was officially established.

It must have been cold that first winter. There were no houses in town. Frisco railroad workers commuting from Cape Girardeau took to calling it "rag city" as the only people who stayed overnight did so in tents and coalhouses. The "labor" train from Cape Girardeau to Chaffee ran until January of 1908, as railroad workers and the real estate company built a town from scratch. Malaria threatened to overwhelm the laborers. During construction, pools of water formed on lower level ground near the freight yards. It soon became a breeding ground for mosquitoes. After the local Frisco physician identified the source of the malaria epidemic, the water was either drained or filled in with gravel.[83] When construction was completed in Chaffee, the Frisco had a new roundhouse and turntable, passenger and freight depots. It was now possible for railroad mechanics and laborers to work on steam engines, repair railroad cards, store freight, and invite passengers onboard trains to travel practically anywhere in the country. For the boom and bust railroad industry, these were salad days. Frisco officials knew the dramatic swings in fortune as well as anyone.

The St. Louis-San Francisco Railway Company represented "aspirations rather than eventualities."[84] The company's tracks never made it out to the Bay Area. However, California played a role in its founding. Shortly after gold was discovered in the state in 1849, people began to push for a railroad that would cover the distance from St. Louis to the west coast. Construction began on July 4, 1851 on a line that would transverse the state of Missouri. The expectation was that any new line coming east from the Pacific Coast would meet the new tracks on Missouri's western border. There was no railroad west of the Mississippi when construction began.[85] The Pacific Company was chartered to undertake the ambitious project. By 1865, a western line extended to Kansas City and a Southwest Branch terminated in Rolla. A California pioneer purchased the Southwest Branch. John C. Fremont had made his fortune in the gold rush. It was Fremont who proposed a specific line from St. Louis to San Francisco. Fremont's company though, like many others after him, eventually failed. By 1876, the Southwest Branch was owned by Andrew Pierce, who purchased it at a public auction after its previous owners filed for bankruptcy. This company was the first known as the St. Louis-San Francisco Railway Company. It lasted for twenty years, a time in which track mileage increased six-fold to 1800 miles.[86] During this time, the Frisco extended its coverage to include Arkansas, Kansas, Oklahoma and Texas.

A second Frisco company was formed in 1896. A Frisco subsidiary was created in 1902. This line would provide the connection between St. Louis and Memphis, with the goal of eventually going all the way to New Orleans. The final gap between the two cities was from Nash to Lilbourn, Missouri. That link ran right through Chaffee.

As in most real estate transactions, location was one of the main attractions for the Frisco Railroad. Chaffee was roughly halfway between St. Louis and Memphis. According to early newspaper reports, Frisco promised that no lot would be sold to anyone wanting to sell "intoxicating liquors." The temperance movement would soon be sweeping the country, resulting in the 18th amendment in 1919. But the promise of no liquor in Chaffee was soon broken. Saloons were among the early businesses in town.

Chaffee's early churches demonstrated the differences in attitudes toward alcohol. The Baptists held the first church service in town, and the Methodists soon followed. By 1907, the Catholic Church had assigned a priest to the town and established its own grade school by 1918. In Chaffee and throughout northern Scott County, the German-Catholic heritage is strong. The casual acceptance of alcohol in their community did not exist with their Protestant counterparts. In an otherwise homogenous community, religion would serve as a source of tension.

Early Chaffee had all the markings of a frontier town. Gambling became such a problem that a private detective was hired to investigate.[87] Even as late as the 1920's, domestic disputes were often settled at the end of a gun barrel. In 1925, railroad worker Ivo McDaniel was shot three times. The reason? He was "caught paying undue attention to the wife of a prominent Chaffee man." McDaniel survived the shooting and was taken to a Cape Girardeau hospital for treatment. Police said the husband of the woman was responsible, but "no arrests have been made."[88]

Almost from its beginning, the railroad offered passenger service and the ability for townspeople to explore the larger world. It also offered others a chance to visit who might not otherwise. Six passenger trains departed Chaffee daily. Just who was coming and going at the town's new depot? "...In small towns the passengers remained chiefly local people on local errands; strangers who came to town most frequently were still the traveling salesmen who drank at the local taverns and stayed at the local hotel. Gypsies and traveling circuses also brought images of the outside world to small communities, the latter coming by train, the former still in their wagons drawn by horses."[89]

But larger forces than gypsies and traveling circuses had a way of intruding on life in the small town. When America entered World War I in 1917, Andrew Aubuchon of Chaffee answered the call of his country. He became the first person from Southeast Missouri killed in the war.[90] Aubuchon died as he lived – working on the railroad. Aubuchon was a Frisco Fireman before the war. In December of 1917 the Chaffee soldier was operating a locomotive engine over rails leading up to battle lines in France when he was killed. A young marine from Chaffee, James Alsobrook, was killed during the war as well. The town's American Legion post is named in their honor.

By 1914, just after World War I began and just eight years after incorporating, Chaffee was close to being the largest town in Scott County. The local paper boasted of the progress made in less than a decade.

"The city of Chaffee is logically and unquestionably the gateway to Southeast Missouri. Only eight years old, it is today a most important railroad center. Chaffee is a beautiful city of over 3,200 people and has more brick and concrete businesses, houses and substantial residences than other city of its age in Missouri."[91]

In the census of 1910, Sikeston had 3,327 residents. The cotton boom of the 1920's would begin to dramatically tip the balance to the southern end of the county.

In 1922, the cornerstone for the new high school was laid. The following school year, Chaffee High School students published their first yearbook, "The Mogul," inspired by the railroad.[92] In early yearbooks, the students showed a fascination with the technology of the age. In a senior prophecy, one student wrote that, "Tonight I sit here listening to this machine which puts the whole world within my reach." The description of radio mentions listening to KDKA in Pittsburgh, WHB in Kansas City, WGY in New York City and KSBW in St. Louis. The prophecy concludes with the realization of how the Internet of the 1920's had changed lives. "Radio....eliminates vast stretches of space and puts the familiar voices of old friends back together."

The first yearbooks also showed an entrepreneurial business community. Advertisers included Essner Brothers, which described itself in early ads as a 1920's version of a Super Wal-Mart, "dealers in everything to eat, wear and use," while the Chaffee Hardware & Undertaking Company proudly called itself, "Exclusive Dealers in Our Line." Indeed.

Early on, the school established sports teams. Basketball at Chaffee High can be traced back to at least 1915. In that year, Chaffee played at Sikeston and lost 99-11. Perhaps the new surroundings played a role. It marked the first time Chaffee had ever played a game indoors. The football team started play in the fall of 1921. The Chaffee "Bull Dogs" played to a six-six tie with Dexter on a rain soaked Chaffee field. Although there was no official playoff competition at the time, the Chaffee basketball team played in the semi-finals of a state tournament in 1922 against a team from Mexico, Missouri.[93] The Chaffee team lost the game 24-22 to McMillan High School, and legend has it the team from Scott County was so impressed by their northern rivals jumping around in their bright red uniforms, the team decided to change its name. From that day on, the Chaffee nickname became the Red Devils. The Red Devils football team became the first in Southeast Missouri (college or high school) to have a lighted football field in 1928.

For those no longer in school, amateur teams offered exercise and an escape from everyday work life. Baseball was the big amateur sport of the early 20th century, with nearly every town having a team. Often played on Sunday afternoons, the games were no walk in the park. In 1921, what was described as a "riot" broke out in a game between Chaffee and Cape Girardeau. It started after an umpire ruled a player safe on a play at second base. Words were exchanged and the argument quickly escalated. By one account, a Cape Girardeau player (Stauder) called a Chaffee player (Escal Daughtrey) a liar. When the two began fighting, all hell broke loose.

"It was then that the fans rushed on the field and under the circumstances, nothing less than a free-for-all could have been expected.
For a big ruffian like Stauder to attack Escal Daughtrey of the Chaffee diamond was like slapping the King of England."[94]

The Cape Girardeau manager had his nose broken during the brawl. While the Chaffee paper "deplored" the action, it also wasn't quite ready to end the feud with its neighbor to the north. It harshly criticized the way the incident was portrayed in the Cape Girardeau newspapers and suggested a boycott might be in order. "Business only goes where it is invited and stays only where it is well treated. Truth crushed to earth will rise again."

The first two decades of the town were exciting times. With new schools, thriving businesses, and a growing population, the landscape had changed dramatically since the days workers filled pools of water with rocks to stop the malaria plague. But Chaffee was, above all, a railroad town. Nothing reinforced that impression like the 1922 rail worker's strike. When it was all over, Chaffee would have another new item to add to its list of changes: murder.

**

The railroad industry of the 1920's served a unique role. Before jet airline travel, the interstate highway system and the trucking industry, the railroads did it all. For people, raw materials and manufactured goods, even the U.S. mail, there was only one way to quickly cross the country. Because of its powerful and unique role, the federal government regulated nearly all aspects of the industry, including how much workers were paid.

A government agency, the railroad labor board, set wages. It was calling for a ten percent pay cut for workers belonging to shop crafts. That meant that hourly wages would drop from 77 cents to 70 cents an hour. There were other issues at stake as well. "Besides the wage cut, the grievances included the virtual abolition of the 8 hour day and the contract labor system, which took thousands of jobs out of the railroad shops and beyond the reach of union contract protection."[95] Even in 1922, outsourcing was an issue. The striking workers were composed of "railway machinists, blacksmiths, sheet metal workers, boilermakers, electrical workers, and carmen and their helpers."[96] Collectively, they were known as "shopmen." On July 1, 1922, the vast majority of the nearly 400,000 shopmen across the country walked out at exactly 10 a.m. In Chaffee, an estimated 350 men walked out of the Frisco shops with only three men refusing to join the strike. [97]

The railroads were quick to note that the strike was isolated to the shop craft workers. The people who actually traveled with the trains, - engineers, firemen, conductors and so forth – were still on the job. But with the trains still running and the shopmen on strike, trouble would soon follow. One of the first places it surfaced was in Slater, Missouri.

Slater was founded in 1878. In that year, railroad tracks reached the town. The Saline County community, a hundred miles east of Kansas City, was established alongside the tracks of the Chicago and Alton railroad, which ran from Kansas City to Chicago. Just like Chaffee, it was a town controlled by the railroads. By the turn of the century, the trains employed 1,000 men in the community, many of them working in the shops. Because of the railroad, the town grew rapidly. By the early 1920's, it had a population of around four thousand, with three banks and two factories. With the railroad dominating the town's commercial life, a shop strike was destined to cause issues in the community.

Just a few days into the labor standoff, strikers seized control of the shops in Slater and placed a group of nonunion men on the first train out of town. Another group was hauled to the edge of town in cars and told to "beat it." The replacement workers, "scabs" in the eyes of union men, would get no sympathy from city officials. Even the mayor of Slater worked as a clerk in the shops. The shopmen patrolled the railroad yards and stopped every train coming through town, searching for strikebreakers. Upon discovering one such group, violence nearly erupted. "A negro porter on a sleeping car where the strikebreakers were quartered was threatened with hanging by the crowd, a railroad official said, and on his knees pleaded for his life."[98]

While the mayor of Slater insisted there would be no violence, rumblings among the railroad men suggested otherwise. "There is loose talk tonight in the streets of Slater, among the groups of union men, who stand on street corners. Some men think that violence is sure to follow any attempt by the railroad to operate its shops. All are agreed that operation will not be allowed. The town is in accord on this point."[99]

All sides in the impasse had reasons to be concerned. While railroad workers began their walkout in July, striking coal miners had been on the picket lines since the spring. Just days before the Slater takeover, twenty-one strikebreakers near the Southern Illinois town of Herrin were "shot, hanged or got their throats slashed"[100] by a mob of union sympathizers.

This time, government officials weren't taking any chances. While the governor of Missouri considered sending National Guard troops to Slater, the federal government didn't wait. On July 8th the Department of Justice ordered U.S. Marshals to the Missouri town.[101] Even with the protection of the federal government, life didn't improve noticeably for the replacement workers. "The strike-breakers are somewhat apprehensive. They are not having a very happy time of it. They were short tobacco and none could be found in Slater for them. An effort to buy 10 loaves of bread to feed these men also failed. A Negro janitor from the local train master's office was sent to buy the bread. The strikers saw where the Negro came from, and stores refused to sell him any bread."[102] Saboteurs struck a few days later. A crank shaft broke when machinery was turned on. Investigators found emery dust mixed in lubricating oil. [103]

Three hundred miles away, in the Bootheel of Missouri, a similar situation played out alongside the tracks in Chaffee. The same week striking shopmen took control in Slater, railroads began requesting help from the government over mail delivery. Frisco officials in St. Louis "requested that some action be taken at once. 'Serious trouble' was reported from Chaffee, Mo."[104] On Sunday night, July 16th, 150 Missouri National Guard troops arrived in town. By Monday morning, troops patrolled the Frisco yards and shops with machine guns mounted upon coal chutes and the roundhouse.[105] Citizens protested both the attention and the action.

"Globe-Democrat, St. Louis, MO.: Gentlemen – Your statement in today's paper that there is serious trouble at Chaffee, MO., is absolutely false. Everything is quiet here."[106]

The Mayor of Chaffee, P.L. Cordrey signed the telegraph. Local doctor and school board secretary W.O. Finney, with the blessing and backing of others in town, invited a St. Louis reporter to come to Chaffee to investigate. [107] A petition was sent to the governor of Missouri requesting the removal of the troops. The editor of the Chaffee paper was outraged over the presence of the state militia, disavowed any interference with U.S. mail, denied any mob violence had taken place, and compared the situation to an act of war, "The residents of Chaffee are all American citizens, and white citizens too, if you please, and all speak and write the English language."[108]

With both railroad workers and coal miners on strike, pressure began to build on the federal government to step in. Citing concerns over interstate commerce and the U.S. mail, the administration of President Harding began to put pressure on all sides of the railroad strike to come to an agreement. Their efforts paid off. By September, the strike officially ended and many of the shopmen across the country came back to work.

The Frisco workers at Chaffee didn't come back as quickly. By November, rumors were flying that the Frisco was considering transferring its entire operations elsewhere.[109] That same month, the machinery used to repair cars was transferred from Chaffee to the Frisco's operations in Cape Girardeau. Citizens feared the worst. One local resident said he had it on good authority that "Frisco officials have decided to move all operations from (Chaffee) and that the people were confronted with a very serious condition."

Eventually, striking workers in Chaffee went back to work. The roundhouse stayed. To a railroad-dominated town, the strike came with a heavy cost. The walkout "was accompanied by the removal of many families from town, some of them being among the very best citizens."[110] Patsy Finley Porter, a college student from Chaffee, writing a term paper at Southeast Missouri State more than two decades later, also mentioned this; "A man was murdered, and everyone else in town was afraid it would happen again." While the identity of the man is not known, the Chaffee Historical Society has visual evidence of whom it believes to be the victim of the crime. The picture shows a man hanging beneath a large tree, head slumped to one side, his hat still in place. Some think the man came to town to work as a replacement for the striking shopmen. He was removed from the local hotel by several men and subsequently hanged. "Law enforcement was unable to gather sufficient evidence to bring any suspects to trial."[111]

During the strike, the local economy stagnated. "Evenings found almost no activity on the streets because all the people were at home with doors and windows barred." Three years after the strike began, the worst fire in Chaffee's history destroyed ten downtown businesses.[112] One of two Chaffee banks, the Security Savings bank, closed its doors in November of that year.[113] As the Great Depression set in, the town's only other bank shutdown. Another local bank wasn't organized for six years.

Right at the beginning of this era, the Frisco began offering its employees the ability to purchase stock. The October 1929 announcement came one week before the great stock market crash.[114] By July of 1932, the market had declined by nearly 89%. That same year, the Frisco again declared bankruptcy. The railroad continued to operate under the auspices of trustees until the company reorganized in 1947.[115]

The bleak depression days offered few opportunities for celebration. One of the brighter days of the decade occurred after President Roosevelt took office and prohibition was repealed. It was once again legal to buy and sell alcohol. The occasion was marked by a parade in Chaffee. Three local retailers made arrangements to begin selling beer. Before the repeal, the local populace took legal and illegal actions to satisfy their urges. "Cola Beer" was marketed to residents. Ads from the 1920's describe it as being available "in bottles and at soda fountains." The drink was made in Chaffee. At the same time, there were strong suggestions that a local speakeasy flourished. "The Signal is informed that a certain joint in this town kept open all night last Saturday night, and the place is neither a café, hotel or store. Here is where a night cop would come in handy."[116]

On December 7th, 1941, everything changed. The day after the Japanese bombed Pearl Harbor Chaffee students listened on the radio as President Roosevelt addressed the nation. World War II brought dramatic changes to everyday life. "Soon there were no bananas in the stores, sugar was almost impossible to obtain, gasoline was rationed and tires were unavailable."[117] Nearly every day, Frisco trains would bring raw recruits and other solders, passing through on their way to boot camp and other destinations unknown.

> *"The servicemen had a great time whistling and yelling at the girls who just 'happened to be in that area'…but it was all innocent and good natured. Sometimes the men dashed to a drug store nearby to stock up on candy bars and cigarettes and they would always throw little scraps of paper with their names and addresses to girls passing by, hoping to receive mail. I would go down to the railroad tracks every chance I got to watch these men, wonder where they were going, and wish I was old enough to be the recipient of even one of these scraps of paper, but while they'd yell 'hi' at me, they just weren't interested in anyone as young as I was."[118]*

Patsy Finley Porter was eleven years old when the United States entered World War II. Born during the depression, she saw the impact the war had on the local economy. "At the beginning of the war, Chaffee was still reeling from the effects of the depression, and war brought prosperity of sorts. Trains were running night and day and there was work for everyone." With roundhouse operations, hundreds of railroad employees, and daily trains back and forth between St. Louis and Memphis hauling troops and machinery, citizens believed they could be the target of an attack by the Nazis. City fathers took the threat seriously. Blackouts were practiced on a regular basis.[119] As chronicled by one citizen-soldier in the winter of 1944, hundreds of the town's young men answered the call to duty.

> *"After the United States had been at war a year she (Chaffee) boasted of having a representative in every branch of the armed services. One-sixth of her entire population has answered the call to arms.*
>
> *Two years at war have brought lines to Chaffee's face. Dead are some of her favorite sons, wounded are many more and hundreds are serving on land they call not their own."*[120]

Bob Capshaw was born in 1919, the son of a Frisco railroad conductor. In the spring of 1942, he entered the army and spent three and a half years with the 31st Infantry Division. After the war, he plunged into a lifelong passion, local politics. A city councilman by 1947, he ran for county wide office three years later. He attempted to consolidate the voters on the northern end of Scott County, reminding his audiences that two other candidates for the County Collector's office were from Sikeston. He also sought to appeal to crowds based on a common heritage. Addressing an audience in a nearby town, Capshaw reminded them of the connection. "I feel perfectly at home in Illmo and Fornfelt because I know I am among railroad people. The reason that I feel at home here is the fact that my father was a railroad man for 32 years."[121] Northern Scott County did not unite in the election of 1950. Capshaw finished third in a four person race. Undeterred, he continued to run for public office, eventually winning an election as Chaffee's Mayor in 1967. He served in the post sixteen of the next twenty years.[122]

Bob and Juanita Capshaw's second child, and first son, took his father's name. Bob Capshaw, Jr. fell in love while attending the University of Missouri and later married his college sweetheart. The marriage didn't last, but Capshaw's ex-wife continued to use the last name professionally and gained fame in 1984 as Wilhelmina 'Willie' Scott in the movie, "Indiana Jones and the Temple of Doom." She later married the director of the movie. Today Kate Capshaw is best known as the wife of film-maker Steven Spielberg.

When World War II came to an end in 1945, Bob Capshaw and other sons of Chaffee returned home. A baby boom and a booming economy soon replaced world war and depression. By 1950, the town still had a population of around three thousand people. But it had three doctors who made house calls, its own hotel and theatre and daily passenger train service that connected it with anywhere in the country. Working downtown in his family's business, a teenager had a front row seat to the unfolding changes. To a first time visitor walking its streets in the 21st century, the Chaffee he remembers seems a world away.

***

It all started in the village of Rockview, just a few miles north of Chaffee. William and T.A. Essner opened for business in 1909. The slogan for Essner's General Store was "from the cradle to the grave." It wasn't just words. Shoppers could find both baby cradles and coffins inside the establishment. With the railroad town growing rapidly, the Essner brothers moved their store to Chaffee in July of 1910, becoming one of the community's first businesses. For the next seven decades, members of the Essner family would be selling something in downtown Chaffee.

William Essner had three children, two boys and a girl. When he died, the two boys took over their family business and split it into two sections, a grocery store on one side and a hardware store on the other. Their sister, Ethel, and her husband had a dry goods and men's clothing store next door.

Ethel Essner married Charlie Kielhofner in 1928. For the first eleven years of their marriage, the couple lived in an upstairs apartment in her parent's home. They had two children, both boys. Bob was the oldest, born in 1935. David came two years later.

Growing up, Bob Kielhofner spent many afternoons and weekends working in the family business. But there was also plenty of time for mischief. Each year at Halloween, he participated in one of the favorite activities of young boys, knocking over outhouses. Indoor plumbing was not universal in small town America in the 1940's.

Kielhofner also remembers one of the legends of Chaffee, passed down through generations. The story has been told in various versions through the years, but the basic gist is this: a black man was killed and hanged on a hillside overlooking the town. The Ku Klux Klan may have been involved. Given the lack of evidence, it's possible the story is apocryphal. But like other stories spread down over time, there are shreds of truth to the tale. The Ku Klux Klan did have a presence in the area.

In July of 1922, the KKK addressed a full house at the Malone Theatre in Sikeston. Klan leaders claimed 35,000 members in the state, including organizations in several Southeast Missouri communities. Chaffee was one of those towns.[123] Three months later, the Klan took out an advertisement in the Chaffee paper. The goal of the ad was "setting forth their plans for constructive methods of rectifying some of the violations of law and order." It was later noted, "Some of their recommendations are progressive."[124] That same month, a KKK messenger showed up at the Baptist Church in Chaffee attired in Klan garb. After handing the minister an envelope containing $40, he read aloud from a manuscript. While "the messenger was not revealed...the donation was well accepted and bespoke a worthy ideal."[125]

The railroad strike and subsequent hanging in town occurred during this identical timeframe. It's possible that people begin to combine elements of two separate stories. But there's also this. In 1924, three black men presented a petition to the Chaffee School Board "declaring it necessary that room was needed for negro children of Chaffee."[126] According to school law, there had to be at least fifteen black children of school age for the board to consider such a measure. Fifteen names appeared on the petition. While it's unclear if any of them actually lived in town, it was noted that "there are several negro children of school age now residing in the school districts of Rockview, Wylie, Blomeyer and Delta (neighboring towns) who will attend this school."[127] Did the possibility of an all-black school in Chaffee lead someone to take dramatic, violent action?[128] While the story of a second hanging lacks solid evidence, all of the tales indicate an attitude of hostility toward black people in the town. Kielhofner confirms that sentiment was alive and well a quarter century later when he was growing up. "No blacks would ever stay in town after six o'clock or after dark, you know. Very few came through during the daytime."

Even within the all-white community, Chaffee was not without its divisions. After class ended each day at St. Ambrose Catholic School, Kielhofner would take back alleys to his grandmother's house. Just down the street from St. Ambrose was the public elementary school. "They were always raising hell with us," remembers Kielhofner, "holler 'cat licker' at you, throw rocks at you, do stupid stuff like that." While not nearly as overt, this tension was just below the surface throughout the community. "I don't know if you could call it a bad, bad situation, it just seemed like it was there. There was this little feeling, even in the adults."

There's evidence that the Ku Klux Klan added to this tension between Catholics and Protestants. The Klan held a meeting just outside of Chaffee in 1931. About 200 people attended, including a contingent from St. Louis that took a Frisco train down to the Bootheel community. One of the organizers of the event was a local reverend. The Klan put a torch cross on the grounds of the Catholic Church.[129] Six years before, a thousand people attended a Klan picnic just south of town. A pastor from the Christian Church of Sedalia, Missouri addressed the crowd for about an hour.[130]

For his part, Kielhofner credits a priest, Father Walter Craig, for turning the situation around. When the priest arrived in town, he organized sports teams for the kids; basketball in the winter, cork ball in the summer, Kielhofner recalls. Catholic school kids would compete against their rivals from the public schools. As has happened untold times through the years, the field of athletics began closing old wounds. "It healed it," said the former St. Ambrose student, "it really got better right away." Father Craig was active throughout the community, even serving as President of the local Chamber of Commerce for a period of time. "That guy was a magician with people."

Father Craig was also unafraid to voice his opinions on issues outside the Church, even if it meant butting heads with city leaders. When funding for proposed recreational facilities for teenagers failed to materialize, the Catholic priest blamed the town's mayor. In a feud that played out on the front pages of the local paper for weeks, the two men fired charges back and forth over the facility that was to be called "Teen Town." Father Craig saw the funding failure in moral terms and wondered why the mayor couldn't see it in the same vein. "Is he ignorant of the fact that gambling houses are doing a fine business in Chaffee? Is he ignorant of the fact that minors can buy 5% beer contrary to state laws in some spots in Chaffee? Is he ignorant of the fact that certain places will sell contraceptives to 15 year old kids?"[131]

No one has called Bob Kielhofner a teenager in fifty years. After graduating from high school in 1953, Kielhofner went to the University of Missouri where he graduated from the School of Journalism. He served in the Navy until 1962 when both of his parents were killed in a car wreck. He came home to Chaffee, ran family owned businesses for a short while and briefly owned the hometown paper. He left the private sector in the early 1970's, serving as Scott County Clerk for more than two decades. Retired and living just outside the north Scott County town of Kelso, his boyhood memories are still crisp and richly described a half-century later. This is a brief piece of what he remembers; the Chaffee of the late 1940's and early 1950's, a time when the town had a different pace and pulse, a certain character, a particular energy, a time when downtown was the soul of the city.

***

It is late on a Saturday afternoon. Already, area farmers and their families have arrived and parked their vehicles in downtown. They may spend some time shopping for groceries in one of at least half a dozen stores, all of which deliver, or spend a few dollars with area merchants, many of them staying open to nine o'clock tonight, perhaps later. But primarily, they've come to town to visit with family and friends. Often, they'll just sit in their trucks, listening to the radio, people watching and patiently waiting until they see someone they recognize. The end of the long workweek is near.

The informal Saturday night social takes place every week on the downtown streets. In a few short hours, there won't be a parking spot left. At the Dinner Bell Café, outside speakers blast the day's special. Just down the street at the corner of Main and Yoakum, two enterprising teens have invested in a popcorn maker and sell the snack to passersby. Across the street is the Byrd Hotel. Frisco officials stay here when they come to Chaffee. Downstairs in the hotel is one of the town's finer restaurants. Next to the Byrd is the Horstman Theatre, providing first run movies, weekly serials and news from around the world. Until television arrived, the only images of World War II battlefields that townspeople saw originated here. In 1938, then Senator Harry S. Truman delivered a speech at the theatre, becoming the only future, former, or current President to make an appearance in the Bootheel community.[132]

The movie theatre is owned by the Montgomery family. Like Bob and David Kielhofner, Morris and Paul David Montgomery are sons of a downtown merchant. Their job on a Saturday afternoon is to make the popcorn for tonight's moviegoers. They often enlist Bob's help. The teenagers will spend hours completing their task. The finished product will be sold for a nickel a bag tonight. They rush to finish their work so they can go home and get ready to go out. The Horstman will have two showings this evening, and if a teenage boy is lucky enough, he will take his date to the late show and sit in the best possible seats — up in the balcony.

When the movie ends, the teenagers cruise the streets of town. Heading down north Main Street, they'll pass the Gray Motor Company, which proudly displays the new Plymouths and Desotos. It's not far from the Chaffee Ice and Coal Company. The coal heats the home furnaces in the winter months, while blocks of ice keep refrigerators cold year round. Turning around and heading back down Yoakum, named after a former Frisco general manager and chairman, stops may include Slaughter's for an ice cream soda or a milkshake, or perhaps on out to Highway 55 for a game of pinball at Johnny's Koffee Kup.[133] If they're feeling really adventurous, and perhaps a bit mischievous, they'll climb the walls of the city swimming pool for a late night dip.

The late night hours mean downtown merchants can finally dim their lights. Charlie and Ethel Kielhofner have closed the family store and are now gathered around their kitchen table. In the summertime, the windows are open; there is no air conditioning. While the dropping temperatures have provided some relief, the air is still thick in the former swampland of Southeast Missouri. Occasionally, the stillness of the night is pierced by the whistle of a passing Frisco train. They count the receipts from the week's business. Their income will depend on how well their store has performed. The couple relaxes with a few beers and snacks. Both their sons, Bob and David, are in bed but not asleep. They strain to listen to every word their parents are saying. They're talking about the day at the store, trading the latest gossip, maybe making plans for a Sunday gathering. Perhaps a radio is on in the background; television has yet to broadcast in Southeast Missouri.[134] It is these quiet family moments that a son remembers most. Tomorrow means mass at the Catholic Church and the one day the entire family can relax and be together. Early Monday morning the six-day workweek begins anew.

***

As a teenager, Kielhofner spent many afternoons and weekends working in the family grocery and hardware stores. He'll never forget the day when a man came into the back of the store and made a confession. "(I was) putting together wagons and lawnmowers in the backroom of the warehouse. And this old man came in there and sat down with me and said, 'I just stabbed a guy down at the tavern.'" It was O.T. Turner, the man who stabbed former sheriff John Hobbs. The teenager could tell Turner had been drinking, but didn't know what to make of his claim. "I thought he was harmless," remembers Kielhofner. "I didn't say nothing." The store was just down the street from Hobbs bar. Turner soon left and it wasn't much longer before he was arrested just outside of town.

Like a lot of Chaffee boys, Kielhofner played football in high school. He also shared another trait with some of his teammates. He had to sneak out of the house to start practice his junior year. His mother didn't want him to play the sport. Football also meant a break from work at the family store, something Kielhofner did after school and on weekends. So did his good friend Bob Miller. One year apart in school, Kielhofner and Miller both attended St. Ambrose. Starting their freshman year, Kielhofner attended Chaffee High School while Miller commuted to St. Mary's, the Catholic school in Cape Girardeau. Kielhofner remembers his friend as lightning quick on the basketball court. It was Miller's athletic ability that made him a natural as a running back, thought Kielhofner. One summer, he badgered his buddy about going to school at Chaffee and trying out for the football team, a sport not offered at St. Mary's. Miller eventually relented. The pestering by Kielhofner and other teammates paid off. Miller would go to Chaffee that fall and join his friends in two-a-day August practices. The experiment didn't last long. "He checked out his equipment and he went to two practices," said Kielhofner, "and here comes his mother and jerks him off the field, sent him back to Cape." Miller returned to St. Mary's. It would be one of the few times that basketball would win out over football in Chaffee.

One Saturday in late November, 1951, the two teenagers were working together downtown at Essner's Grocery Store but managed to take off work early. Basketball season had started and the finals of the Delta Tournament were that evening. The two Chaffee teenagers made the ride over together in Miller's Mercury. Kielhofner would watch the game from the stands. Miller would be playing for St. Mary's. Their opponent was the Puxico Indians, the defending state champions. Just as impressive, the Indians had won an incredible forty-five games in a row. The Puxico talent and their unique style awed Kielhofner. He had seen them play in the finals of the state tournament in Cape Girardeau the season before. On the short ride over to the gym, he thought about the task facing his friend. Nobody can beat Puxico, he thought. Nobody.

CHAPTER THREE
Wonder Boys of Stoddard County
1945-1952

"I never had a pair of shoes that weren't all hand-me-downs
and daddy's morning coffee came from ol' left over ground
My mama wore no jewelry or any store bought stuff
And home was on a hillside forty miles from Poplar Bluff"

"Forty miles from Poplar Bluff"
Written by Larry Kingston and Frank Dycus
From the album "Porter Wayne and Dolly Rebecca" (Porter Wagoner
and Dolly Parton)

In August of 2003, residents in the town of Puxico, Missouri gathered to dedicate the naming of their high school gymnasium. Puxico, a town of 1,145 situated about twenty miles from Poplar Bluff and roughly forty-five miles from Sikeston, had long had a proud basketball tradition. The hundred or so attendees in the crowd that night, many of them elderly, came to remember a man who died more than thirty years before and whom some of them probably hadn't seen in a half-century. One by one, speakers came to the podium to praise the coach their gym was now named for: Arnold Ryan. Puxico graduate and former player Forest Arnold described it best for many in the crowd when he said, "coach Ryan was ten years ahead of his time. He was playing fast break run and gun basketball years before it ever had a name."

Ryan coached at Puxico in the 1940's and '50's, and his legacy lives on in high school gyms across the region. To this day, there are people in Southeast Missouri who will tell the story that "Hoosiers," the 1987 movie starring Gene Hackman as the coach of a small town Cinderella basketball team, was actually inspired by Ryan and one of his Puxico squads (it was not – the movie is based on a 1954 team from Milan, Indiana). But Ryan's exploits need no embellishment. While his accomplishments never made it to the silver screen, one cannot tell the story of Missouri high school basketball history without including the Puxico Indians and its coach. Looking back now decades later, their story has added significance. When Ryan's teams were blitzing teams throughout the state more than fifty years ago, a young Puxico boy by the name of Ronnie Cookson was sitting in the stands. Two of his older brothers and a cousin were in uniform.

When Ryan arrived to coach basketball at Puxico in the fall of 1945, he was starting a new career. He had never coached a basketball team in his life. The new coach had a lot to learn. So did his players. The previous coach, described as a "bachelor and ex-marine" liked to treat his team to cigarettes at halftime and beers after a win.[135] He lasted all of one year in Puxico, Missouri. There would be no more smokes or cold ones for Puxico players once Arnold Ryan arrived. If you wanted to play basketball for the Indians, there was only one way – the Ryan way. A local newspaper once described the rules the coach had for his players: "1. Be in bed by 10:30 and sooner if possible. 2. Eat plenty of oranges; 3. No soda or candy; 4. No drinking or smoking. Dating was authorized so long as it falls within the training regulations and doesn't interfere with basketball." [136]

Ryan was also devoutly religious, insisting that his players attend a church service every Sunday. Morning, noon or night. Weekdays or weekends. It didn't matter. To play basketball at Puxico meant being under the watchful eye of their coach. It wasn't just the players. Years later, former player Grady Smith remembered that era. "There was a period of time there that Mr. Ryan had 99 percent control of the cheerleaders, the athletes, the student body, the parents, the whole community."[137] The community of Puxico didn't know all of this in the fall of 1945, but just as World War II was coming to a close, it was about to enter a golden age of high school basketball.

Arnold Ryan was born in 1916. His family owned farmland in Mississippi, but as the boll weevil ravaged crops and farm prices dropped, the Ryans went in search of richer soil. First in Arkansas and then in Missouri, the family worked on farms, helping grow and harvest crops. Arnold spent many hours in his youth picking and chopping cotton. He graduated from high school in the New Madrid County town of Marston and wanted to go to college, but the family couldn't afford it. Ryan chose to join the Army. After a short stint in the military, he returned to Missouri. By this time, his parents had bought a farm near Puxico. Looking for a job in the area, he found one as a teacher at a one-room schoolhouse, making seventy-five dollars a month. A local farmer, Odus Cookson, recommended Arnold for the job because he knew his father.

In the spring of 1939, Arnold married the former Nola Perkins. In August, the newlyweds moved in with the Cooksons as Arnold started his teaching career. It would be six more years before he began his coaching career. Odus and wife Agnes had three sons living at home at the time; 13-year-old Joseph Thomas (J.T.), eight-year old Ancel, and four-year-old Carroll. A fourth Cookson son, Ronnie, would arrive in 1944.

The Cookson name is both popular and longstanding in Stoddard County. James Cookson settled in the area after the Civil War. He married three times, outliving his first two wives. He had children by all three. Odus was one of his sons by his second marriage. James farmed the land of Stoddard County, eventually acquiring 200 acres.[138]

While farming has always been an important part of the rural economy, it was the timber industry around Puxico that attracted the attention of businessmen and the railroads. Occupying Stoddard County in 1862, Confederate soldiers took notice of the trees. "Some of the timber is of remarkable size, many tulip trees exceeding six feet in circumference, six feet above the ground." It was claimed that 83 different varieties of timber grew in the area.[139] With the railroad making its way through the region in the early 1880's, the town of Pucksekaw was established. But because the name was "not only hard to remember, but hard to spell," it was changed to Puxico. By 1884, the T.J. Moss tie company had established its headquarters in Puxico, eventually becoming the state's largest supplier of railroad ties.[140]

With the vast Mingo swamps nearby, large tracts of land were uninhabitable in Stoddard County around the turn of the century. Local residents established their own drainage district. But attempts to drain the land "were never completely successful. Mingo never did dry up."[141] During the depression, the Mingo Drainage District went bankrupt. The land was eventually sold to the federal government and the Mingo National Refuge was created in 1945, the same year that Arnold Ryan began coaching at Puxico.

The family that helped him get his start would eventually supply him with players but the Cookson's oldest son was not among them. J.T.

did not play basketball. His parents believed he should spend his time working on the farm, not playing sports. As a teenager, he dreamed of owning a car. When he was 17, he bought a 1934 Chevy with the help of his parents. One night on the way to Poplar Bluff, J.T. let a friend drive while he and his girlfriend were passengers in the backseat. On a hillside curve, the driver lost control of the vehicle. The car went off the road, flipped over, and J.T. was sent crashing through the soft top of the vehicle. He couldn't move. The accident severed his spine and paralyzed him. He would spend the rest of his life in a wheel chair. He spent months in the hospital, first in Poplar Bluff, and later in St. Louis. During his stay in Poplar Bluff, Ryan "visited him everyday.....everyday," according to Carroll. Before he made his daily trek to Poplar Bluff, Ryan, who no longer lived with the Cooksons, would check in with Ancel and Carroll to make sure the boys were all right. The young Cookson boys lived at home by themselves during this period, as their parents spent the night with J.T. in Poplar Bluff. Before he ever played for him, Carroll had a deep respect for the high school coach.

Ancel would be the first Cookson to play for Ryan. He was a freshman during Ryan's first season at Puxico. There was just one problem. At less than 100 pounds and under five feet tall, Ancel was so much smaller than his teammates, the coach was afraid of what might happen to him during a game. He made him the team ball boy instead. Ancel was disappointed but went along, anything to be at the gym and with the team. Returning home after a Friday night road game, the team was unloading the bus when Ryan noticed something was missing. The ball boy had left the balls behind. The next day, Ryan drove out to the Cookson farm. Ancel and his father were working outside. Ryan told them he'd been out that morning retrieving the basketballs left behind the night before. He told Ancel there was just one thing left to do. Ancel expected punishment. Instead, he got a uniform. He was now a player for the Puxico Indians. Ancel would play basketball for Ryan for the next four years. He eventually started his senior season, but not before getting a dose of the Ryan discipline. The night before the first game, Ancel broke the 10 o'clock curfew, arriving home ten minutes late. The next night, he watched the game from the bench. At one point, he stood up and yelled at the cheerleaders, "How about a cheer for the boys on the bench?"[142] Later that season, he scored 32 points in a game (the school record at the time). That record breaking game would be the last win for the '49 Indians. They would lose their next game and not make it to the state playoffs.

During Ryan's first four seasons, the team had a winning record each year. The '48 team made it to the state playoffs, but lost in the first round. Ryan's goal of a state championship had proved elusive thus far. That was about to change. When it counted the most, one of the Cookson Clan played a pivotal role in the biggest game of his life.

Puxico entered its sixth season under Ryan in the fall of 1950 as a favorite to win state. In September, the St. Louis Post-Dispatch profiled the Indians and prophesied great days ahead. "...here's a good tip, it (Puxico) will be the home of a state champion if coach Ryan and Winfred Wilfong have anything to say about it."[143] The season before, Puxico had fallen just short, losing in the state semi-final game to eventual champion Ozark. The Indians best player, Winfred Wilfong, had played that game with the flu, and fouled out near the end. Puxico would win the next night and claim third place in Class B (small schools). Wilfong was a freshman on the '48 team that lost in the first round of state play. Ryan was so upset by that experience that he left the next day with his freshmen players (the upperclassman were allowed to stay behind to watch the tournament). The day after returning to Puxico, they scrimmaged on a Saturday morning for three hours. Those freshmen were now seniors, and that was a big reason why they were expected to perform so well. They didn't disappoint.

Even by today's standards, the 1950-51 Puxico Indians produced eye-popping statistics. They averaged 89 points a game and broke the 100-point barrier thirteen times. The '51 University of Kentucky team coached by Adolph Rupp won a college basketball national championship that season averaging slightly less than 75 points.[144] They called it "run-shoot-run", Ryan's fast break style of basketball. Coupled with his full court pressure defense, Ryan's teams generated numbers that are still hard to believe. They won a game that year by the score of 148 to 16. Their next three games they scored 131, 131, and 142.

True to its timber heritage, Puxico played its games in a log gymnasium. Completed in 1936, the building was "made from native cypress timber and was reportedly the largest log structure in the world."[145] The gym had seating for around 500 people, large enough to accommodate most of the town's 749 residents at the time. It wasn't big enough. By the early 1950's, the gym couldn't hold the crowds that were showing up to see the Indians play. In the 1952 season, the team only played ten games on its home-court. The overflow crowds that followed the Indians forced them to move their games to bigger courts such as those in Poplar Bluff and Cape Girardeau.

Fans literally shattered glass to see Puxico play basketball. Newspapers across the state followed their exploits. "The St. Louis Globe Democrat called Puxico 'that magic name' and called the Indians the wonder team of Stoddard County.'"[146] Just how good was this team? Decades later, Mike Eisenbath of the *St. Louis Post-Dispatch* put it in perspective. "All five starters (on the '51 team) played basketball on the NCAA Division 1 Level. Two were drafted by National Basketball Association teams."[147] Every year, Ryan would talk to his players at practice and during class about winning a state championship. In his sixth season at Puxico, that dream would come true.

In the fall of 1950, Ryan began his days as he had the previous seasons, opening the gym at 6:30 a.m. From early morning until often late at night, someone would be dribbling and shooting basketballs at Puxico High School. When practice ended, the coach would shuttle any player who needed a ride home. After going home for dinner, Ryan often returned to the streets of Puxico, making sure his players met their ten o'clock curfew. It was almost never a problem. These players had been around Ryan since junior high. They knew the rules and knew what he expected of them.

On those early mornings years ago, a parade of talent would meet Ryan at the gym that included two future NBA draft picks. Winfred "Win" Wilfong was the best player in the state of Missouri his senior season. The 6' 2" forward scored 54 points in one game and only played about two quarters. Forest Arnold knew next to nothing about the game of basketball when his family moved to Puxico his freshman year. He once asked his coach, "What's a zone?"[148] Like with many of his players, Ryan helped Arnold put up a basketball goal at home. A good leaper, the 6' 5" Arnold could easily dunk a ball.

Although not a starter, one of the best shooters on the team was a 5'7" guard and another member of the Cookson Clan. Leon Cookson grew up on a farm outside Puxico. He was one class in front of his cousin

Carroll. Leon's dad worked as an engineer on the Frisco Railroad. Leon first met Arnold Ryan when he was in seventh grade. At the country school he attended, Ryan taught grades 5 through 8. Ryan's wife Nola taught the younger students. It was in seventh grade that his new teacher introduced him to the game of basketball. That season also marked the beginning of Ryan's coaching career at Puxico. Each day after classes ended, Ryan walked from the school into town to begin basketball practice. But before he arrived at the log gym, he had already spent hours coaching and thinking about the game he loved. According to Cookson, many of the plays and drills he remembered in high school began on the dirt court outside the one room schoolhouse. "It was at that school that he designed a lot of his plays. The warm-up play that we had in high school he developed while I was in 7th grade." That particular drill consisted of players in six different spots on the court and focused on the fundamentals: passing, cutting, screening and shooting. It was a warm-up exercise that Cookson never forgot. Later in life, when he became a coach, he had his teams use the identical drill.

Talk to any of the Ryan men and a consistent story emerges. Their coach made the game fun for kids and kept them constantly motivated. One of the ways Ryan did this was by a chart that he kept on the wall as his players entered the gym. The chart had everyone's name on it and that particular week on the calendar. Players had to track how many shots they had taken. "When you looked on the chart and some of your buddies had shot seven-hundred or eight-hundred or a thousand shots and maybe you'd been busy and hadn't got around to shooting much and had around one-hundred or two-hundred, that looked bad," remembers Cookson. "The peer pressure kind of kept us all working on our shooting games."

Shooting a basketball was the one fundamental that Ryan stressed the most. To accommodate his players, Ryan kept the gym open year round. Even in the summer time, scrimmaging took precedent over dating on Friday and Saturday night. "All summer long, there would be fifteen, twenty, twenty-five people – it varied – kids up there playing ball. We'd just choose up, five on five, we'd play like a quarter and the winners got to stay on the floor." After a few hours of playing basketball, Cookson recalls, "we'd get with our girls then. We'd go to a drive-in theatre or the local drug store."

By the end of his sophomore year, Cookson began to get serious about basketball. In the summer of 1949, he decided to do something many of his teammates had done: put up a goal at his house. The task was made difficult by the situation at home. "My father was working away all the time on the Frisco railroad during the week and my mother was there with four younger brothers and sisters and myself. I just kind of did what I did on my own."

Cookson started from scratch. The first thing he needed was a goal post. He spotted a white oak tree on the family farm that was about the diameter of an electric pole. He chopped it down and trimmed all the limbs off. He then got his grandfather's tractor and pulled it up close to his house. With a drawknife, he peeled all the bark off. After letting the post sit in the sun for about a week, he painted it white. He made a square backboard from some cypress boards that were sitting down by the barn. With the post painted and a backboard in place, all he needed now was a goal. Nothing around the farm fit the description of what he needed. He decided to have one made. "I went down to the local blacksmith shop there in Puxico. Mr. Green was the blacksmith, and I asked him if he could make me a goal." The blacksmith said he could. He charged Cookson three dollars. Leon painted his new goal bright orange. He mounted it to the backboard and took precise measurements on the post before it went into the ground. He wanted the height to be exactly ten feet. He got an old net from the high school and secured it around the goal with tape. With the help of an uncle, he put it into the ground. For the next two years, Cookson would shoot baskets on the dirt court outside his house. On a clear moonlit night, he would shoot for hours. The geography also made him focus on following up. "I would have to shoot on a hill. It was relatively level where I shot. But if the ball bounced just right, it would roll down the hill. I would really follow my shots so I wouldn't have to go all the way down that hill chasing the basketball."

Leon's senior year, the 1950-51 season was not without controversy. Junior Grady Smith joined the Indians that season, transferring from nearby Advance. Grady's move to Puxico also brought charges of illegal recruiting from other coaches and towns, especially his former school. The drama would play out over many months. After Puxico finished third in the state his sophomore season, Smith made it known that he had an interest in transferring. Smith would later admit that residents of Puxico, including a school board member, showed up at his house, trying to convince his parents to make the move.[149] When school started in the fall, he went to Advance the first day. By the second day, he had changed his mind and boarded a bus to Puxico (where his family lived was close to the school district borders). Carroll Cookson says he remembers Smith getting off the bus that morning and being greeted by Arnold Ryan. Ryan told him, according to Cookson, that he could go to school at Puxico, but he couldn't play ball there. If any type of recruiting was involved Cookson believed the coach didn't have anything to do with it. But when Advance officials refused to sign for the transfer, he wound up back at his original school. Finally, the matter seemed settled when Smith's parents made it official and moved to the Puxico School District. Grady would be eligible to play in the middle of December.

The Grady Smith recruiting controversy would be the only blemish on an otherwise perfect season. The season tipped off with what would be a common occurrence – a blowout victory. After beating Piedmont by 55 points, a reporter told Ryan he had the best team in the state. "No sir", Ryan quickly fired back. "I have the two best basketball teams in the state. My second team can beat anybody."[150]

The Piedmont game served as a warm-up for a much-anticipated rematch with Ozark, the 1950 state champs. Puxico had revenge on its minds after the loss the previous season. Puxico won the game by ten points; an early indication that it would be a force to reckon with all year long.

In their third game that season, Puxico defeated Lutesville and did something they would do 12 more times that season – score 100 points. In their next twenty-six games, only twice did they win by less than ten points. A game against Fisk was the closest all season. Puxico played without both Forest Arnold and Grady Smith and won the game 58-53. In a second rematch with defending state champion Ozark, the Indians won by nine. The Puxico Indians ended the regular season 29-0.

The march to the state championship in Missouri back in the 1950's consisted of three rounds of play; the sub-regional, the regional, and the sweet sixteen state tournament. High school basketball's second season was and is a one and out affair.[151] Winners survive to play another day; the loser's have a long off-season to think about what might have been and to get ready for next year. Coaches have to take into consideration the impact of not only the game their team is playing that day but keeping the team motivated and sharp for their next opponent. Part of that preparation means that starters need to play, to stay in shape, and keep their edge. In post-season tournaments, first round games, where the highest seeded and best teams take on the lowest seeded and worst teams, often produce blowouts. It's a pattern we will see later on with both Carroll and Ronnie Cooksons' teams. But perhaps the mother of all blowout basketball games occurred when Puxico took to the floor against Greenville in the first round of the sub-regional in 1951. The Indians led 34-4 after one quarter. Their offense stayed just as hot during the second quarter and their defense got better. It was 71-5 at the half. Win Wilfong scored 54 points, playing in two quarters. Greenville was overwhelmed by the Puxico press with Wilfong frequently stealing the inbound pass, quickly scoring a bucket and just as quickly, returning the ball to his stunned opponent. With Wilfong on the bench for much of the second half, Puxico scored even more points. The final score was 148-16. It's a game that's still a source of resentment and bitterness for some. Years later, Carroll Cookson had a school official at Poplar Bluff tell him he never liked Puxico for what it did to Greenville that day in 1951.

The onslaught continued. Puxico scored 131 each time in its next two games, beating Naylor by 87 points and defeating Bunker by 84. In the sub-regional championship game, Ryan's team came close to matching their output against Greenville. Puxico won by a score of 142-41 over Annapolis. In regional action, the Indians only cracked the 100 point barrier once, in a 104-54 win over Oran, but no one came within twenty-seven points of Ryan's team. Puxico entered state play with a 36-0 record. Only four games stood between them and an undefeated state championship season.

The Puxico Indians arrived at Cape Girardeau's Houck Field House on Monday, March 6, 1951 with hundreds of fans watching their every move. There was no ballgame Monday night, just a late afternoon practice session. With a perfect record, a fast paced style, and talent on par with any high school team in the nation, Puxico basketball had created a buzz not just around the Bootheel but all over the state. Over the next several nights, fans would jam Houck Field House to see a team that was averaging 90 points a game while allowing its opponents only

43. Their overwhelming style of play demoralized their opponents early. Rarely had Puxico played a fourth quarter that had any meaning. That would soon change. In the interim, run-shoot-run was once again off to the races.

The Indians opened play on Tuesday night against Dixon. Before the game, the Dixon players commented, "We'll give them all we got. We're not afraid of them."[152] It didn't take long for the players to realize that all they "got" wasn't good enough. With an estimated four hundred people turned away from the gate and a standing room only crowd inside stacked "like cordwood," Puxico doubled up Dixon in the first half, leading 36 to 18. With the Indians fast break and full court pressure overwhelming their opponent, Puxico won the game going away 80-45. One eyewitness account of the game provided a description of the Indians style.

> *"Spectators got a thrill from their style of play that keeps the opposing team under constant pressure. The Indians meet them under the defensive end of the goal and play them over the whole court, not simply half of it.*
> *Time after time, a Puxican would steal the ball from a Dixon player, and each time a shout would go up. There was the underdog sympathy for Dixon apparent in the crowd, but it can't be denied that playing in their home territory, the Indians were the darlings of the show."*[153]

The "darlings of the show" moved on to the quarterfinal round against Skidmore. Different night. Same results. This time, Puxico racked up a tournament record for points as the Indians easily outdistanced their opponent 97-43. Once again, Ryan's team attacked from the opening tip, leading 31 to 9 at the end of the first quarter. The only thing that prevented the Indians from breaking the century mark was a fourth quarter stall by Skidmore.

With Puxico routing its opponents in the state tournament much like it had done during the regular season, there was considerable speculation that week in Cape Girardeau about whether the Class B champion (small schools) would play the Class A (large schools) winner in a one game playoff. Ultimately, the decision was made not to pursue it. Citing "undue commercialization of the game and the boys who play it" as well as extending the season "beyond reasonable limits,"[154] the Missouri State High School Activities Association nixed the idea.

During that same week, the *Southeast Missourian* put a picture of a high school basketball team on its sports page. John S. Cobb High School in Cape Girardeau had qualified for state tournament play. However, the team would not be playing in front of the hometown crowd. Cobb High School was all black. The team was traveling to Jefferson City to the campus of Lincoln University to play in the Negro high schools' state tournament. Cobb lost its first round game to Joplin, the eventual Negro league champion. But while the buzz in Cape Girardeau that week wondered if the Class B winner would face the Class A champion, no one speculated about any of these all-white teams playing a championship black squad. It simply would not happen. Separate but equal was still the law of the land in 1951. It applied to academics and to athletics.

Two games away from an undefeated season and a state championship, the legend of Puxico basketball continued to grow. Two hours before the doors even opened to the Indians semi-final contest against Morehouse, another Bootheel team, fans started lining up outside the entrance doors. When the doors finally opened with an estimated one thousand spectators waiting outside, the crush of movement was overwhelming. As fans rushed to get inside, plate glass in two of the doors shattered. At least two people were cut by the shards.[155] On one side of the stadium, a window was broken as people rushed to get inside any way they could. Carroll Cookson remembers even the Indians resorted to novel tactics to help get people inside the gym. One of Arnold Ryan's relatives needed a way into the game. "We had those old army duffle bags that we used to bring in basketballs," remembers the Puxico guard. When the Indians arrived to enter the stadium, one of the duffle bags was used to carry different cargo– the coach's nephew.

When Puxico and Morehouse finally got underway in the jam-packed stadium, the Indians found themselves briefly trailing their opponent. Morehouse opened up with a 4-0 lead. But by the end of the first quarter, the Indians had caught and surpassed their Bootheel rival, whom they had already beaten three times that season. A seven point first quarter lead was stretched to a thirteen- point lead by halftime. Puxico won its fourth match-up with Morehouse and its 39th game of the year in convincing fashion, 85-61. Only one game separated the Indians from a perfect season.

The Waynesville Tigers entered the championship game against Puxico as a heavy underdog. Even against the best the state had to offer, Puxico had demonstrated that it was in a different league from its opponents. During the first three rounds of state tournament play, the Indians had averaged slightly more than 87 points per game that produced an average margin of victory of nearly 38 points, numbers not at all unlike what they put up during the regular season. No one could play the whirlwind, non-stop, up and down the court style like the Indians. Even Waynesville recognized that. That's why they didn't even try. The Tigers employed a slow down brand of basketball Puxico fans didn't recognize. But what Waynesville didn't realize was that the Indians had a secret weapon on the bench – a member of the Cookson Clan.

Leon Cookson knew from his warm-ups that night that something special might happen. "We were out there just after we ran our warm-up and just shooting. I was shooting my long set shots. I shot a one handed set shot. I shot about NBA range. I liked to have a lot of room; I didn't like to be hurried. I had shot out there that night and I remember thinking I'm hot tonight." Cookson began keeping track of how many he could make in a row. "I hit ten straight out there - I counted them. I hit ten straight before I missed one."

When the game got underway, Cookson was in his customary spot on the bench. Typically, the 5' 7" guard would enter the game in the second quarter. Not on this night. With Waynesville ball handler Kenny Foster handling the Puxico press, and the Tigers zone defense causing trouble for the Indians, Arnold Ryan made his move early. Just as Morehouse had done, Waynesville jumped out to a 4-0 lead. With his team struggling, Ryan told Cookson to get into the game, much to his surprise. "I was startled," remembers Cookson. "He said get your shot – take it." It didn't take him long. "I came down the floor and got a shot. They were sitting back in a two three zone. They (Waynesville) didn't know me, they knew about all these other players, so naturally they're going to let me shoot. It's not a high percentage shot. So I fired away out there, and it didn't hit nothing but the bottom of the net." The Stoddard County teenager who spent countless hours shooting baskets by moonlight got his chance to shine in the spotlight. Another Puxico trip down the court, another long-range shot by Cookson. It too was good. The Arnold Ryan move had paid immediate dividends. The first quarter ended in a tie, 9-9. Cookson wasn't done.

"I remembered the ball went out of bounds on a possession we had when we were right in front of our bench. Win Wilfong in-bounded the ball to me. I'm about a 45-degree angle from the goal, approximately 22 feet from the basket. I faked like I was going to shoot." Cookson really had no intention of shooting the ball. Just then, he heard a familiar voice from the bench. "I heard coach Ryan right behind me say, 'Shoot it!' I kind of reloaded and bent my knees and put it up there and it didn't hit anything but the bottom of the net." Adding a fourth jump shot and a free throw, Cookson's nine first half points help spark his team to a 25-14 halftime lead. But Waynesville refused to give in.

The Tigers rallied in the third quarter, outscoring Puxico by twelve points to cut the lead to six. Cookson's first half shooting may have come as a surprise to Waynesville, but they were prepared in the second half. "I played a little bit, but not much. They came out on me. They got more aggressive with their defense." The combination of the Tigers defense and their ability to break the Puxico press frustrated the Indians all night long. With two minutes to go in the game, Waynesville trailed by three. Sitting on the Puxico bench, a thought occurred to Leon Cookson that hadn't crossed his mind all season. "That was the first time all year long I thought we could get beat. It was close." The tenacity of the Tigers forced Puxico into doing something it had never done before. "We were holding the ball trying to run out the clock for the first time that whole season." The stall worked. Waynesville never got any closer. Their valiant bid for an upset came up just short. Arnold Ryan's Puxico Indians had a perfect 40-0 season and a state title, winning the game 42-38. Puxico's best player, Win Wilfong, led the Indians in scoring with 11 points. Second highest on the team was Leon Cookson's nine point effort off the bench.

The end of the 1951 season broke up one of the greatest collections of talent in high school basketball history. The next season, Win Wilfong would be playing basketball at the University of Missouri. As a sophomore, he achieved All-Big Seven conference honors. Drafted into the Army, Wilfong later returned to college ball at Memphis State. During his senior season, Wilfong became the Tigers first All-American while leading Memphis State to a second place finish in the NIT tournament. The St. Louis Hawks selected him in the first round of the NBA draft in the spring of 1957. His first year in the pros, he was part of an NBA championship team. Wilfong died in 1985 at the age of 52, a victim of cancer. He was remembered by St. Louis Globe-Democrat columnist Rich Koster. "Before and after his professional career, Wilfong was a Puxico High School Indian. He was *always* a Puxico Indian."[156]

Leon Cookson started his college basketball career at a junior college in Mississippi. He later transferred to Memphis State but never got the opportunity to play for the Tigers. He was drafted into the army during the Korean War. Returning home to Puxico after the service, he taught school for a brief period and did some factory work in St. Louis. Eventually, he decided to get serious about his education and returned to Memphis State, graduating with his degree in the summer of 1958. Looking for a teaching job in Southeast Missouri, the first person he thought about calling was Arnold Ryan. Cookson recalls his former coach's reply to his request for help. He said "we'll go to Missouri, spend the weekend, I know three or four superintendents and we'll see what we can come up with." What they discovered was a job opening for a grade school teacher in Scott City. Cookson signed a contract to teach fourth grade for $3,400 a year. The next year, he moved up to teach junior high and also start the school's junior high basketball program. Eventually, he became the high school coach.

The first Cookson vs. Cookson high school basketball game in the Bootheel didn't involve Ronnie, but rather Carroll against his cousin Leon. It happened during Carroll's first year at Advance. The game turned on an unusual play. "There was a jump ball and I think they had the players turned wrong. Nobody called it or saw it, but anyway, they scored a basket in our goal and as the game wore on we ended up winning by one point. He (Carroll) always said, we won that game for you," Leon remembers with a smile. That would be the only time the two coaches would meet. The following season, Leon took a job at Fox High School in Arnold, where he taught and coached the rest of his career. He still appreciates his days as a Puxico Indian and the coach that made it all possible. "Coach Ryan was always influential in my life. Seems like he was always around when I needed him to be."

***

In the fall of 1951, with Leon off to college, it was time for another Cookson to emerge. Carroll saw little playing time as a junior. That would soon change. A profile of the Indians that season described him this way. "A Lilliputian among a host of Gullivers, (Cookson) is the sparkplug that helps make the team go. His height, 5 feet 6 inches, may look out of place, but ability places him as tall as any of the giants he competes with."[157]

Leon agreed with the sparkplug description of his cousin. "He was quick, he had good ball sense, he loved to play. He teamed up with Gene an awful lot on the pressure defense – knew how they were going to trap. Carroll was a scrappy, quick, competitive, little guard. I think that's what Arnold liked about him."

Gene was Gene Wilfong, Win's younger brother. Carroll and Gene would form the new backcourt tandem for the Puxico Indians. With three starters graduated and everyone in the state gunning for Ryan's squad, their task was formidable. How do a team and a coach top an undefeated championship run? For one thing, it ventures outside the borders of the state. The Show-Me Kings would soon leave a mark in Razorback Country.

The 1951-52 Puxico Indians opened their season with home and away match-ups against Greenway, Arkansas. On November 16, 1951, the Indians tipped off their season at the log gym in Puxico against the Greenway Tigers and Ryan's team let everyone know the basketball cupboard wasn't bare. Puxico won the game 90-25 with eleven different players scoring points for the Indians.

Exactly one week later, the teams met on a Friday night in Piggott, Arkansas. The game was moved from Greenway to the larger gym in Piggott to accommodate the overflow crowd. The day the Indians arrived in town, the front-page headline in the *Piggott Banner* read, "Best High School Team in Nation To Play Here." Greenway coach Troy Walls told the paper that everyone should come out to watch Puxico. "They play clean and beat your ears off doing it. They rarely ever foul and put on the finest scoring show you ever saw in high school. My team will know a little more about them, but fans should not come out expecting us to beat them for better teams than mine lost to them last year by wide margins. We are just going to give them the best scrap we can."[158]

In a steady downpour of rain that afternoon, fans started arriving from all over Northeast Arkansas and Southeast Missouri. Well before the 7:30 p.m. scheduled tip-off, the gym was "packed to the rafters."[159] The Greenway coach describes the setting. "There was so many people there at six o'clock," remembers Walls. "Couldn't play on the whole court there was so many people there. They had to lock the doors to keep everybody out. They could have had twice that many."

When the game finally got underway, Puxico sent signals this night would be a repeat of the previous Friday. At the end of the first quarter, the Indians led 23-2. At this point of the game, with his team already down by 21 points and having lost to Puxico already by a large margin the previous week, Greenway coach Walls made a decision that would stick with him the rest of his life. He addressed his players in the team huddle. "I told them - I don't mind getting beat but we're not going to get humiliated." What Walls decided to do would have Puxico fans irate by the end of the game. Driving up from Mississippi where he was attending college, Leon Cookson was in the bleachers that night in Piggott. "There was a lot of hostility in that gym after the game was over."

Troy Walls grew up in Senath, Missouri. Born in 1924, he remembers growing cotton on the family farm just outside of town. He was one of ten children. "That's the reason that dad bought as much land as he did. We had enough in the family to pick all the cotton. We used to start at daylight, quit at dark, six days a week." A 1943 graduate of Senath High School, Walls played basketball growing up. He also honed his talents at another sport. "I started boxing rather than playing basketball, me and another guy. He and I won a Golden Glove tournament in Cape Girardeau. We were the two champions. "

Graduating high school in the middle of World War II, Walls had dreams of being a pilot. A failed hearing test quickly vanquished those dreams. After spending a year working in Detroit, Walls was drafted. Leaving the service in the late 1940's, he attended Arkansas State in Jonesboro. Greenway was his first head coaching position. He would later leave the Arkansas school and coach in the Bootheel town of Bragg City. He sang in a barbershop quartet, often entertaining the crowd at halftime. While coaching at the small Missouri high school, he met his future wife at a basketball game. "She was sitting up on the top bleacher. I just happened to look up there and boy she was a beautiful woman."

Walls immediately turned to his assistant coach and made a prediction. "You see that lady sitting up there between those other two girls – that beautiful lady? He said yeah. I said that's the lady I'm going to marry right there." Peggy O'Neal was teaching at Cooter – the rival team that Bragg City was playing that evening. Peggy and Troy eventually started dating, got married and had two children, a boy and a girl. Like his father, Troy Walls' son's most memorable basketball game would involve a member of the Cookson Clan.

But on this rainy November night in 1951, Troy Walls was a single man, 27 years old, coaching against the "best high school team" in the country. Walls was familiar with Puxico before he ever coached against them. He drove to Cape Girardeau the previous season to see Arnold Ryan's team play. "Forest Arnold, he'd jump up there and grab that ball sometimes, and (Winfred) Wilfong would run down the middle of the floor. Arnold (would) throw that thing the length of the court and Wilfong would put it in. Wilfong was probably the greatest high school basketball player I'd ever seen."

Win Wilfong was no longer a member of the Puxico Indians. But his younger brother Gene and his teammates had put on a clinic in the game's first eight minutes. Down by 21 points heading into the second quarter, Walls was determined not to get blown out again. He told his team to start stalling, dribble and pass the ball as much as possible, but not shoot it. With Greenway making no attempt to score, Puxico started fouling. But in high school basketball of the early 1950's, teams could refuse to shoot free throws, opting instead to take the ball out of bounds. Each time a Puxico player fouled his opponent, Greenway chose ball control over foul shots. In the short amount of time that Puxico did have possession, the Indians managed to score one point on a free throw. The score at halftime was 24-2.

To the dismay of nearly everyone in the gym, the Tigers got possession of the ball at the third quarter tip-off and the stall continued. By this time, Arnold Ryan and the Puxico fans had seen enough. Ryan told his team to no longer challenge the Greenway players. Instead, the Indians players sat on the court, sometimes laying "flat on their backs, making no effort to get the ball or try for a basket."[160] Fans became restless and started tossing coins onto the court. At one point in the third quarter, someone pulled the plug on the lights. When order was restored and the lights flipped back on, the play on the court didn't change. Greenway players stood and tossed the ball back and forth while the Puxico players watched the action sitting down. The Tigers missed the only shot of the quarter at the buzzer.

At the beginning of the final quarter, Puxico got the ball at the tip and roles reversed. The Indians went into a stall with the basketball, refusing to attempt a shot. Once again, eight minutes ticked off the clock uninterrupted. Puxico fired up a shot in the game's final seconds. The ball went through the bucket. For the first time since the first quarter, someone had made a field goal. The game ended with Puxico defeating Greenway 26-2.

While the ballgame may have finished, the action on the court was not over. Upset fans stormed the Greenway bench, wanting answers from the coach. "They just had me surrounded," remembers Walls, who quickly zeroed in on the group's ringleader. "He said when you come outside coach we'll teach you our stall." With his team still sitting on the bench beside him, the former Golden Gloves boxing champion issued a challenge. "The dressing room is right here behind us. Our kids are sitting right here – there's nobody in there. So if you want to whip me by yourself, you got all night to do it. Go in there and I'll give you all the time you need." The challenge worked. The ringleader backed off and the angry crowd dissipated. There would be no fights with the coach that night in Piggott, Arkansas. But the events of that evening would stay with Walls for years.

Coach Walls Greenway Tigers were not an untalented group of basketball players. They just had the unfortunate experience of going through the Puxico buzz saw twice in eight days to start their season. The 1952 Greenway team finished third in the state of Arkansas in Class B, losing to the eventual champions in the semi-finals. A few weeks after the season ended, Walls and a friend decided to go fishing at Duck Creek near Puxico. They stopped at a Puxico diner and ordered food. It was then that Walls spotted a calendar on the wall. In big bold letters, someone had written the Puxico basketball team's single game high and low point totals. The 26 points against Greenway was the Indians lowest output of the season. Walls told his fishing buddy it was time to go. "I said I better leave a tip and let's get out of here. Someone might recognize me and that might be the end of the road."

Even more than fifty years after the game, people were still reminding Walls of what went on at the Piggott gym that night. Playing golf one day in 2003 near his home at Cherokee Village, Arkansas, Walls heard a familiar voice. "Hey coach, I'm thinking about wrapping this driver around your neck." The voice belonged to a former basketball coach in Jonesboro. Walls looked up and asked his former colleague the reason why. "He said I drove all the way up to Piggott to see that ballgame from Jonesboro and all I got to see was a first quarter."

***

Starting their season at 2-0, the Puxico Indians had little time to rest. Three nights after the second Greenway game, the Indians started play in the Delta tournament. A blowout of Bloomfield and a convincing twenty-four point win over Advance put Puxico in the championship game against St. Mary's, a private school in Cape Girardeau. With a forty-five game winning streak and a tournament championship on the line, a standing room only crowd packed the Delta gym. Bob Kielhofner from Chaffee had made the drive over with his buddy and St. Mary's starting point guard, Bob Miller. "I stood there against the wall, behind some seats. I don't know how I got into that damn place. It was loaded with people." For the majority of the game, Puxico seemed in control. With three minutes to go, the Indians led by ten points, 60-50. In the game's remaining moments, St. Mary's players would attempt six shots. They made all six. A last second shot by Gene Vandeven was the game winner. Bob Kielhofner recounts the winning shot. "It was a desperation shot in the corner. He (Vandeven) was deep in the corner. He jumps up and hits this two point jump shot. He just threw it, swished it. It was over. The place went nuts." St. Mary's defeated Puxico 62-60. The Indians winning streak was history. Bob Miller from Chaffee, who nearly stayed at home that year to play football for the Red Devils, scored 17 of St. Mary's points.

The 1951-52 Puxico Indians would not be an undefeated team. But there was still plenty to play for. Many considered Puxico the favorite to repeat as a state champion. After the two-point loss at Delta, the Indians started playing like one. Ryan's team won its next twelve games in a row, breaking the century mark on three occasions. The streak included a rematch with St. Mary's in the semi-finals of the Christmas Tournament in Cape Girardeau. There would be no last second dramatics this time.

Puxico avenged its only loss of the season to date with a convincing 63 to 31 win. The next night, the Indians claimed the tournament championship for the second year in a row with a twenty-two point victory over Cape Central. On New Year's Day, Puxico routed Lutesville 94-33. Gene Wilfong led the way with 25 points. In stringing together a dozen wins in a row, no team had come closer than nineteen points to the Indians. But with a record of 16-1, Puxico was about to get its biggest challenge of the season; the first of two games against the John Burroughs Bombers.

More than five thousand fans packed the gym on the campus of Washington University in St. Louis to see the first Puxico-John Burroughs match-up. They got their money's worth. The undefeated Bombers matched the Indians bucket for bucket. A field goal late in the game put John Burroughs up by one point, 54-53. But with time running out, Puxico guard Gene Wilfong was streaking with the ball to the other end. There was one defender between him and the goal. The outcome of that match-up would determine the fate of the game.

***

Gene Wilfong grew up on the family farm outside of Puxico. He remembers the town of his youth. "I guess it would make some people mad the way I would describe Puxico. I guess the best way to describe it was that it was a beer drinkin', tobacco spittin', log haulin' town." Gene was born in 1935, two years after, but only one class behind, his brother Winfred. "My senior year in high school, when I graduated, I was sixteen." Working on the farm as a kid, there was little time for sports. He didn't know anything about the game of basketball. "We'd gone to a country school and we didn't know a thing about basketball until my brother started at city school in the eighth grade." Win Wilfong's eighth grade teacher was Arnold Ryan. He would be Gene's teacher the following year. The teacher and coach introduced the brothers to a sport that became a lifelong love. Win and Gene would soon put up a basketball goal in their barn. On Sundays, the Wilfong boys would play basketball with their neighbors down the road, the Cooksons. "That was our Sunday afternoon thing to do. Carroll's brother (Ancel) and myself would take on Carroll and my brother. We were always in some kind of mischief."

Like so many others who grew up around Puxico in that era, Wilfong's introduction to organized basketball came his freshman year, playing Junior Varsity ball for Ryan. That year, Wilfong was introduced to the Ryan discipline when he disobeyed his coach's orders at lunchtime. The freshman team had a ballgame scheduled right after school. "They had potato cakes that day and Arnold said don't eat the potato cakes, they'll be sitting on your stomach. Course, they were awfully good to me and I was eating some," Wilfong recalls. "Guess who sat right down beside me? Coach Ryan. He said it would probably take until half time for those potato cakes to settle." Wilfong did get to play that day, but not until the third quarter.

What Wilfong still appreciates about his former coach is how he made the game enjoyable for everyone on the team. "Number one, he was a good motivator and he motivated you by playing. And he motivated you by the competition against the boys on his own team." Some of the best games and most difficult teams the Puxico players of that era took part in were against each other in practice in the log gym after school. "We scrimmaged everyday. He had two teams divided up and he had Forest (Arnold) and Win (Wilfong) against each other. At the end of the quarter, he'd say, 'Win you beat Forest's team by two points, now you and Forest swap and see if you can get that team to beat this team.' Everyday it was competition, everyday it was fun, and everyday we scrimmaged." Wilfong believes the daily scrimmage was an integral part of the team's success. He sees a coach and his team as being analogous to a driver and a car. Some teams, like certain cars, can be driven faster over longer periods of time before beginning to break down. Like the driver, the coach has to find the optimal speed. "The coach has to decide if he wants the team to play at 50 miles an hour without making turnovers or can they play at 60 without making many turnovers? At what speed can they play?" When other teams would be playing at full speed, Ryan's teams still had another gear or two to go. "We probably played at an 80 mile an hour level and most everybody else played at 40. They just didn't know it. Didn't know where the whirlwind hit them," remembers Wilfong. It was the daily scrimmage that made this frenetic pace possible. "If you don't do those things everyday, you can't do those things."

Ryan always made the gym accessible to his players. In the summertime, he had the gym open at night. When the coach wasn't around, players would seek out a janitor who had a spare key. "Any of us that wanted to go to the gym could go by the (janitor's) house anytime and get the keys." It was that player's responsibility to make sure everything was in order at the end of the night. "I can't ever remember there ever being an incident in that gym where kids got into fights or things broken or torn up. Everybody just took care of things like they were supposed to." The game of basketball quickly became a part of Wilfong's daily habit. "It was just a way of life to us."

The Puxico guard remembers two lessons that Ryan constantly preached in practice. The first was a focus on shooting the basketball. Like the rest of his teammates, Wilfong worked on his shot year round. " Common sense tells you that if you can hit (forty out of hundred), that's forty times you don't have to rebound, that's forty times you don't have to make a pass, forty times you don't take a chance on passing. So common sense tells you that the thing you need the practice the most on is shooting the basketball." Shooting the basketball would never get a player in trouble at Puxico. Not playing defense was another story. "Anybody could take a shot who wanted to. Where he (Ryan) did frown on it was if you didn't hustle on defense to get that ball back. He put his emphasis on that." In fact, Ryan's defense was an integral part of his offense. The full court pressure applied by the Indians often resulted in easy lay-ups. That same formula would later be employed by teams coached by both Carroll and Ronnie Cookson.

***

Back on the campus of Washington University in January of 1951, it was a lay-up that Gene Wilfong was after. Down by one with just seconds to go in the game, the Puxico guard had the ball and was driving toward the goal. With five thousand fans screaming in the stands, Wilfong put up his shot as time ran out. It went in. Puxico began celebrating a 55-54 victory. What few fans had heard was a referee's whistle as Wilfong went up for the shot. He was called for charging. The bucket was taken away. Clinging to a 54-53 lead, John Burroughs made one free throw and won the game by two points, 55-53. Puxico had been dealt its second defeat of the season. Wilfong recounts the game's final moments. "They called a charge on me. Best I remember I made the basket, but they didn't count it. Whoever it was went down to the other end and shot free throws and beat us. Whether I charged or not —who knows?" One thing Wilfong is certain of, however, is that no player on the Puxico side argued the call. "It was one of those things that we weren't allowed to be involved in or participate in. All he (Ryan) let us do when we were fouled was raise our hands and go on with the game."

The Puxico Indians were now 16-2. But just as they had the opportunity to avenge the loss against St. Mary's, Ryan's team would have another chance against John Burroughs. It happened seven games later in early February. In the interim six ballgames, Puxico never won by less than thirty points. The Bombers took the train down from St. Louis while Puxico players rode the bus up to the contest. The two teams met in Cape Girardeau. The match-up at Houck Field House was sold out nearly a week before the game. John Burroughs was still undefeated but would play without their leading scorer from the first contest. Bill McCarthy had a fractured leg. A two-point game at halftime tilted decidedly to Puxico in the third quarter. At one point, the Indians had a sixteen-point lead. Ryan's team got its revenge. Puxico defeated John Burroughs 69-58.

Before sub-regional action tipped off in late February, the Indians reeled off an additional six consecutive victories. For the final regular season match-up, Puxico once again traveled to Arkansas where the Indians defeated Jonesboro. With basketball's second season about to start, Ryan's team had a record of 28-2. Seven games stood between Puxico and a return to the sweet sixteen, scheduled once again in Cape Girardeau. Only once during those seven games did an opponent come within 15 points of Puxico. The closest contest came in the regional semi-finals, the third match-up of the year with St. Mary's. The Bulldog's Bob Miller led his team with 21 points, but it wasn't enough to stop the rampaging Indians. Puxico won the game 73-58.

The 1952 Puxico Indians did not enter the state tournament undefeated. It did not score 100 points nearly as often. But when measured against the best in the state in the crunch time of tournament play, there is no doubt this version of Ryan's squad was equally as dominant. Teams, fans, and the media once again converged on Houck Field House for the nearly weeklong tournament. At least three players received extra scrutiny because of their basketball talents: Forest Arnold and Grady Smith of Puxico and Norman Stewart of Shelbyville. All three would be playing Division I college basketball in the fall. For one night in the winter of 1952, the three players would share the court. But it would take three victories for both clubs to make that match-up possible.

Puxico opened tournament play with a blowout win over Atlanta. Ten different Indians players scored points for Ryan's team. Gene Wilfong led Puxico with 15 in the 89 to 46 victory. With John Burroughs defeating Pattonsburg, it set up the highly anticipated third match of the year between the Indians and the Bombers. In their first game, Bill McCarthy for John Burroughs scored 24 points in the Bombers two point victory. Missing the second contest with a leg injury, Puxico easily won in Cape Girardeau. With McCarthy back in the lineup, the two clubs met for the opportunity to advance to the semi-finals of tournament play. Regardless of the outcome, many people believed the winner of the game represented the best of Missouri high school basketball.

Last year, there was always the feeling, "Wonder what would happen if Puxico (Class B state winner) and Normandy (Class A winner) could get together?" There's no doubt in these parts what would have happened, but it couldn't materialize. But if either Burroughs or Puxico goes to the B championship, there is no question about the winner's superiority over Class A champion in 1952. Burroughs is conqueror of St. Louis University High, the A winner at Columbia last week and DeAndreas of St. Louis, the A runner-up. That proves Burroughs ability. Puxico has split its first two games with the Bombers.[161]

Make that two of out three for Puxico. The Indians took advantage of poor shooting by John Burroughs while hitting nearly 55 percent of their shots from the floor. They dominated at every turn and stretched their lead in every quarter. Puxico led by seven points at the end of the first quarter, lengthened it to 12 by half, increased it to 19 points by the end of the third period and won the game by the twenty seven points, 88-61. Gene Wilfong and Grady Smith combined for 48 points for the Indians, while Forest Arnold shutdown the Bombers Bill McCarthy, who scored only three points before fouling out. Reflecting an era in which far lower scores were predominate, a person at the scorer's table remarked after the game, "imagine making 61 points and not winning the ball game."[162] Earlier that same day on the court at Houck, Norman Stewart sank a late free throw as Shelbyville won its quarterfinal contest, edging Fayette 54-53. The Shelbyville Pirate's record stood at 38-1.

The semi-final games followed form: a Puxico blowout and a narrow Shelbyville victory. With center Forest Arnold leading the way with 26 points, Puxico beat Wheaton 76-55 in a game a lot closer than the final score indicates. The Indians didn't take their first lead of the game until late in the second quarter. With Stewart once again providing late game heroics, Shelbyville won by a single point. Stewart was fouled late in the game. "The 6'4" postman grinned as he stepped to the free throw mark, but missed the try."[163] Stewart captured the ensuing moments in his memoirs years later. "I step to the line and miss the free throw. Before I can really react, my teammate George Chase jumps up and slaps the ball off the backboard. No one blocks me out, and the ball comes right back to me. I shoot it right back in the basket and we win the game."[164] Stewart's bucket with three seconds left on the clock was the difference in a 49-48 win. It would be once beaten Shelbyville against twice beaten Puxico in the finals.

With thousands of people pouring into a Cape Girardeau for the basketball tournament for the second year in a row, the local paper kept track of all the action, on the court and in the stands. Just who was showing up to attend?

"There are no people at the tournament games who are exactly feeble, but numerous old folks join right in. One Grandpa Fan has been seen at each session, and he usually has a choice seat. Some ladies well past 30 are seen in the crowds, too."[165]

University of Missouri basketball coach Sparky Stalcup was in the crowd at Houck Field House. So too were many of Arnold Ryan's former players, including one who now played for Stalcup, Win Wilfong. The star of the 1951 Puxico club was joined by former teammates Leon Cookson and Frank Hoggard. Why were the Indians such a motivated group of basketball players? "They'd walk through fire for him," commented Hoggard. "He respects the men and they respect him."[166]

The group of men who would walk through fire for their coach had played him now for four seasons. They had already been part of one state championship team and had celebrated seventy-eight victories over the last two seasons. On the night of March 16, 1952, the Puxico Indians would claim their second state title and victory number seventy-nine. If the best basketball team in the state of Missouri was ever in doubt, this game erased all hesitations. Arnold Ryan's Puxico Indians were one for the ages.

It was 7-0 Puxico before Shelbyville could score a point. The Pirates were overwhelmed by the full-speed, full-court Indians. Down by fourteen points at the beginning of the third quarter, Shelbyville attempted to stall the basketball. For nearly three minutes, Norman Stewart stood near the half court line with the basketball as boos from the partisan Houck Field House crowd reigned down upon him. The stall came to an end when a Shelbyville player was whistled for a three second violation. The end of the stall marked the end of any shot that Shelbyville had of keeping the game close. Puxico led by twenty-seven points at the end of the third quarter and didn't let up in the game's final eight minutes. The final score was 85-37. In the fourth quarter, Puxico coach Arnold Ryan did something for only the third time that season: call timeout.[167] In four state tournament basketball games, Puxico had scored 338 points to their opponents 199, an average margin of victory of nearly thirty-five points. Shelbyville's Stewart would go to the University of Missouri where he played both basketball and baseball. Achieving all-conference honors in basketball, he also pitched for the 1954 national champion Missouri baseball team. He would later return to Columbia as the head basketball coach. Norm Stewart won more than 600 games coaching the Missouri Tigers. His first experience with Bootheel ball was a memorable one. About the game against Puxico, Stewart would later say, "We were never in the game, never."[168]

Puxico's celebration of its second state title was short lived. The Indians defeated Shelbyville on Saturday night. On Monday, Puxico made front-page news. Not because of its team, but due to its coach. Arnold Ryan was resigning. While vague about his future plans, he intimated that he had another job somewhere, for more money than what he was making at Puxico. He left Puxico to become an assistant coach at Memphis State. Center Forest Arnold would join him at the school in the fall. After four years and 1,856 career points for the Tigers, Arnold was selected in the 1956 NBA draft. He never played a day of professional basketball, opting for a career in the ministry instead. Puxico's other top college prospect, Grady Smith, went on to play basketball at St. Louis University.[169]

Ryan's departure represented the end of an era. During his last two seasons at Puxico, the Indians went 79-2 and won back-to-back state titles. In the process, they transformed the game of basketball in the state of Missouri and electrified fans across the South and Midwest. Just how special were Arnold Ryan's Puxico Indians? Former Poplar Bluff newspaper reporter Bob Gray once related this story to the *Southeast Missourian.* Gray's son ran into legendary North Carolina coach Dean Smith one time at an airport. The two men struck up a conversation and Smith asked him where he was from. When Gray told him, Smith replied. "Oh yeah, I know where Poplar Bluff's at. I went there one time to watch Win Wilfong play basketball game when he was at Puxico"[170] In the early 1950's, Smith was playing college basketball for Forrest "Phog" Allen at the University of Kansas in Lawrence, some four hundred miles away at a time when no interstate highways existed.

In St. Louis, in his same column where he eulogized Win Wilfong, columnist Rich Koster remembered Puxico basketball.

"If you are old enough to have been aware of sports in Missouri in 1951, you must remember the basketball fable of the Puxico Indians. Of the sleepy little farm town on Highway 51, halfway between Poplar Bluff and Cape Girardeau, which captured headlines and imaginations for two exciting winters.

...Basketball fans in St. Louis could recite the names of the kids from Puxico as readily as they could those of Kentucky's Fabulous Five.

...It was a marvelous, magical story. It was more than two championship seasons. It was a source of sustained pride for a community, confirmation of its rural values."

While the legend of Puxico basketball spread west to Kansas and north to St. Louis, it also left vivid memories south of Missouri. Like Dean Smith, Troy Walls heard about Puxico basketball while living in a neighboring state. More than fifty years of watching the game hasn't changed the mind of the former Greenway, Arkansas coach. "Best high school team I've ever witnessed in all the years that I've watched basketball, in college and everywhere else. I tell you what I believe – I believe they could beat Arkansas State, Cape Girardeau (SEMO), they may have beat St. Louis U – I'm not kidding you."

CHAPTER FOUR
Brothers
1952-1975

"I saw a joke one time that said you know if you're from Southeast Missouri if you played basketball for one of the Cooksons."

Terry Wills – Advance class of 1973

In the summer of 1952, with Arnold Ryan heading off to Memphis State to become an assistant coach, several of his players joined him. Carroll Cookson was one of those who made the journey to the Tennessee city. Carroll was a year younger than many of his classmates and stood 5'6". His growth spurt was still to come. He would play college basketball at 6' 2". However, it would not be at Memphis State. The lifestyle in the southern city was not for the boy from small town Southeast Missouri. He went back home at the end of the summer and worked for a while in his brother's TV repair shop.

After he turned eighteen, he moved to St. Louis and worked at a Fisher Auto Body plant. One night while working, Carroll heard a knock at the window. He looked up and saw a familiar face, that of his former teammate Gene Wilfong. He told Carroll he needed to borrow his car and a place to stay. Cookson threw his keys out the window and told him he would see him later that night back at his apartment. Like Carroll, Gene soon took a job at the factory. The company later transferred both of them to their plant in Arlington, Texas.

It was in Texas that Cookson met his future wife, Nelda Rozelle Daniel, in 1955. Carroll and Rozelle were married a year later. Thanks to basketball, Carroll would keep his new bride busy. He worked the assembly line by day and played basketball at night. Cookson played AAU basketball with his company's team and he would play in another league, often playing multiple games in a week. "I would wash four uniforms a week," Rozelle recalled years later. The teams would travel all over the state to play ball, often taking off for the weekend to drive to Houston, San Antonio, or Abilene. There was no distance too far if basketball was to be played. Carroll and his brother Ronnie would follow the same philosophy when they started coaching years later.

One of Carroll's best friends on the AAU team was a talented young athlete by the name of Sammy Fountain. Sammy played college basketball at Arlington State and tried to get Carroll to do the same. "He kept wanting me to go back to college to play basketball. I messed around and didn't do it. I had a family and this and that, and I didn't do it." Carroll recalls his friend was also a gifted baseball player who signed a professional contract. Staying at a hotel on a road trip, Sammy fell asleep by the swimming pool. He woke up and started walking to the room. Groggy and disoriented, he proceeded to fall in the water. For all his athletic ability, Sammy couldn't swim. He drowned in the hotel pool.

Another shortened life precipitated Carroll and Rozelle's move back to Missouri. Cookson's oldest brother, J.T., was in failing health. The teenager who nearly died at the age of seventeen following his car accident had defied the odds for another seventeen years. He passed away in May of 1961. While Carroll lost his oldest brother, his move back to Missouri reunited him with his youngest one. Ronnie was a small boy when Carroll left home to work in St. Louis. He was now preparing to start his senior year in high school. In the intervening years, Ronnie had bonded with his oldest brother. "My brother J.T., now he was an exceptional person," the youngest Cookson brother remarked years later. "He had a TV repair shop and worked on cars. I saw him crawl out to change a tire. We were really close. He was something special."[171] Ronnie never knew J.T. before he became wheelchair bound. When he started teaching and coaching, people would recall his sensitivity toward kids who were either physically or mentally challenged. He learned that sensitivity at a young age.

One year later and getting ready to graduate from high school, Ronnie didn't know exactly what his future would hold. He did make one decision. He wanted to go to college somewhere to play basketball. It was a game he almost gave up on years before. As a freshman at Puxico, Cookson barely played. "I was set to quit after getting about three seconds of playing time as a freshman basketball player."[172] His father wouldn't let him, telling him it was important to finish what he started. The source of Cookson's ire was a decision by his coach to play sophomores in a freshman game. "One of those sophomores took my place in the lineup." Recounting the story for the *Southeast Missourian* in 1988, Cookson told the newspaper his coach's behavior made a lasting impression. "To this day I make it a point to tell all my players that if they work hard in practice, they will get in the game at one time or another."[173]

Ronnie only has vague memories watching his brother Carroll play in the log gym at Puxico. One story told through the years involves an incident with Arnold Ryan. Six-year old Ronnie took off sprinting down the court one afternoon at practice, wearing nothing but mistletoe held with one hand above his backside. The Puxico coach paddled him with a tennis shoe and sent him home. Ryan and the log gym were both gone from Puxico by the time Ronnie played his high school basketball. The gym burned down in February of 1958.[174] Like his older brothers, Ronnie developed a love for the game at an early age. "I was a gym rat. I was always there. I had a key to the gym when I was in the seventh grade and as long as I promised to sweep the floor and keep the trash picked up inside, nobody said anything."[175]

After the Puxico Indians were knocked out in the regional finals his senior year, Cookson began to search for a college where he could play basketball. Southern Baptist, an Arkansas junior college, had a tryout session one day in Fisk, Missouri. The Puxico player didn't exactly set the world on fire. "The coach didn't even talk to me." Undeterred by his unimpressive performance, Cookson decided to make another attempt. Southern Baptist had scheduled another tryout session, this one on its campus in Walnut Ridge, Arkansas. His older brother Carroll made the 100-mile drive with him. When they arrived at the gym, one of the teams was shorthanded. An extra pair of basketball shoes was located and Carroll joined his brother on the basketball court. While he may not have realized it at the time, Carroll was also auditioning. When it was all over, the coach wanted both Cookson brothers to play for him and offered scholarships to each of them. Ronnie arrived as a typical eighteen-year old single college student. When Carroll and Rozelle arrived at Southern Baptist Junior College that fall, they brought their three children with them: four year old Steve, two year old Lesa, and youngest child Lorie, all of one week old when her dad started college. For the next eight years, Carroll and Ronnie would be virtually inseparable, either in the classroom or on the basketball court.

At Walnut Ridge, the Cooksons played for coach Jake Shambarger. The small Arkansas junior college didn't have a team bus. They had to drive themselves to away games; Shambarger drove one vehicle while the coach asked his twenty-eight year old freshman to take the keys of the second one. "I think he sort of respected me, "remembers Carroll. "I respected him, and to help take care of things I always drove the other car."

On one road trip, the Cooksons had to share a hotel room with their coach much to the dismay of the younger brother. "We would go on these road trips and Shambarger would starve us to death," remembers Ronnie. "He wouldn't let you eat." Carroll's wife had made the brothers chocolate chip cookies to take along with them. They packed one duffel bag with their basketball gear while the second one was full of cookies. They didn't want their coach to find out about the additional food supplies they brought along. To avoid having their snack taken away, the two took turns eating cookies in the hotel bathroom. It would be the only time the brothers had to room with their coach. Ronnie explains why. "We went out and got beat that night. He swears that we elbowed each other, talked to each other in our sleep, played the whole game again in our sleep, kept him up all night. 'Pass the ball; why in the hell didn't you pass me the ball?' He later told the team, 'I'll never stay again in the same room with those two.'"

Richard Pyland played two seasons of college basketball with the Cookson brothers.[176] The former Gideon star came to Southern Baptist one year after Carroll and Ronnie arrived. He credits the elder Cookson for being a big influence on his teammates. "Carroll taught us how to play the game," remembers Pyland who later coached against both Cooksons. "Ronnie was like the rest of us. He was green." When all three men began their high school basketball coaching careers a few years later, Pyland was not surprised by the success that Carroll enjoyed. He recalls with a smile one game where Cookson's team was beating his squad by 25 points. "He felt sorry for me so he took all his starters out of the game." Big mistake. Pyland's team rallied to win the game.

But of all his coaching opponents over the years, it's the younger

Cookson's success that caught him off guard. "Ronnie was radical," said Pyland, who remembers his teammate on the court as being "the hatchet man." One season in college, Ronnie was named the team's defensive player of the year. His assignment was to shut down the opponent's best shooter, any way he could. Carroll recalls one game where an opposing player tried to intimidate the Cookson brothers and their teammates with his physical style of play. "I was underneath the goal and he hit me underneath the chin and he knocked me over. When I landed, my feet were all the way out to the circle." A referee ran over to Cookson and asked him what happened. "I couldn't talk. I still have trouble with my throat." Payback for the incident came the next time the two teams met. "They had to come to our place and Ronnie took care of business. He ran him into the wall. That goes on when you play college ball."

Ronnie was always quick to take up for his older brother. Ron Cook used to hear the stories when he was assistant coach at Scott County Central. "I think Ronnie almost got into a lot of fights. People called Carroll 'old man' – he had premature gray hair."

After two years at Southern Baptist, Carroll and Ronnie transferred to the College of the Ozarks in Clarksville, Arkansas.[177] The style of play was especially physical in the AIC conference and the Cookson brothers took it as well as they gave it. Carroll claims he never took a yearbook picture in college. Each year at that time, he would typically have a black eye or a swollen face from getting roughed up during a game. "They played just like they coached," said Nick Lanpher, who played and coached against both of the Cookson brothers. "They were real aggressive." Carroll has vivid memories of an encounter against Lanpher. He was driving to the basket for a lay-up when Lanpher tried to prevent it. A 6'2" forward for Ouachita Baptist, Lanpher would find himself in Southeast Asia a few years later with the military police, helping to escort convoys through the jungles of Vietnam. Cookson didn't make the lay-up. "He buried me on the wall," said Carroll. "He was like a bull in a china shop." Cookson and Lanpher are friends today and laugh at the memory, but both remember the competition in those days as particularly intense.

Lanpher would later coach at Kelly High School, just outside of Benton. His teams played in the same conference as Ronnie's Scott County Central Braves. He remembers another facet of basketball in 1960's Arkansas as integration on college campuses across the South was just beginning. Ouachita had one black player on the squad. When they traveled to play other schools, particularly in Louisiana and Mississippi, their coach would have to ask permission to eat at a restaurant. If management allowed black patrons, they would stop. Lanpher would join the isolated teammate in the back of the restaurant.

The athlete who would break the color barrier in Arkansas college basketball was a 6'1" guard/forward by the name of Sylvester Benson.[178] He played at the College of the Ozarks. Ronnie and Carroll were his teammates. One night, the brothers who grew up in the all-white town of Puxico, received a first hand experience in racial intimidation. It happened after a game against Southern Arkansas. Near the town of Malvern, coach Sam Starkey and his team decided to stop to eat at a restaurant. While the group waited for the food to arrive, Ronnie began playing pinball. His older brother looked around the restaurant and noticed that other than the team, everyone else had departed. "I went over to coach (and said) something's going on. We looked out the window. Then he (Starkey) said, I'd better go tell Ronnie to not say anything, no telling what Ronnie would do."

What Carroll and his coach saw as they looked through the window were local residents gathering outside. This was no welcoming committee. "Those guys had their trunks up. They were getting their chains out and their tire tools." The coach told the team they were leaving, to get back on the bus, and to ignore the mob that had formed two lines on either side of the restaurant's door. "We put Syl (Benson) in the middle of us and walked out right between them and got on the bus and left," remembers Carroll. As for his younger brother, he kept his mouth shut as they walked outside, but once on the bus, delivered a message to the group that began to shout at them. "As we got ready to pull out of the parking lot, I raised my arm and gave them a signal," recounted Ronnie years after the incident.[179] The signal was his raised middle finger.

While at Southern Baptist, the Cookson brothers helped their team win more than forty games during their two seasons at Walnut Ridge. They made an immediate impact in Clarksville as well. One of the reasons the two chose the College of the Ozarks was because of how poorly it performed the year before. For Carroll and Ronnie, the worse the team, the greater their odds of playing. "College of the Ozarks had won one game in two years. I think we wound up third or fourth in the conference," said Carroll. Ronnie recalls the impact their teams had. "We beat Arkansas Tech. First time they had beat them in 25 years. It was chaos. We'd win 15 or 16 games, and you would have thought we had gone 39-0. They just weren't used to winning. And that really changed the atmosphere around the school. And the community as well."

During his senior year in college, Ronnie fell in love with a freshman cheerleader. Ann Marie Cookson, better known as "Dee," remembers how the two became husband and wife. "I came back for my second year of college and called Ronnie and told him I didn't want to be there. He said, 'Then let's get married now.' I was 18 and my parents had died while I was in high school, so I didn't have anyone to talk me out of it."[180]

After four basketball seasons and taking every class together, Carroll and Ronnie had their college degrees. Both men knew they wanted to coach the game they had played all their lives. In April of 1966, the school board at Advance High School, a Stoddard County rival to Puxico, offered a job to Carroll. He accepted. It made front-page news on the pages of the *Advance Advocate*.[181] The paper introduced Cookson to its readers by adding "The former Puxico man will be remembered as being one of a basketball team that won wide recognition some 16 years ago." Brother Ronnie joined him as the junior high coach and as an assistant on the high school squad. That summer, Carroll, Rozelle and their three children packed their bags and moved back to Missouri. Dee joined Ronnie in Advance that fall. The new coach had to rearrange his schedule. "I canceled a volleyball game so we could get married."[182] Ronnie and Carroll had embarked on their coaching careers. To a generation of Advance players, the Cookson brand of basketball would be the only game in town.

***

One of Richie Walker's earliest memories is of the log gym in Puxico. He was only three or four years old at the time, but remembers being inside the legendary home of the Indians before it burned down. Walker's father was a big basketball fan, and he would take his son with him to games all around the area. He grew up in Advance, and when the 1961 Hornets made the state tournament, Walker begged his father to go. His dad offered to pay him money to stay home with his grandmother. Walker wouldn't accept it and off he went to Columbia with his father to watch basketball.

Walker's father was born in 1916 and was quite an athlete himself. At the age of 16, the lefthander pitched in a semi-pro baseball game against Satchel Paige. The legendary Paige was the fastest pitcher the elder Walker had ever seen. He compared Paige's pitching to trying to hit an aspirin tablet with a broomstick. Paige beat Walker that day – three to nothing. The Cincinnati Reds later drafted the young lefthander, but he hurt his arm his first season and had to give up his baseball career.

Walker settled in Advance, got married and had two boys. Richie was the youngest. Starting junior high school in the fall of 1966, the Cookson way of playing basketball was the only way Richie Walker knew. Ronnie was his junior high coach and Carroll coached his high school teams. The two of them together made a vivid impression on the young athlete. He remembers practices where the team would form a line underneath each goal. One person would stand at the end line with the ball while another player would take off toward the other end like a wide receiver in football. The purpose of the drill was to catch the ball on the fly at the other end and make a lay-up without ever dribbling. The Cooksons did not want players to dribble if possible. Throwing the ball down the court was always a preferred alternative. Punishment came if the lay-up was missed; standing with players at one end of the gym with a whistle strap was Carroll, at the other end of the court stood Ronnie waiting with a paddle. Walker remembers players literally trying to climb the walls behind the goals in order to avoid a swat on the butt. He also remembers something else; there was a purpose to the punishment. The Cooksons wanted their players to have total concentration. If a player cannot make a lay-up in practice, how can he be expected to make a key shot in a big game?

Walker began to notice other things about the brothers as well. While in Junior High, he remembers going to the gym on weekends and working on his shot. Even then, he had a goal of winning a state championship. His coaches noticed. While they liked the idea of him devoting the extra time, they told him it was his responsibility to bring in other team members and get them to be just as motivated as he was. The whole idea of a team meant something very specific to the Cooksons. It wasn't just a group of kids practicing together and putting on the same colored jerseys and playing games. The coaches wanted to know about their lives off the court as well. Does this guy get along with his teammates? When did that player start dating the cheerleader? Who needs help in certain classes? The Cooksons wanted their players to be just as a cohesive unit off the court as on it. When players struggled with homework, they encouraged players to have study groups and work through class problems as a team. Absolutely no smoking or drinking was allowed. Curfews were strictly enforced. So were haircuts. Walker remembers getting a haircut one season and walking into practice one day and being told it wasn't good enough. He had to return to the barber chair before he could get back on the gym floor. In practice, the brothers from Puxico were extremely verbal. They would yell and scream and get in players faces if they did something wrong, often blowing the whistle and stopping everyone dead in their tracks. The paddle always lurked as possible punishment, be it in practice or a game. Whatever the punishment, Walker always thought the brothers dealt it out in an even-handed fashion. "I never in my lifetime of playing for these guys – I never saw a time they were unfair, ever. Everybody was treated the same."

Another thing about the Cookson brothers the players noticed was their love for the game. It's what they did as a job, but also for fun. When they stopped playing, they started coaching. When they weren't coaching, they were talking about it in class to their students. When they couldn't talk about it, they would think about games, practices, and their players, anything they could do to get an edge on an opponent. This passion for the game meant that Ronnie and Carroll's teams were going to play basketball, regardless of what the calendar said. From their playing and coaching days, they had developed an extensive contact list of coaches, not just in Southeast Missouri but throughout the region. On summer weekends, they would load up the teams in two vehicles – Carroll would drive one car and Ronnie the other one – and take off for the southwest part of the state, Arkansas, Kentucky, or Illinois; anywhere a gym and an opposing team awaited. Walker remembers arriving at the gym one night in Ballard County, Kentucky. What they thought was an out of season scrimmage looked more like a full-scale regulation game. The gym was packed and the concession stand was doing brisk business. Walker thought there were more people inside that gym than could ever fit into the one at Advance. He remembers the words of his coach. "I'm sure glad we're out of state!" said Carroll as they walked in.

In 1971, the Advance Hornets finished their season with a loss in the regional semi-finals to Parma. It marked the first year that the Cookson duo had been broken up, with younger brother Ronnie departing for Scott Central to take the head-coaching job the previous fall. But Carroll Cookson knew his squad for the next season had the potential to be special. He took his players to the state tournament that year. He wanted to give them a glimpse of what could be theirs if they only wanted it enough. The '71 high school season had not officially ended, but Cookson's Advance team was already thinking about 1972.

The next season marked Cookson's sixth season at Advance. While his teams had never even made it to the state tournament, that season he felt they could win it all. Richie Walker remembers a huge difference between that team and the previous ones he had played on. He went into every game that year thinking he was going to win. He had never felt that way before. Walker thought of basketball like dancing. The really good teams had the ability to play with a certain rhythm on the court. They didn't have to think about their next move, they just did it, honed by relentless hours of practice. In 1972, Walker and his teammates found their rhythm. For the next four years, the Advance Hornets could dance.

Point-guard Walker was one of two senior starters. Forward Richard Hitt was the other. According to their coach, those two players were the cornerstones of the team. "Richie Walker was the glue of the 72 team, and Richard Hitt was the best player – he could jump center, play anywhere." The Hornets entered state tournament play with a record of 23-5. Of the five losses that season, the one that stands out in Walker's mind was a game against the Oran Eagles; not for just what transpired on the court but also what happened later that night at home. With just a few seconds left, Advance trailed by one point. An Oran player had a one-and-one free throw opportunity. Cookson called timeout. If the player missed either shot, the idea was to get the rebound as quickly as possible and kick out to a guard for a last second shot to either tie or win the game. The Oran player made the first free throw. He missed the second one. The Hornets trailed by two points. Just as they had planned, an Advance player got the rebound and delivered a pass to Walker at half-court. Taking just a few steps, Walker fired a shot toward the goal. The last second desperation shot went in. The game was tied and headed to overtime. But on this night the Eagle's star player, Robert Earl Gibson, could not be contained. Oran beat Advance in overtime. It was Oran that Advance later defeated to win the regional title to move on to the state tournament. Gibson was hurt for that game and did not play.

Returning home after the overtime loss to Oran, Walker sensed something was wrong. The light was on in the kitchen and his father was sitting at the table. Usually, his parents were in bed by the time he returned home. Walker remembers what his father told him. "My dad said to me, 'Well Rich, I just wanted to tell you that was a wonderful shot you made to tie the game up tonight.'" The senior guard appreciated the compliment but was still scratching his head as to why his father waited up to tell him. Then he added this: "If you're gonna do that, you might as well go on and win it." With those words, Walker's father got up from the table and went to bed. The Advance Senior realized then his father couldn't sleep until he had gotten that off his chest. Walker remembers the incident because it was one of the few times that his father ever made any comments following a game. That's the way it went with the Cooksons. "Our parents, none of them, I don't think there was a parent on that team that when we went home they didn't say, 'you should have done this, or why didn't you do that.' You just played and they kept their mouths shut." They kept their mouths shut because they respected the coach. "I think the parents knew that the Cooksons gave everything they had to that game. And there wasn't a damn thing they could add to improve you or the outcome."

Playing Couch in the first round of state tournament, the outcome was very much in doubt after two quarters of play. Advance led by only three points, 29-26. Carroll Cookson would say after the game, "I woke'em up at half."[183] Both Carroll and Ronnie's motivational antics are legendary. Walker witnessed many of their halftime tirades first hand. "They had a philosophy that when they would go in at halftime, it was a show." Usually the brothers looked for something they could kick. "Ronnie would always look for trashcans – he had a thing for trashcans. I've even heard him say, 'go get me a trashcan.'" Walker recalls another night where Carroll was looking for a trashcan, but couldn't locate one. He kicked the next best thing he could find– a bathroom stall door. "I think he kicked it harder than he thought and of course, it was on hinges and it swung the wrong way and it just pulled the screws right off and the door did a big flip and made a big noise." The bathroom door that was now lying on the floor briefly caught the coach by surprise, but he quickly recovered. "He looks at over the assistant coach and says, 'fix that.'" Yelling, screaming, or kicking, the coaches' messages usually got through to the players. "I will borrow the term 'shock and awe,'" said Walker. "And it worked quite well."

Whatever Carroll Cookson said or did on this night worked out quite well. Leading Couch by three points at half, Advance "put the game away with a blazing fast break offense spearheaded by a full court press and precision ball handling."[184] The Hornets poured in 65 second half points to blow out Couch by the final score of 94-66. Stan Whitson, the Couch coach and former basketball player at Southeast Missouri State, was impressed by the Hornets and complimented their coach. "They are well drilled on blocking out underneath the basket and in every other phase of the game."

Advance moved on to quarterfinal action. So prolific was the Hornets style of play that the local media started calling them by a nickname that matched their uniform color. "The Big Orange Machine" rolled into the town of New Haven to take on Wright City. With three minutes to go in the game, Advance looked firmly in control. The Hornets led by 17 points when junior forward Terry Wills fouled out. As he can with seemingly every other moment of his senior season, Richie Walker vividly recalls the game's final moments. But he also remembers another incident involving Wills, their coach, and ultimately the entire team. It still brings a smile to his face.

It wasn't uncommon for a basketball player to suffer from a cold in the winter months. So it came as no surprise when Wills came down with one. Vicks Nyquil had recently come out on the market and Wills bought some down at the local drugstore. He was impressed with the results. "Terry bought some Nyquil, come back, he was bragging on it, said that was the best night's sleep," remembers Walker. "Somebody else got a cold and said you oughta get that Nyquil. And before long, everybody on the team was taking Nyquil. Carroll come down with a cold. And I think it was Terry who said you gotta take that Nyquil." Cookson took his player's advice and took a dose of the cold medication. The next day at school, their coach was nowhere to be seen. Finally, at the end of the day, with practice already started, Cookson arrived. He told everyone to go sit on the bleachers. As recounted by Walker, the coach then explained his absence to the team. "The reason I wasn't at school today wasn't because of my cold. I've been drunk today," Walker remembers Cookson saying. The coach discovered a day after taking the medication that Nyquil contained alcohol. He could hardly move when he woke up. To the tee totaling, Arnold Ryan disciple, the alcohol was a shock to his system. He then wanted to know how many of his players had taken Nyquil for their colds. Walker will never forget the response. "I don't think there was a hand that wasn't raised," recalls the Advance player. "I'll never forget the expression on his face when everybody raised their hand. And he just looked down and shook his head." Nyquil was immediately outlawed by the Advance coach.

There would be a memorable round of cold and flu illnesses the following season and that time no one would be laughing. But back in the quarterfinals against Wright City in 1972, Carroll Cookson was shaking his head at his team's performance on the court. A 17-point lead was quickly evaporating. Over a two and a half minute timeframe, Wright City outscored Advance 17-4. With thirty seconds to go in the game, Advance led by four points, 82-78. While Terry Wills could only sit on the bench with his five fouls, the other starters quickly checked back in. The rally started to create some doubts in the mind of the Hornets team leader. "When you don't have your momentum anymore and you're back in there with a little 'doubted seed' if you will, you're having to fight." Walker and his teammates had to fight right to the end. Wright City missed an inside shot and the first attempt of a one-and-one free throw. Still trailing by four points as time ticked away, they were forced to foul. Advance made two late free throws and hung on for an 84-78 victory.

With the new Hearnes Center still under construction on the campus of the University of Missouri-Columbia, the final four teams met in Rolla. Advance drew the North Harrison Shamrocks as their semi-final opponent. The Shamrocks had only lost one game all season. They were about to lose their second. The Hornets sprinted to a 10-point lead at the end of the first quarter only to see North Harrison close the gap to one by halftime. But as they did against Couch to open state tournament play, Advance came out firing in the third quarter and pushed the lead up to eleven. Five different Advance players scored in double figures as the Hornets prevailed 86-70. One game to go.

It had been exactly twenty years since Carroll Cookson had participated in a state tournament championship game. Two decades had gone by since the days of Arnold Ryan's "run-shoot-run" created a basketball buzz across the state. In the intervening timeframe, Cookson had grown from a 5'6" boy to a 6'2"man. He had worked at the family television repair shop, performed assembly line work in St. Louis and Texas, gotten married, graduated from college, raised and supported a family of three children. Doing what he loved, he was on the verge of following the identical path of his mentor: win his first state championship in his sixth season as a head coach. His wife and children would be there to witness it, as would his brother Ronnie, now in his second season at Scott County Central. One man wouldn't be there: Arnold Ryan. After leaving Puxico to take an assistant coach's job at Memphis State, Ryan quickly returned the high school coaching ranks. Over the years, he coached at Brentwood, Lilbourn, Manila, Arkansas, and Woodland High School, in addition to a second tour of duty at Puxico. Taking a job at Charleston in the fall of 1969, Ryan coached both the basketball and baseball teams. On a baseball diamond before a game in the spring of 1970, Ryan was warming up with the team when a ball rolled in from the infield. He stooped to pick it up and "at that moment, another ball was thrown in from either third base or left field striking him behind the left ear." Ryan collapsed on the baseball field. He was rushed to the hospital in Sikeston where he was pronounced dead on arrival. Arnold Ryan was fifty-three years old.[185]

No one respected or carried on the Arnold Ryan tradition more than Carroll Cookson. His team played an up-tempo style, pressed their opponents on the defensive end, and conducted themselves on and off the court under a rigid set of rules. On March 4, 1972, all the years of hard work paid off. The Advance Hornets, for the first time in the history of school, became state champions.

It wasn't easy. Their opponent, the Morrisville Panthers, matched them shot for shot throughout much of the contest. The score was tied at ten different points in the game. With the game tied at 53 with a little more than five minutes to go in the fourth quarter, the Hornets finally began to break away. A free throw and a ten-foot jump shot put them up by three points. Leading by four points with two minutes to go, Richie Walker hit a fast break lay-up. At that point, the Advance cheering section erupted. "We're number one!" We're number one!" The Hornets held on to win the game 69-61. Appropriately, Walker and teammate Richard Hitt, the glue and the top gun at Advance, led the team in scoring with 22 points apiece. Walker and Hitt were Cookson's only two seniors. After the game, someone asked Cookson about his chances of repeating. One reporter captured his reply and the look in his eye.

"It's possible. We've got some good sophomores.'" Suddenly, a far-away look emerged in his eye, and he hadn't even begun to celebrate the title already in hand."[186]

Just as he had done the season before when he took his team to watch the state tournament, Carroll Cookson was beginning to look ahead to next year. He had reasons to be optimistic. With Walker and Hitt lost to graduation, three other starters returned for their senior season: forward Terry Wills, center John Rhodes, and guard Darrell Croy. This trio would lead Cookson's squad back to the state championship game. As they always did when Carroll coached at Advance while his brother was at Scott Central, the two teams met in the first game of the year. Carroll won this round of the battle of the brothers, winning 69-54.

Playing junior high basketball for one and high school basketball for the other, Richie Walker knows the two coaches well. "They were definitely out for one another - neither one wanted to lose to the other one." The relationship mirrored that with their players; hyper-competitive during the game, but relaxed, friendly and die-hard loyal off the court. Ronnie would find ways to needle his brother during the games as well. Often, when he needed a timeout, he would yell down at his sibling to call one, especially when he didn't have any left. Carroll would almost always comply. One season, Carroll's son Steve, was nursing an ankle injury. It was in the fall before games started. Carroll had to drive him to Memphis for treatment. The Advance players didn't miss any practice, however, as Ronnie filled in. He started the afternoon with his team's practice. Once that ended, he made a quick dash over to the Stoddard County School. "I would get in the car and drive as hard as I could to Advance and I would practice his bunch over there. I practiced them for about a week and I mean to tell you I didn't cut them any slack either. I worked their asses off," remembers the Scott Central coach. His

Advance players never forgot the contributions he made to their program. "When Ronnie left, it hurt, I can remember feeling. We knew we lost something," admitted Walker. "When we won the state championship, I went to Ronnie and said we would have won that for you. I know that had to hurt him. But it showed you how much that hurt me when he left. I think that's something I don't think I've ever told anybody. "

Just as Walker had done, the seniors on the 1973 Advance team played their junior high ball under Ronnie. Terry Wills remembers just how seriously their coach took the games. "He spent a lot of time with us in junior high. He hated to lose in junior high as much as he hated to lose in high school."

Ronnie Cookson's Scott Central team was their first victim of the new season. It was far from the last. After winning the Bloomfield Christmas Tournament, Advance had won 26 games in a row dating back to the previous year. Four additional victories in the month of January pushed their record on the season to 19-0 and their winning streak to 30 games. It came to an end one night against their bitter rival, the Puxico Indians. Puxico slowed the ball down, throttled the Advance fast break, and forced the Hornets into several turnovers. The last turnover of the game would be the difference. With Advance leading 45-44 and controlling the ball with just seconds left, the Indians were applying full-court pressure. Puxico guard Jim Davis remembers what happened next. "What was funny was that Red Smith who was our point guard, was supposed to be on the back of the press. Red was the one who deflected the ball and I was at the top of the circle and it just came to me." With the ball in his hands and just a few remaining ticks on the clock, Davis launched the ball toward the basket. "The shot went up and the next thing I saw it go off the top of the square and it fell through just before the buzzer went off. It was just unreal." Puxico had won the game and snapped the Advance winning streak. A disappointed Carroll Cookson said after the game, "We deserved to get beat."[187]

With one winning streak snapped, Advance promptly started another one. The Hornets ripped off ten consecutive victories to start state tournament play with a record of 29-1. Meeting Parma in the first round at Bloomfield, Advance won by 15 points. Terry Wills led all scorers with 35. In the quarterfinal round with John Rhodes and Darrell Croy combining for 46 points, the Hornets beat Clopton 73-66.

Advance was back in the final four. But while the team was winning games, it was losing the battle against the flu. "There was concern by the nearly 1,000 AHS followers before the game as to how the Hornets would perform with the flu bug setting in on the team. Terry Wills, who netted 35 points in the team's first round romp of Parma Monday night, was physically weakened and pale because of the illness."[188]

Two things were certain. The Hornets were headed to Columbia and no one would be taking any Nyquil. Attempting a repeat, comparisons between Cookson and his former coach Arnold Ryan were now inevitable. Sportswriter Ron Jaynes of *The Daily Standard* put it in perspective for his readers.

"The greatest sports yarn since the epic of the 1951-1952 Puxico Indians is being spun this weekend as the defending Class S state basketball champions seek to become only the second team from the Bootheel region of Missouri to claim back to back championships."[189]

Advance began state play at the newly opened Hearnes Center in Columbia with a convincing win over Mound City, 80-65. Since January of the previous season, the Hornets had gone 43-1. With only one game left against Forsythe, the Advance team also battled a flu bug that was spreading. While Terry Wills was recovering from his illness, teammates Darrell Croy and Kenny Emerson were now sick. That meant three of the top six Advance players were under the weather. The talented Forsythe team was able to do something that few opponents had been able to that season: beat the Advance press and stop the fast break. Forsythe won the game 63-60 in a game the *Columbia Daily-Tribune* called an "upset." Freshman Steve Cookson saw action that day. His father put him into the game to do one thing – foul one of the opponents reserve players. The strategy backfired. The Forsythe player went seven for eight from the free throw line, and the Advance Hornets had to settle for second place. But the Advance JV squad went 21-1 that season. The Hearnes Center hadn't seen the last of Carroll Cookson. Terry Wills and the rest of the class of 1973 were left to ponder what might have been. A last second shot and a spate of illnesses at the end of the year were all that separated them from a possible undefeated season. "We shouldn't have lost a game; we should have gone 34-0." But the Advance forward still cherishes the experience of playing not for just one, but two members of the Cookson Clan. "Their wives are great. Their whole families are great. They have had a great impact on people. I saw a joke one time that said you know if you're from Southeast Missouri if you played basketball for one of the Cooksons."

***

Ironically, Advance played its final game that season on the same court and on the same day that history was being set at the University of Missouri. Mizzou's John Brown set what was then an all-time school scoring record that afternoon at the Hearnes Center. The "blond bomber" scored 43 points in a Tigers victory over Oklahoma State. Brown came to Columbia from Dixon, Missouri, where he played on an undefeated championship squad in 1969. An unusual call in the final game that season still has a generation of Bootheel basketball fans talking. Decades later, a Bootheel ballplayer is still answering the same question about his role in the event.

Fred Johnson was born in Scott, Mississippi in 1950. When he was just a few months old, his family moved to Missouri. Johnson's grandfather was a farmer and a dispute with a neighbor over the cotton crop led to the move. "The gentlemen next to my granddad was a white landowner and he didn't have a very good crop, so he thought it would be fine to go over and cut our crop." As a small child, he also lived briefly in Helena, Arkansas, but when his mother decided to move to Chicago, she left Fred with her parents. He moved in with his grandparents at their house just outside Oran. When he was five years old, Fred and his uncle John, started working in the cotton fields of the Missouri Bootheel. His grandfather worked on ground owned by E.P. Coleman, the land baron who helped transform the region back in the 1920's.

Johnson's first memories of farm work are carrying water out to the fields. His grandfather worked the land with mules. He and his uncle John, the same age as Fred, weren't allowed down into the cotton fields because they were too small. Instead, they would pick cotton off the end of the rows. By the time the two were nine years old, they were chopping cotton. "We would chop a row together. Of course, it was tough work but when we got tired, we was able to rest instead of continuing to work. And we got tired quite often. By the time we was eleven years old, we was carrying our own row."

Fred attended a segregated country grade school. He played sports growing up, primarily softball and baseball, not basketball. "The first time I ever saw a basketball in my life I was in eighth grade. I had no idea what a basketball was." The eighth grade coach at Oran wanted Fred's uncle, John Johnson, to tryout for the team. The principal told the coach that if he took John, he had to take anyone else who wanted to tryout. Fred decided to tag along. Once he got on the basketball court, he had no idea what to do. "I would bounce the ball once and pick it up and run with it like a football." That first weekend, Fred followed some relatives and friends down to the dirt court at their country schoolhouse. While everyone else played, Fred stood on the sidelines and watched. When a player sprained his ankle, one of his uncles ordered him into the game. "We were always taught the oldest in the family, the male, was just like the dad when he was gone. Of course, I didn't say anything. I just got up and got myself out there and started playing with them." When he took his first shot, the other players had to stop the game because they were laughing so hard. His teammates told him all he had to do was play defense. But later in the game, one of the players missed his shot. Fred rebounded the ball and put it into the goal. "That was the first bucket I ever scored in my life and then after that, I said shoot, I can play this game, so I started watching and I started playing." A fire was lit. From then on, people would know Fred Johnson as a basketball player.

From their living room in Southeast Missouri, Fred and his uncle John, raised like brothers, began watching basketball. The broadcasts were carried by the local ABC affiliate in Southern Illinois, and reception of the games wasn't always the best. In the days before cable television, Fred and John would improvise. "We used to go outside and hold the antennae. I would go out and hold it for awhile and John would watch TV and then I'd go in and he would hold it and I would watch." Fred remembers watching Jo Jo White of the Boston Celtics and Walt "Clyde" Frazier of the New York Knicks. White, the former standout from St. Louis McKinley High School, and Frazier, the former college star from Southern Illinois University, made a strong impression on the basketball neophyte, particularly on the defensive end of the court. When Frazier was at SIU, Oran coach Gene Bess took his team over to Carbondale to watch him play. From Frazier, Fred Johnson learned a move that became his calling card throughout his career – the art of taking a charge. "What

I would do was work my butt to set the man up and if he got close enough, I'd grab his shirt and pull him up on top of me. I would just put my hand under (his jersey) and just kind of slide him over so he wouldn't hurt me. It worked." It worked so well, in fact, that Johnson only remembers two charging fouls where someone actually made contact. Both incidents sent him to the hospital. While the second incident happened well into his college career, the first one took place in high school. Johnson attempted to draw a charge against Notre Dame standout and future University of Missouri player Greg Flaker. The resulting collision sent Johnson to the intensive care unit. Flaker, showing the sensitivity and compassion that would ultimately lead him to a career as a surgeon, went to the hospital as well. It's a gesture that Johnson will always remember. "He couldn't sleep. He would come to the hospital and sit there and wait."

Fred and John Johnson started playing varsity basketball their freshman year at Oran. From not knowing how to shoot or dribble in 8th grade, Fred made tremendous strides in one short season. He remembers playing three first halves of junior varsity games. His uncle didn't play JV basketball at all. Playing for the recently integrated Oran High School, not every town in Southeast Missouri welcomed the team with open arms. In the middle of the 1960's, certain restaurants in the area would refuse service to the black players. When that would happen, the team would move on to another eating establishment. Johnson recalls what coach Gene Bess told his team. "He said where one eats all eat." Once inside the gym, the team found it often had to battle three opponents: the other team, the fans, and the officials. "Some officials, I don't know if they saw color or not, but if the call was close, we didn't get it." Playing in a few towns, the team had to endure a stream of racial epithets from the stands. "We were called everything except our name." The abuse from the crowd only strengthened Johnson's resolve. "You shut people up by what you did on the court. That's what people remember."

In the winter of 1966, Johnson's freshman year, the Oran Eagles entered state play with a record of 28 and 3. Their first round opponent was Howardville, an all black school in New Madrid County. Playing at Houck Field House in Cape Girardeau, the game was close to the end. With just a few minutes to go in the contest, Howardville guard Lennies McFerren had the basketball. McFerren saw an opening and started driving to the basket. An Oran defender stepped in front of him. The whistle blew. McFerren was called for charging. It was his fifth and final foul of the game. The defender on the play was freshman Fred Johnson. "He really didn't touch me," remembers the Oran player. "I faked it." Oran would go on to win. McFerren, a senior for Howardville, had played his final high school contest. But as we'll find out later, Bootheel ball had not seen the last of the Howardville guard.

Oran's season ended the next game in a match-up against Bloomfield. The Wildcats had a young assistant coach at the time who would go on to make a name in the college ranks – Charlie Spoonhour. The coach had gotten his start at Rocky Comfort, a small school in Southwest Missouri. When coach Tom Hewgley left Exeter, a nearby school, to take over at Bloomfield, Spoonhour joined him in the migration across the state. He noticed a difference after coming to Stoddard County. "The Bootheel had better athletes than Southwest Missouri," he once admitted. The 1966 Bloomfield team finished fourth in the state. The previous season, the Hewgley-Spoonhour crew claimed third after losing to state champion Buffalo in the semi-finals.

The game against Bloomfield was the farthest coach Gene Bess's team had ever advanced in state play until 1969. That year, Fred Johnson's senior season, the Oran Eagles streaked through an undefeated regular season. After winning the regional championship and the first two rounds of state tournament play, Oran made its way to the final four at Brewer Field House in Columbia. The Eagles defeated Pembroke Day to go to the finals. In the other bracket, featuring two undefeated teams, Dixon defeated Hermann.

Although the finals pitted two teams with identical 35 and 0 marks, the contest wasn't expected to be close. Dixon's John Brown stood 6'7" and not only would he go on to set scoring records at the University of Missouri, he was also a future number one NBA draft pick and played several seasons of professional basketball. The tallest player on the Oran squad stood 6'1". The team was called the "running runts of the Bootheel."[190] Johnson knew Brown would cause match-up problems for the shorter Oran Eagles because they always played a man-to-man defense. Still, he was confident his coach would have them ready to play. "Coach Bess had us conditioned in our minds that we just didn't pay that (Brown and his height) any attention. We had a job to do and you go do your job." Doing their job right started in practice. Johnson will never forget the night he and his teammates blew out an opponent and seemed satisfied with their effort, perhaps a little too satisfied. "Coach Bess told us don't get dressed, brought us home that night and we practiced – got off the bus, went into the gym and practiced." The late night practice served as a wake-up call to the team; never become overconfident. "That sure did bring us down to earth," said Johnson.

Back on earth and in the state finals, Oran found itself trailing Dixon at halftime by the score of 49 to 43. In the third quarter, Oran rode the hot shooting hand of Fred Johnson, who poured in 10 points in the quarter, to take a 62 to 59 lead. Back and forth the game went, with the lead changing hands three times in the fourth quarter.

With 12 seconds to go in the game, Johnson was fouled. Down by two points, he had the opportunity to tie the game. Handed the ball at the free throw line, he took his time before he shot. He remembers the yelling from the crowd and the Dixon cheerleaders stomping their feet on the court. Focused and methodical, Johnson finally released the basketball. He made the shot. Oran now trailed by one point, 75-74. The next free throw would tie the game. Repeating his successful habit from his previous attempt, Johnson again contemplated his shot. With all eyes on the Oran senior, the crowd noise swelled and the foot stomping renewed. Johnson prepared to shoot the most important free throw of his high school career. He never got the chance. Before he could shoot, the referee blew the whistle and took the ball out of his hands. Johnson thought at first the official was halting the action to warn the crowd. It took him a few seconds to realize the call made by Gene Barth. The referee, who would go on to have a 20 year career as a National Football League official, ruled that Johnson had exceeded the 10 second time limit at the free throw line. Johnson lost his attempt at the second free throw and the ball was returned to Dixon. The rarely called infraction by the official who would later referee Super Bowl XVIII effectively ended Oran's season. A late free throw by Dixon made the final score 76-74. Ever since that day, Johnson has been asked about the call. For more than thirty years, his answer has been the same. "Did I take too long at the line? I took longer on the first one," recalls the former Oran star. The single loss, second place team remains the best in Oran history.

Following that season, coach Gene Bess left Oran to become an assistant coach at Three Rivers Community College in Poplar Bluff.

His star player followed him to the junior college. As we'll discover, like many athletes in the Bootheel, Johnson's career would eventually intertwine with the Cookson Clan. But he recognizes he will always be known for the events that transpired that fateful day in Columbia on the Brewer Field House basketball court. "Had I known, I probably would have shot it quicker, but the thing is I wouldn't have gotten the notoriety I've gotten for not shooting it. It's been since 1969 and people are still talking about it."

***

Upset in their bid to become back-back-state champions, Carroll Cookson's Advance Hornets would make two more final four appearances in Columbia. In the semi-finals of 1974, a controversial decision at the beginning of the second half helped turn a game against Cookson's team. Advance went into the locker room at halftime with a one-point lead, or so its coach and players thought. When they came back out for the second-half, they looked up the scoreboard to discover they were trailing by three points. The four-point swing occurred when the official scorer accidentally credited Advance with two free throws that belonged to Greenfield. The error was corrected during the halftime break. Cookson sought an explanation. "I said what is going on here? He (Missouri state high school official) said, 'Well everyone agreed to it.' I said I was in the dressing room. I was just so mad." Greenfield went on to win the game by five points, 70-65. After the game, Cookson told reporters, "Never in my coaching career have I seen an official scorebook changed."[191]

The following season saw the emergence of Carroll's son on the Advance team. A junior in 1975, Steve was four years old when his father went off to college to play basketball. For the past twelve years, his dad was either playing or coaching the game. Being the coach's son made life more difficult for him both at practice and in games. "I would say most people would definitely say it was harder. He expected more out of me." One time in practice, Steve was chastised by his father for dribbling the basketball too much. The son thought he would teach the father a lesson. "From that point on, I didn't take another dribble. I just passed it." It wasn't long before his father and coach tired of his antics. He kicked Steve out of practice. "The bad thing about it was when he sent people home, they got to go home and they didn't get to see him until the next day. I got to see him later on that night." As punishment, Steve didn't start the next game. "It got my attention. He could get my attention."

One thing that got the attention of the entire Cookson Clan was the traditional season opening match-up. Once again, Scott Central and Advance opened the season against one another. Ronnie Cookson's Braves, with junior forward Otto Porter beginning to display talents that would make him a dominant force in Bootheel basketball, defeated the Hornets. As January of 1975 began, Advance had three losses matched against ten victories. In addition to Scott Central, the Hornets had lost to Poplar Bluff and Kelly. The games against the Kelly Hawks pitted Cookson against his rival from his college basketball days back in Arkansas, Nick Lanpher. Cookson's former players tell the story of when they arrived at Kelly one night only to find the windows open and the heat shut off in their locker room. The players had to get dressed in ice-cold conditions. When Cookson sought out Lanpher for an explanation, he told him the heater was broken. The next year at Advance, Cookson returned the favor, telling the janitor to turn off the heat in the visiting locker room early in the day. Anticipating additional shenanigans back at Kelly the following season, Cookson took preemptive action. The team arrived with electric heaters in their bags.

Regardless of conditions in the locker room, Cookson's team began to heat up on the basketball court. Entering regional play at the end of February, Advance had won eleven straight. Three more victories put them in the regional finals against Delta. In the other regional tournament held in Southeast Missouri, Ronnie Cookson's Scott Central team had also advanced to the finals. The brothers were one game away from facing each other in the first round of the state tournament. It didn't happen. While Advance took care of business by beating Delta, the Braves were defeated by North Pemiscot. After five seasons at Scott Central, Ronnie Cookson had only won a single regional tournament.[192] His record in state tournament play stood at 0-1.

Carroll Cookson's Advance team returned to the final round of sixteen teams for the fourth year in a row. Cookson knew his first round opponent, North Pemiscot, would be a formidable opponent. After all, they had done something already that the Hornets failed to do – defeat Scott Central. But on this night, the North Pemiscot Mustangs had no answer for Advance center David Tropf. The 6'6" post-man poured in 36 as Advance won the game 66-55 and moved on to the quarterfinal round. "We beat one good team," commented Cookson afterwards.[193]

Two nights later in Flat River, Advance met a Crocker team that had won 23 games in a row. Shooting 65 percent from the field and forcing 16 Crocker turnovers in the first half, the Hornets led at one point in the game 34-9. Ten Advance players scored points in the game as Cookson substituted freely. Four players scored in double figures as the Hornets won the game by 20 points.

The 27-3 Hornets were on their way back to the Hearnes Center. They would go up against probably their most celebrated opponent of the past four seasons, the Glasgow Yellowjackets. Not only was Glasgow the defending state champions, but they had won a phenomenal sixty four games in a row. That winning streak tied a state record set by Bradleyville back in the 1960's. One more win and the state record would belong to Glasgow exclusively. Advance knew a record was on the line. The Hornets were ready. It all started with an article in the paper. "Our kids had read the St. Louis paper and they saw an article which said they're going to break that record in a certain ballgame. We got to counting up and figured out that was us," recalls coach Cookson. Son Steve has a slightly different memory of the event. "Dad had put up on the bulletin board that year – the St. Louis Post-Dispatch went and done a big article on them. He underlined some quotes."

Glasgow was led by their 6'3"forward Lawrence Butler who was averaging 32 points a game. The only way to beat Glasgow was to somehow put the brakes on their one-man scoring machine. Advance had the solution. Once again, a member of the Cookson Clan stepped front and center in state tournament play. It was Steve Cookson's responsibility to guard Butler. "We were able to frustrate him," remembers the Advance player. "I was able to draw three charges on him." The *Columbia Missourian* summed up Cookson's performance and the Advance strategy.

"The Advance Hornets, led by junior guard Steve Cookson, coach Carroll Cookson's son, used an effective combination of conservative offense and gambling defense to snap the Glasgow streak.

Hornets forward Ron Oller led all scorers with 15 points, but the real story was Cookson and the Hornets defense that

forced 15 Glasgow turnovers in the first half alone (and 24 for the game).
The Yellowjackets Lawrence Butler, who had scored a total of 76 points in two previous tournament contests, scored only 13 points and fouled out with just more than five minutes remaining in the game."[194]

The 13 points for Butler was his lowest output of the season. Advance won the game 59-50 in a ballgame that wasn't as close as the final score indicated. With two and a half minutes to go, the Hornets led by 18. The Yellowjackets winning streak was snapped. Glasgow had lost its first ballgame since February 28, 1973. The Glasgow coach admitted the streak had become a burden. "These kids have lived under a lot of pressure, "said coach Dick Royston. "After it was all over, they said something like 'We're glad it's over'. It's like someone has taken a weight off their shoulders."[195]

Star player Lawrence Butler was distraught. "I might still be remembering this game for a long time," Butler told a Columbia newspaper. "I may never forget it. I lost more than a basketball game out there today. I lost my pride."[196] Butler may have momentarily lost his pride, but he didn't lose his incredible basketball talent. After high school, he played four years of college basketball, first at a junior college and then at Idaho State his final two seasons. In 1979, Butler's senior season in college, an Indiana State forward by the name of Larry Bird captured the nation's imagination as his team advanced to the NCAA finals against Ervin "Magic" Johnson's Michigan State Spartans. Bird averaged nearly 29 points a game that season. He didn't lead college basketball in scoring however. That honor belonged to Lawrence Butler who led all NCAA Division 1 scorers with an average of 30.1 points per game.

Defeating Glasgow in the semi-finals almost made the final game seem anti-climatic. When asked about the possibility of a letdown, Cookson told reporters, "We'd just like to play another good ballgame." The Hornets had now won eighteen straight games since a loss to Kelly on January 10. Their opponent, the Northeast Nodaway Bluejays, hadn't lost a game all season. Against Advance, they slowed the ball down and packed into a 3-2 zone defense that denied the Hornets their outside shots. Only at the very end did Advance pull away. Outrebounding their opponent 16-5 in the second half, the Hornets won the game 55-44. For Advance and Carroll Cookson, it was their second state title in four years. For Bootheel basketball, it was a third state basketball championship of 1975. In addition to the 1A Hornets, the 2A Lilbourn Panthers and 3A Charleston Bluejays walked away from the Hearnes Center with championship hardware. Two things were written on the chalkboard in the Advance locker room. "Relax and play hard!" and "SEMO (Southeast Missouri) Power".

With his second state championship, Carroll Cookson's teams had completed an amazing four-year run; one that bore eerie similarities to his former coach and mentor. Like Arnold Ryan, Carroll would win his first state title in the sixth year of his first coaching job. In Ryan's last four years at Puxico, he compiled a record of 143 and 11 and won two state titles. From '72 through '75, Cookson's squads won 111 while only losing 21, also with two championships. After their second title, neither man won another one. Just as Ryan did, Carroll would leave his first coaching job, later return, and leave again to coach other teams in the area. But the magic of those early years could not be recaptured. The biggest highlight of Carroll Cookson's coaching career was over. Younger brother Ronnie was just getting started.

CHAPTER FIVE
Season Number Six
1970-1976

"I think I can honestly tell you that as a senior I'm not sure I got tired in a game."

Point guard Richie Walker – Advance class of 1972

"We practiced so hard that game days, Tuesdays and Friday, oh, it was just so easy. We didn't even break a sweat."

Point guard Jeff Limbaugh – Scott Central class of 1980

As the winter of 1971 began, Paul McCartney was bringing court action against John, George and Ringo, his fellow Beatles band members. McCartney was demanding the band be legally dissolved. The Beatles would never tour again nor release another album. Journalists named the aborted Apollo 13 mission as the top news story of 1970, edging out shootings on the campuses of Kent State and Jackson State Universities and a war in Vietnam that had spread to Cambodia. As American GI's died in Southeast Asia, the American economy and culture were gradually but permanently shifting on the heartland. In Sikeston, Missouri, Woolworth's announced it was shutting down its Front Street location. The dime store chain had come to town in 1932. The store would close its doors in April, after a thirty-eight and half year run. Just a few blocks away, moviegoers in the area could take in the Russ Meyer film, "Finders Keepers Lovers Weepers." The ad in the Sikeston paper mentioned the *Yale Daily News* called the X-rated flick the "Best film of 1969." Author Tom Wolfe has identified the year 1970 as a cultural divide in American history. Before that year, NASA would not accept divorced astronauts. After 1970, marital status didn't matter. American society had changed in another small way; exactly two to the day before the Russ Meyer film debuted, the same theatre in Sikeston was showing the MGM re-release of "Gone With The Wind." But why it took until 1971 for the best film of 1969 to make its way to Missouri Bootheel wasn't exactly clear.

Everything seemed to move a little slower back in the days before cable TV and the Internet. A check of the January 1971 TV listings shows that both the local CBS affiliate in Cape Girardeau and the NBC station in Paducah, Kentucky ran no programming either overnight or early in the morning. On Sunday afternoons, other than sports programming, local television viewers' only choice was the Sunday Double Feature on the ABC station in Harrisburg, Illinois. Crossing the Mississippi River Bridge at Cape Girardeau into Illinois proved to be a popular Sunday afternoon activity. Shoppers were out of luck in Southeast Missouri. Blue laws prevented stores from opening. North of Sikeston along Highway 61, the gym was always open at Scott County Central High School, regardless of the day of the week. Ronnie Cookson was in the middle of his first season as a head basketball coach. There was also another reason that attracted Cookson to the small school. It offered something that not every basketball program in the region could. "I know that Ronnie left (Advance) because he wanted some black athletes," remarked his coaching rival and friend Ed Arnzen. "I think that's the reason he went to Scott County."

Scott County Central High School (Scott Central) was formed in 1959. It joined students from the towns of Morley, Vanduser and Haywood City. The combined population of the three towns is less than 1,500. Morley, located just off Highway 61, is the largest of the three communities. It's here the topography of the county changes with the Benton Hills beginning north of town. Looking south from Morley, a visitor would have a hard time distinguishing the landscape of this part of the Bootheel from that of eastern Arkansas. When black sharecroppers staged a protest alongside Highway 61 in 1939, Morley was the northern most point of their demonstration. Vanduser and Haywood City are both smaller and more remote.

Owing its origins to the cotton craze of the 1920's, black people lived in only certain areas of the county. But while cotton fever had long since died and Scott County farmers produce a variety of crops, the population demographics still retain a certain correlation. The northern half is almost exclusively white. Even in the southern portion, African-Americans were historically confined to the Sunset Addition in Sikeston and a few surrounding areas. In 1947, a new town south of Morley was formed in the area known as "the Sands." Originally called Hay-wood City, it officially incorporated in 1960. Outside of Sikeston it was and is the only town in the county with a substantial black population. By the early 21st century, it had the distinction of being listed as the poorest community in a four county region.[197] Other than a "few day cares and a tiny candy store," there are no businesses.[198] While both isolated and impoverished, starting in the 1970's, it produced a generation of high school athletes that came to dominate the newly integrated school, the Bootheel and ultimately the entire state. A new coach at the school was highly influential in their development.

He arrived at Scott Central in the fall of 1970 full of hope, energy and confidence. He also arrived with a set of basketball rules laid down by Arnold Ryan, learned first hand by brother Carroll and since hardwired into the fiery, first year coach. He kicked two members off that first team for not cutting their hair. There was a new sheriff in town, and his name was Ronnie Cookson. He almost didn't get the job. After four years at Advance, both Kelly High School and Scott Central had job openings. Cookson interviewed both places, and Scott Central had offered the position to someone else. But that person turned it down, and Cookson signed a contract with the school south of Morley "before they could change their minds."

Denny Alcorn was a senior guard Cookson's first season. He remembers basketball before the Cookson era. "Up until that time, we were pretty much a laid back team." The head coach the previous season had resigned from the school mid-year. A high school math teacher finished out the year at the helm. Then Ronnie Cookson arrived. "It was quite a drastic change when Ronnie came along," said Alcorn, "mainly in the discipline area. That's all something we really hadn't experienced."

Alcorn was 5'10", relied on his quickness, his shooting ability, and his dribbling skills. So comfortable and adept was he at dribbling a ball that Cookson would sometimes line up a player next to Alcorn with the two racing to the other end of the court. The senior guard would dribble the ball as he ran while his competitor just had to worry about sprinting. Alcorn and Cookson both remember he never lost a race.

Alcorn honed his dribbling skills on the streets of his hometown. At the time, where he grew up in Morley, the streets were gravel. The street in front his parent's house wasn't paved until he left for college. The teenager would dribble his basketball over the gravel roads to downtown Morley, out to Highway 61, turn and head south and then make a left back onto the road that led to his home. Ronnie and Dee Cookson lived on the same road at the time. Alcorn can remember Dee bringing out lemonade to him during the hot summer months.

The coach's wife, who also taught at Scott Central, made a big impact on the program, according to Alcorn. One of the biggest challenges confronting Cookson when he took over the program is that many of the black athletes didn't play basketball. "We had a couple of boys my senior year that were as good as ballplayers as anybody," recalled Alcorn. "But their parents made them work. They couldn't go out for basketball." Through the years, Ronnie and Dee Cookson began to change that. "Dee would pick up kids from practice, shuffle them to Sikeston to McDonald's or Hardee's for work and sometimes even go back and pick them up. They (Ronnie and Dee) did that so they could play ball. They gave every kid an opportunity that wanted to." In Cookson's first year, six of the ten players on the varsity squad were black. In time, black athletes would come to dominate basketball at Scott Central. In the fall of 1970, however, the integrated school district was relatively new. While Cookson brought with him a color-blind attitude toward his athletes, change in the community came slower. Each year the team had a dinner for the players at a restaurant in Sikeston. One year, a group of parents in Haywood City decided to host a dinner as well. That night made an impression on Alcorn. "I was the only white kid who showed up."

That separation began to erode under Cookson. "When I came over here, it didn't matter any difference what color you were, if you could play basketball, you could play. The black kids over here realized I was that way. They realized I would kick their ass just as fast as I would someone else's ass," said the coach. The mantra was clear — everyone was to be treated the same.

Even his unintentional acts could result in better discipline. Alcorn will never forget one such incident early in Cookson's first year. One afternoon at practice Cookson was explaining the finer points of a box-in-one defense. The idea of such a scheme is when one opposing player is so dominant on offense, the defense has one guy assigned to guard him, wherever he goes. The other four defenders remain stationary in a zone setup. The coach was standing at the top of the key on one end of the court with a basketball in hand. Two of the players stood near the goal. Occasionally, they would turn and face the other direction as they were talking and laughing at the same time Cookson lectured. A big mistake. The coach warned them once, demanding they turn around and listen. The players complied for a short period of time, but soon, they were again with their backs to the coach. Cookson decided a basketball in the back would get their attention. But just as he released the ball, the players turned back around, facing their coach. Instead of the basketball hitting one of them in the back, it landed on his face. The blood started flowing immediately. Cookson had a group of players rush their injured teammate to the Sikeston hospital. Once inside the hospital, the diagnosis was delivered and assistance was needed. "They come in there and tell me – his nose is broke, we got to fix it," remembers Alcorn. "It took about four of us to hold him down, but they got his nose lined back up." According to the Scott Central guard, the accident had another effect on the team. "From that day forward, everybody listened."

In addition to breaking down racial barriers and injecting a dose of discipline into his team, Cookson made another change at his new school. In the years prior to his arrival, "we'd go out and practice basketball and that was about it. We might run a couple of wind sprints," said Alcorn who also recalled the dramatic differences under Cookson. "All of a sudden, every basketball player had seventh hour PE. We shot free throws and got some of the basic things out of the way. As soon as the bell rung, you were on the line running wind sprints for 30-45 minutes and then you played basketball. It was all about conditioning." That conditioning would soon start reaping rewards for the Scott County Central Braves.

Shortly after the new year began, Cookson took his team to Sikeston to play the Bulldogs. January 5, 1971 proved to be a memorable evening. Scott Central won the game by one point in overtime, but that's not what players and coaches remember most. Two incidents off the court stand out to Denny Alcorn. "I was dating one of the cheerleaders and one of the Sikeston girls tried stabbing her in the bathroom." After the game, the unrest moved outside as some Sikeston fans directed their anger at the departing Scott County Central transportation. "They broke out all the windows on the bus," said Alcorn who also recalls the lasting legacy of that evening. "Scott Central and Sikeston have never played against each other again since then." Cookson finished his career with a 1-0 mark against the Bulldogs.

Despite an impressive victory over the much larger school, Cookson's first ball club was struggling somewhat as the season reached its midpoint. After a loss to Lilbourn in mid-January, the team's record stood at 7-7. The season had opened with a win at Advance. Ronnie Cookson's first career coaching victory came against his brother. Denny Alcorn led the Braves with 20 points in their 88-76 victory. Richie Walker topped all Advance scorers with 22. This was Walker's junior year, the season before Advance won its first state title. Playing against his former coach was an intimidating task. "I remember being scared in that game. I was scared to lose. That's not the focus you want."

The next time out, Cookson took his first loss. Ed Arnzen had taken over the reigns of the Notre Dame program the same year Cookson started at Scott Central. Opening against the Braves in Cape Girardeau, Arnzen's team won the game by twenty-two points. Meeting for a second time at the Christmas Tournament in Cape, Notre Dame won that contest as well; setting a pattern that plagued the Braves throughout the 1970's. As we'll see later, the two coaches had memorable battles throughout the decade. But while Cookson's greatest teams were still to come, Arnzen thinks his first edition may have been his best. "That might have been, talent wise, the best club that we had."

Since opening the season at 1-1, the Scott Central Braves had seemingly fallen into a pattern of alternating wins and losses. Things soon began to change. Entering the Scott-Mississippi Conference tournament, the Braves were not expected to win. Kelly High School was seeded one in the tournament and after the first two rounds, the Hawks and the Braves met in the final. After the game, the Sikeston paper took notice of the new coach and offered a prediction.

"If coach Ronnie Cookson of Scott County Central high school doesn't accomplish anything else the rest of the season with the Braves basketball team, he's already done more than any of his predecessors have. The first year head mentor, former

*Advance assistant, directed the sharp shooting Braves to its
first Scott-Mississippi conference championship Saturday
night, knocking off the top seeded Kelly Hawks 81-62.
The 1970-71 edition of the Scott Central Braves have now
but to advance to the State Class S tournament to equal the
other accomplishments of former SCCHS quintets....And
you know that might not be too hard to accomplish if they
continue their present talents on the hardwood."*[199]

Cookson and his team weren't about to rest on their accomplishments.
They closed out the regular season with seven more victories bringing
their winning streak to ten games. The rest of the Bootheel began to take
notice. The Braves entered regional play as the number one seed. They
beat College High 112-65 to start post-season play. The output was far
from the highest of Cookson's career. As we'll see later, the Braves played
another first round regional tournament game reminiscent of Arnold
Ryan and his Puxico team's blowout of Greenville. Things began to get
more difficult after the first round for Cookson's team. Scott Central beat
Oran by nine points, they edged Matthews by five, and in the regional
finals, squeaked out a one-point victory over Parma.

After beating Parma and winning the regional title, Cookson's team
had reeled off 14 straight decisions. *The Daily Standard* thought it had the
answer. Cookson hadn't lost "since he began to sport the same shirt, suit,
socks and shoes to every game." The coach vowed the superstition would
last "until we lose."[200] Cookson had clearly put his imprint on the school
north of Sikeston that season and people were beginning to notice.

*"Cookson....has transformed the schools basketball program
from a relatively slow, zoning basketball program to a fast
moving, sharp shooting success."*[201]

The coach and his team would do something that night he would
never do again after gaining a berth in the state tournament – celebrate.
"It was an enthusiastic group of Scott Central players and fans who danced
around the gym Saturday as the cheering section rang out with chants
of 'we're number one!'" That celebration continued after the players left
the court. "The team went out and partied that (Saturday) night after the
(regional) championship," Cookson later admitted.[202]

That celebration would be short-lived. The Braves clinched the regional title on a Saturday night. State play started Monday night in Poplar Bluff. The opponent was South Iron. Their star player was John Matchell. The 6'3" center scored 40 points in the game against Scott Central. His South Iron Panthers would defeat the Braves 90-80. Cookson's team shot only 37% from the floor. After the game, the coach had a succinct answer when asked about his players' shortcomings that night, "We were flat."[203] In his first season at Scott Central, Cookson had a lot to be proud of. His team had gone 21-8, won the conference, the conference tournament and the regional tournament. Still, the spectacle of celebrating a regional championship and then losing in the first round of state play would haunt Cookson. "Until we win the championship, we keep our heads to the grindstone and get after it."[204] It would be five long years before he could begin to exorcise the demons.

***

Three years after taking a team to the first round of state play, Cookson experienced something that would only happen twice during his entire coaching career. He had a losing season. Nevertheless, the early 1970's were a significant time for the Braves coach and his team. In the fall of 1972, a freshman by the name of Otto Porter decided to go out for basketball. Porter's friend, Ricky Thomas, had recently transferred from Oran. He too went out for the squad. Porter and Thomas would be seniors in '76 and form the nucleus of his first championship season.

Porter and Thomas's indoctrination to Scott Central basketball wouldn't be easy. They played in a freshman basketball game their first season against Advance. Steve Cookson was also a freshman that year and remembers traveling to Scott Central one afternoon and getting whipped on the court in the first half. The Braves led Advance by about 20 points when Ronnie Cookson took the time to needle his brother as the buzzer sounded to end the second quarter. Advance players and their coach started walking to the locker room. The Scott Central coach told his team to go get a drink and stay out on the court. They were playing so well there was no need for any halftime discussions. Ronnie made sure he spoke loud enough for Carroll and his team to hear. By the time the Advance coach got to the locker room, he had just one request; somebody needed to get Ronnie's paddle. The whipping on the court wasn't nearly as painful as the one the players received off it. Stinging from their punishment, Advance proceeded to come out in the second half and turn the tables. A double-digit deficit turned into a double-digit victory and now it was Scott Central's turn for the paddle treatment. Ronnie lined up his players along the bleachers before Carroll and his team could walk off the court. With the Cooksons, it was possible for both the losing *and* winning team to get a spanking in the same ballgame.

Otto officially began his high school career in a game at the Bell City B-team tournament. While he had played in scrimmages and pick-up games, this game was something entirely new to him. Uniform on, bleachers full of fans, referees blowing whistles, the young freshman felt disoriented and confused. "I'm kind of lost. I'm kind of like – what do I do? I'm kind of stumbling around there, not knowing where to go or what to do." Cookson called timeout and took Porter out of the game. The freshman took a seat on the bench next to his coach. Cookson grabbed him on the inside of his leg just above the knee. He started to squeeze. "And I mean he held me there. You talking about pain. I was like, man! He was like, 'you better play ball.'" More than anything else his first year, the episode on the bench became Porter's wake-up call. "I will always remember that because it was the one thing that got my attention. I had been paddled before with the whole team. But this was directly at me. He was like 'you better play ball.' That got me going. I will always remember that. I will *always* remember that."

Otto Porter was born in Helena, Arkansas in 1958. When he was a young boy, the family moved to Missouri and settled near Oran. His father was a farmer. David and wife Johnnie Mae Porter later made the decision to move the family to Haywood City. That move would have long-term consequences for Bootheel ball. For nearly two decades, a Porter would be playing basketball at Scott County Central. Otto was the first. Porter comes from a large family. "I'm actually in the middle of the family. There's thirteen in my family. I'm number seven."

When one of Otto's sisters began to date, the Porters began to take basketball seriously. That's because Otto's future brother-in-law, Larry Mosley, loved the game. They would often play on a dirt court in Haywood City. "That's where I got a lot of my experience from. Lot of one-on-one, lot of two-on-two, we played pretty much everyday. Sandlot. It was the type where you couldn't dribble the ball, it was like pass, shoot. That's all that you could do." Mosley's influence was important.

Porter's father was always working on the farm and didn't take the time to enjoy sports. "My dad wasn't really into sports of any kind. He was pretty much a farmer. We played and every once in a while, he would pick up the ball and shoot it. He was not into that."

In Otto's freshman year, his father passed away, leaving a wife and a large family behind. The loss meant everyone in the family suddenly had to pitch in and help out. Otto would take farming jobs in the summer. One year, in the middle of a field on a tractor, he felt a sharp sting on his face. Otto wasn't sure what happened until he started to rub his cheek. That's when pellets from a shotgun shell fell into his hand. "A guy shot me. Of course, he was quite a ways from me but the pellets did hit me in the face." A quail hunter from a nearby field had accidentally fired on Porter. Fortunately, other than the brief stinging sensation and removing a few imbedded pellets from his skin, Porter survived intact. A Ronnie Cookson practice could be more treacherous.

Profiles of Porter over the years invariably mention the fact that he didn't start basketball until his freshman year. In fact, Otto actually went out for the team in seventh grade. He quit. "Didn't have that much interest. I liked the game but it wasn't that much to me at the time." But by the end of his 8th grade year, peer pressure began to get the best of him. Basketball had become cool at Scott County Central. "Once we got into high school, all the other guys was playing –that was the big thing." Like many others, he found his high school coach a bit intimidating. But he soon learned there were two Ronnie Cooksons – the one on the basketball court and the one away from the game. "I think everybody learned that when you're out there playing, he expects certain things out of you. Once it's over with, he's the best person in the world to have around."

In Porter's junior season of 1975, Bootheel ball claimed three state champions. Scott County Central was not among them. However, the Braves did play two of the teams that season. Carroll Cookson's Advance Hornets only lost three games en route their second state title that year. One of the losses was to Scott Central. The Braves also played against 2A champion Lilbourn. The Lilbourn Panthers, under coach Bob Phelps achieved in victory what few opponents of Scott Central over the years even dared to attempt; they outran the Braves. In thirty-two minutes of basketball, the two teams combined for 203 points. Lilbourn won 106-

97. Sitting over on the Lilbourn bench, Assistant coach Leonard Bishop could appreciate the style of play. He was an experienced hand at the run and gun style of Bootheel ball.

***

Bishop grew up in the New Madrid County town of Matthews. Until his sophomore year, he attended segregated schools. But after going to O'Bannon High School in New Madrid as a freshman, Bishop started at Matthews High School the following year. His senior season, the Matthews Pirates, under coach Jim Hart went 34-1 and won a state title. It was the first state championship for a Bootheel team since the 1952 Puxico Indians. Their point guard was 5'10" senior Leonard Bishop. "We played what we called a controlled fast break. We played kind of like a sagging man-to-man defense. We didn't put a lot of pressure out front but we always wanted to stay out in front of our man. We also ran a diamond press."

After high school, Bishop did what many talented Bootheel basketball players of his era did: play basketball for two seasons at Three Rivers Community College in Poplar Bluff and then on to Southeast Missouri State to play for his final two seasons. After graduating from college, Bishop started at Lilbourn as an assistant coach. In both 1974 and 1975, the Panthers won state titles. The 1975 team that blew past Scott Central also defeated Charleston in overtime during the regular season. The Charleston Bluejays, with sophomore sensation Ricky Frazier, went on to claim the state title in 3A, giving the region the three state champions. For the first time in a long time, people around the state started paying attention to Bootheel ball. Writing in the *St. Louis Globe-Democrat*, Dennis Dillon took notice.

"Southeast Missouri, known previously for the Bootheel and the folks who walk around saying, "Y'all," now has to be recognized as a basketball hotbed."[205]

The 1975 Lilbourn team featured all-state guards Earnest McFerren, brother to former Howardville player Lennies McFerren, and Frankie Robinson. "Earnest and Frankie are probably as good as shooters as I've been around in all my days of coaching," remembers Bishop. "If three pointers were in back then, Frankie would have done nothing but shoot three pointers." Just as the black community of Haywood City fed basketball talent to the Scott County Central school district, the town of Howardville played much the same role at Lilbourn. Until the late 1960's, the two schools were segregated and the all-black Howardville Hawks had been a basketball force in their own right.

Bishop later became the head coach at Lilbourn and when schools in the county consolidated, he became the first ever head coach at New Madrid County Central. He might still be coaching in the Bootheel today if it weren't for a trip he took to Texas over New Year's Eve in the early 1980's. There was snow on the ground back in Missouri, but people in Dallas were walking around in shorts. He made up his mind right then he wanted to move to Texas. He was coaching in the Lone Star State the following season. His second coaching job in Texas took him to Lincoln High School in Dallas. In 2002, his team went 40-0. Leonard Bishop was named *USA Today's* National Coach of the Year. His star performer, Chris Bosh, played one season of college basketball at Georgia Tech before entering the NBA draft and being selected by the Toronto Raptors with the fourth overall pick in 2003. When asked if Bosh was the best player he ever coached, Bishop hesitated. "I think he was one of the best but if you say the best? Because I really think that Frankie Robinson had so much potential, so much potential." After high school at Lilbourn, Robinson played college basketball in Arkansas. "He went to Arkansas State and he hadn't played but about five games and they were already talking about they were going to have to retire his number," remembers his coach. According to Bishop, Robinson only played one season of college ball. He left after his freshman year never to play again.

Bishop hasn't called the Bootheel home in more than twenty years. But when it came time for his son to make a decision about where to play college basketball, he decided to follow in his father's footsteps. Three Rivers assistant coach Brian Bess (son of head coach Gene Bess) saw Leonard Bishop, Jr. play in an all-star game following his senior season. "He (Bess) said he was interested in him, not knowing he was my son." In the fall of 2003, Bishop's son began his college career at the junior college in Poplar Bluff.

In the coaching ranks now for three decades, Bishop can draw upon an impressive list of influences. His high school coach Jim Hart had an impact, as did Gene Bess at Poplar Bluff, the all time leader in victories among junior college coaches. He also thinks Ronnie Cookson's Scott Central Braves carved out their own special niche. "One of the things I can remember as far as Scott Central is that they were exciting because they were the first team to run on every possession. The thing about them is—and at that time, I don't think they really understood—is the fact that they played really good defense. They got a lot of baskets off of steals," said Bishop. "I think they were playing basketball ahead of their time."

Ahead of their time, but not always ahead of their opponents at the end of the game. The young Scott Central lineup was inconsistent. "Scott Central runs hot and cold. They might look great for a few minutes and just the opposite for the next few minutes."[206] The Braves finished the 1975 season 23-6, losing in the regional finals to North Pemiscot. But Scott Central showed flashes of its potential in defeating one state champion and narrowly losing to another one. The loss against Lilbourn was a one-point game with a minute and a half left. The junior dominated Braves team, led by Otto Porter, Ricky Thomas, and guard James "Frog" Williams, would all be returning for their final season.

A new player almost joined the Braves in 1976. After Carroll Cookson had won his second state championship in four years at Advance in the winter 1975, Southeast Missouri State University began talking with him about joining the Indians as an assistant coach. Steve Cookson was entering his senior year at Advance, but if his dad was to take the college job, he knew exactly what he wanted to do; move to the Scott Central school district and play basketball for his Uncle Ronnie. The job didn't pan out. It turned out that an assistant college coach at a Division II school (at the time) didn't pay anymore than a high school head-coaching job. Carroll and Steve would stay at Advance.

At Scott Central, Ronnie was set to begin his sixth season coaching at the school. Being around the Advance program for four seasons, he knew what it took to make a state champion. Coaching with his brother, he would constantly strategize about the game, frequently talking basketball with Carroll's former coach. Steve Cookson remembers Arnold Ryan stopping by to chat with Carroll and Ronnie. "I remember him (Ryan) coming over to our house and those three guys sitting around the table talking basketball." Those early years laid a foundation. "Working with Carroll the first four years and talking to Arnold when he would come down to the house, I'd pick up little things. I hunted and fished, but all the time I hunted and fished and was sleeping, there was something about basketball – it was all in your subconscious. Even sleeping, you'd come up with as much stuff sleeping at night as you would in practice."

After starting his own head-coaching career, Ronnie began attending coaching clinics and camps. He discovered he had a talent for working the referees. At one camp, with three NCAA referees calling the action, Cookson and the opposing coach decided to conspire against the officials. With three minutes to go in the game, each coach made a substitution. However, no one from either team came off the court. Both teams played six on six the rest of the way. "We're playing not the last thirty seconds, I'm talking the last three minutes," recalls Cookson. "They never seen it coming. Never picked up on it. The horn went off. We was still playing six on six. Everybody was laughing, all the boys on the bench was laughing. We did stuff like that all the time. I really enjoyed summer camp."

He also experimented with something else during that same game at summer camp. "About six times I put the wrong free throw shooter on the line." It's a trick he would incorporate into his regular season routine. Player A, call him Joe, would receive the foul, but Cookson wanted Player B, call him Jeff, to shoot the free throw. The key moment came right after the referee blew the whistle. While clapping his hands, the coach would yell out onto the court. "I'd stand up on the sidelines and I'd say, 'put it in Jeff, put it in Jeff.'" The tactic frequently worked. "We did it at the state tournament, we did it at regular game, we did it everywhere we could."

Even when Cookson would come under fire from the referees, he knew where to draw the line. After playing for him, Jeff Limbaugh later became a high school official. "He was so good at working referees, he was a connoisseur. I refereed him for ten years, you thought – one more word buddy and you got a technical, even if you are my friend. But that one word never came out." Cookson did receive technical fouls during his career, but he never got the third one that would get him thrown out of a game. Wife Dee remembers the routine. "Ronnie never got tossed. He would get his two (technicals) and then he'd quit. After two, I'd get the keys out to warm up the car, but he'd make it."

But not all experiences with referees were confrontational. Some developed into lifelong friendships. One night, when Scott Central was scheduled to face a Carroll Cookson team, one of the referees called Ronnie to say he couldn't make it. Needing an official to fill in at the last minute, the Scott Central coach called his brother to ask for a recommendation. "I knew there were a lot of referees that Carroll wouldn't want," recalls Ronnie. "I said do you know of anyone we could get? Carroll said, 'yeah, I know a referee we can hire.'" The referee that Carroll called was a friend of his. Jerry Pilz arrived at Scott Central with Carroll on the team bus. "Jerry comes in with Carroll and he's got a pair of Converse tennis shoes tied together like we used to, with two strings, hung over his shoulders, wearing his referee shirt. To tell you the truth, it looked like he had slept in it for a week," remembers the Scott Central coach. "Carroll's giving him instructions, 'now watch this one, he'll jump on your back if you're not careful.' That's how I got to know Jerry Pilz – over that game." Pilz, a school administrator in Altenburg, Missouri at the time, got his introduction that night to the run and gun style of the Cookson Clan. "It was the wildest game, just going up and down the court." It was the first game that Pilz had ever refereed. It was also his last. "I was wore out."

Pilz, whose son Chris later became a Second Team Division II All-American at the University of Missouri-St. Louis, has always enjoyed the game of basketball. After his son played his last college game, he and his wife thought of a way to stay involved with the sport. Each summer, he hosts an annual all-star game featuring recently graduated high school seniors on the campus of the College of the Ozarks in Branson. When he initially thought of the idea for the "Gerald A. Pilz and Friends" game, he knew exactly who to ask to help out. "I think Carroll and Ronnie are the best friends I got," said Pilz. "They were the first two people I called."

***

For those familiar with the success of Ronnie Cookson's teams while at Scott Central, it is hard to imagine the view from the fall of 1975. When someone mentioned coach Cookson back then, they were just as likely, perhaps more likely, to think about his brother Carroll. It was Carroll who had taken four consecutive teams to the final four, winning two state championships. It was Carroll who played for the legendary teams at Puxico under Arnold Ryan. While in high school, Ronnie's teams never made it to the state tournament. As a coach, he had yet to win a game in state tournament play. But just like his brother and Arnold Ryan before him, season number six was his date with destiny. But unlike the other two men, the spotlight on Ronnie Cookson would continue to shine nearly non-stop for the next two decades.

Cookson knew his team could be special. What worried the coach was the lack of depth. The team had five experienced senior starters and not much else. "If we get into foul trouble, we're going to get beat."[207] The best of those five starters was 6'3" forward Otto Porter. Once he finally started to play basketball, he didn't want to stop. "I fell in love with the game and I was playing it because I loved the game not so much because it was going to get me somewhere or it was going to do anything for me." At the end of Porter's freshman season, he broke his arm. The experience proved beneficial. "The breaking of my arm helped me because I played a lot of guys with one arm. One arm in a sling – one on one. That helped me out a lot." By his sophomore season, he was playing on the varsity. His coach loved his work ethic and his attitude. "He's usually in there (the gym) playing ball before classes start in the morning. And if he gets twenty minutes off for lunch, he takes five minutes to eat and spends the other fifteen shooting. That's why he's such an outstanding player."[208] At the end of his junior season, a new student teacher showed up at Scott Central. Oran's Fred Johnson was finishing up his degree at Southeast Missouri State. "We would be in the gym playing pickup games after school," remembers Johnson. "Heck, I was a student teacher. I didn't have anything to do on my off days." Johnson and other former players from Oran would regularly scrimmage against Porter and his teammates. Playing better competition only helped the Braves lineup. "Fred, Robert Earl (Gibson), a bunch of those guys from Oran – yes, (would) come over there and we played them and we held our own. And it only made us better," said Porter.

The Braves would soon find out just how much better they were. They opened their schedule with defending state champion Advance. Carroll Cookson's team had won nineteen straight from the previous season. But they entered the game with a banged up lineup. Several players were injured, including his son and star guard Steve. Cookson had broken his ankle over the summer, and the injury took a long time to heal. Later in the season, the senior would contract hepatitis. The combination of the injury and the illness meant the Advance guard didn't play much his final year. It's something his father and coach still regrets. "Steve's junior year they (sportswriters) wanted to make him all-state and I messed up and should have let it happen. But I thought he'll come back," said Carroll. With Steve and two other players injured, Scott Central was picked to win the game by twenty-five points. The game was tied at half. A second half outburst lifted the Braves to an 89-72 victory. It marked the third consecutive year that Ronnie's squad had defeated Carroll's crew. Otto Porter, who scored 17 points that night, recalls the Cookson vs. Cookson match-ups. "Here you got Ronnie, (who) is younger, trying to beat older brother and there was always this rivalry between the two teams. Of course, it was a big game when we played them and Cookson expected us to beat them. That was just going without saying."

What others soon began saying was that Scott Central had one of best teams in the Bootheel. An overtime victory against Delta put their mark at 7-0. The next game out against Puxico, Scott Central won by 23 points. The trio of Porter, Ricky Thomas and "Frog" Williams combined for 85 of the Braves 95 points. It was the 100th victory of Ronnie Cookson's career. The undefeated Scott Central team received the number one seed at the annual Christmas Tournament in Cape Girardeau. The defending 3A state champion Charleston Bluejays were seeded second. Both teams won their first three games of the tournament and the stage was set for the epic battle of the Bootheel. Not only would the game feature two of the best programs in the region, but it would also showcase the talents of two of its marquee players: Senior Otto Porter of the Braves, and Junior Ricky Frazier at Charleston, who would later star for Norm Stewart's Missouri Tigers. The battle lived up to its billing.

"Early in the game, it seemed like it was set to be a shootout between the two scoring stars, Otto Porter of Scott Central and Ricky Frazier of Charleston. The duo traded basket-for-basket in the first two quarters."[209]

At halftime, the Braves led the Bluejays by seven points, 42-35. Porter led Scott Central with 19 first half points. Frazier had 18 for Charleston. It was Frazier's teammates who made the difference in the second half. At one point in the third quarter, the Bluejays scored 15 consecutive points. Six consecutive points by Scott Central's Ricky Thomas narrowed the advantage. Starting the final quarter, Charleston led by three. They would never trail again. Leading 72-70 with just ten seconds left, a Scott Central player went to the free throw line with a chance to tie. He made the first shot but missed the second. Charleston held on for a one-point victory. Frazier only scored five in the second half, but led Charleston with 23 points. Porter paced the Braves effort with 30 and along with Thomas and Williams, scored 64 of the Braves 71 points. Leading by seven at halftime, the Braves failed to stop the Charleston third quarter run. "We didn't play up to par," remembers Porter. "We played OK but we should have won the game and of course after that happened Cookson was not happy." Now with a record of 11-1, the defeat became a turning point in the season. "It did give us a wakeup call," recalls the Braves star player, "not only from Cookson's standpoint, but from our own standpoint that hey, we shouldn't have let that happen, but hey, it made us better."

In January, Scott Central did show signs it was a better team than previous editions. One example: the Braves defeated both Lilbourn and Notre Dame that season, a rarity at the time for a Ronnie Cookson team. "Notre Dame and Lilbourn always cause us a bunch of misery," their coach once admitted.[210] Scott Central didn't lose a game the rest of the regular season as they reeled off thirteen consecutive victories and entered regional tournament action with a record of 24-1.

Otto Porter had a spectacular regular season, averaging close to thirty points a contest. He was about to have an even better post-season. The Braves blew by Bell City to open regional play. Porter poured in 35. In a blowout 103-40 victory over Naylor, the Braves forward scored 29. In the regional semi-finals against Clarkton, the Braves star had his best outing of the year. Scott Central won the game 100-82. Otto Porter hammered home 22 field goals and five free throws for a total of 49 points. The regional finals saw Scott Central matched up again with North Pemiscot, the team that had ended their season the previous year. The outcome of this game was never in doubt. The Braves sprinted to a 23-9 first quarter lead en route to an 84-62 victory. Porter scored 28 on the night as a Cookson coached team made its way to state tournament play for a sixth consecutive season. Ronnie was all set to meet his brother in the first round of state tournament play but Advance lost to Delta, ending Carroll Cookson's season and Steve Cookson's high school career.

Otto Porter had scored 141 points in the Braves four regional victories. He would exceed that output in the state tournament, as the rest of the state would soon find out what Bootheel teams had discovered; there was no stopping the Scott Central star player. Delta, a conference rival to Scott Central, had already faced Cookson's team two previous times. The first game went into overtime before Scott Central managed to win by three points. In that game, Delta guard Nate Crowden had broken his ankle. Meeting for a second time in the conference tournament without their star player, Delta lost by 16 points. Returning to the lineup in late January, Crowden scored 22 points in the Bobcats upset victory over Advance. Facing Scott Central for a third time, Delta led by two points early in the second quarter. But Cookson switched defenses, going from a man-to-man to a zone. Thanks to a 15-2 run during the second quarter, the Braves led by seven at halftime. Delta matched Scott Central basket for basket in third quarter as both teams scored 19 points. Finally, in the fourth quarter, the Braves put it away, winning 79-57, in a game much closer than the final score would indicate. It took a 13-2 run at the end of the game to finally seal Delta's fate. Otto Porter led all scorers with 35 points.

The Braves marched on to quarterfinal action to face Wright City. Before the game, a Wright City assistant coach told a reporter, "We don't get in much too much of a hurry on offense."[211] While Wright City may not have been in a rush to get somewhere, Scott County Central clearly was. The Braves full-court press forced their opponent into turnovers their first three possessions. With the game barely two minutes old, Scott Central led 10-2. From there, things only got worse for Wright City. It was 45-21 at the half. Cookson's team cruised to an 80-54 victory. "We wanted to shock'em early," said the coach after the game.[212] Once again, the Braves star forward led the way.

"...It was 6-3 senior Otto Porter who really frustrated the Wildcats. Porter put the ball in from all over, scoring most of his 41 points on long baseline shots and offensive rebounds. Left wide open from his favorite spot, number 35 drew oohs and ahs from even the Wright City fans with his long set shots and jumpers."[213]

Ronnie Cookson's squad arrived in Columbia in March of 1976 with two games left to play. Drexel was their semi-final opponent and they would be playing for first or third against the winner of the Plato-Glasgow game. Plato's coach, Bob Chance, played college basketball with Ronnie and Carroll. Before the game, Cookson was asked about the potential match-up. "I'm not picking, but if Plato gets in the finals, we'd enjoy playing them."[214]

He didn't get his wish. Glasgow, the state's number one ranked team, defeated Plato by nine points. It was the closest game of the day by far. Otto Porter scored 39 points and grabbed 22 rebounds for the Braves, as they routed Drexel by 43. Scott Central out-rebounded their overwhelmed opponents 68-33.

The stage was now set for a Scott Central-Glasgow final. For much of the season, the Braves had been the number two-ranked team in the state. The consensus of much of the media and coaches was that Glasgow was the better team. If the Braves didn't carry a chip on their shoulder for the lack of attention paid to them, the Bootheel media did. *The Daily Standard* in Sikeston presented the evidence to its readers.

"One Columbia newspaper devoted three times as much space to Glasgow's semi-final win over Plato than Scott Central's impressive 91-48 romp over Drexel. After all, the Yellowjackets had won 96 of their last 98 games...It just wasn't possible that the powerful Glasgow team would blow it two years in a row."[215]

Carroll Cookson's Advance team had knocked Glasgow out in the semi-final game a year earlier. Now Ronnie Cookson's Braves had their chance in the finals. The game represented one of the last times a Cookson team would come into a championship game as the underdog. Coach Dick Royston's team had lost star player Lawrence Butler and didn't arrive in Columbia undefeated. The Yellowjackets had lost a game earlier in the year to Boonville. But the 31-1 Glasgow team had only two losses in the three previous seasons. Their coach was glad to return to Columbia and relieved that a winning streak record wasn't on the line. "I honestly feel we choked last year (against Advance)," admitted Royston. "We had a super team featuring a superstar (Butler) and the media constantly hounded us all year. Pressure was everywhere we went."[216]

Pressure was everywhere we went. Royston could have just as easily been describing the Scott County Central style of play. The Braves jumped out to a 6-2 lead and led at half by six points. The duo of Otto Porter and Ricky Thomas poured it on in the third quarter as a 10-2 run stretched the lead to 16 points. With Thomas scoring 31 points and Porter putting up 28 points and 25 rebounds, Ronnie Cookson had his first state championship trophy. The Braves won the game 82-71. Porter recalls the celebration with their coach. "I remember him (Cookson) coming over and hugging Ricky Thomas and I and kissing both of us on the side of the face, said we finally got it. It was wild. It was a wild time." Playing against the best the Bootheel and the rest of the state had to offer, Porter scored 284 points over his final eight games. He averaged 29.9 points his senior year.

Otto and the other four senior starters had played their last high school game, but Porter, Thomas and "Frog" Williams weren't finished as teammates. The following year, they would all be playing at Southern Baptist in Walnut Ridge, Arkansas just as their coach had done. Steve Cookson from Advance would follow in his father's path and join the Scott Central trio at the Arkansas school. All would leave Southern Baptist after one year. Porter and Cookson would play their sophomore season for Gene Bess at Three Rivers. Otto finished college with two years at Southeast Missouri State, ending his basketball career with the highest scoring average in conference history. [217] Even as a high school senior, college had yet to enter Porter's mind. His coach was the one who pushed him in that direction. "I would have to say he was a big influence," Porter said. "Even once my senior year had come and we had won state, once I was out of school, I was like get a job, get a car, nothing as far as that goes. Cookson was the one who kind of pushed me over the edge to go to college."

Record breaking performances became expected with Cookson teams. The 1976 squad didn't disappoint here either. Otto Porter set a state tournament record with 143 points over the four games, breaking the mark set by Lawrence Butler of Glasgow the year before. Scott Central and Glasgow set the mark for the most points scored in a 1A championship game. As a team, the Braves scored 332 points over the four games, just one point less than the record set by Carroll Cookson's 1972 Advance squad.

Buried deep in the scrapbooks and memorabilia that Ronnie and Dee Cookson have preserved over the years is a telling sign of modesty. Handwritten on a scrap piece of paper is the dinner order for the state champion Braves the night of the victory over Glasgow. It included ten Quarter-Pounders, six Big Macs and eighteen large fries. Scott Central celebrated by going to McDonald's. The players were also feted with a cake. The Braves returned to Southeast Missouri the next day and a parade was held in their honor. It wound through the towns of Haywood City, Morley and Vanduser. "That parade was a mile and a half long if it was an inch," remarked Cookson, of the nearly 100-car entourage.[218] On Monday, the Braves celebrated with a school program held at the gym. Then it was back to work. The next year, with all their starters gone, the Braves had a losing season. It would be the last one of Ronnie Cookson's career.

In his first year as a head coach, Ronnie Cookson's Scott County Central Braves went 21-8 and local sportswriters honored him as Coach of the Year. (All photos courtesy Daily Standard/Standard-Democrat unless noted otherwise)

Carroll Cookson brought the Puxico "run-shoot-run" style of play to Advance High School.

The 1975 State Champion Advance Hornets. The title was the second in four years for Carroll Cookson and the school.

The 1975 College High Christmas Tournament Team. (L to R) Ricky
Frazier, Charleston. Otto Porter, Scott County Central. James Davis,
Charleston. Lindy Duncan, Chaffee. Mark Beussink, Notre Dame.
Frazier and Duncan went on all Big-8 careers at Mizzou, Frazier in
basketball, Duncan in baseball. Porter set a conference scoring average
record while playing at Southeast Missouri State.

On the road to his first state title, Cookson barks orders in 1976. Son Jay celebrates in the background.

Ricky Thomas of Scott Central scores two of his game high 31 points against Glasgow in 1976 giving Cookson and the Braves their first state title.

Chaffee's Wade Sanders shows off his unique shooting style which led to all-state honors as a junior and senior.

Chaffee basketball coach Nick Walls (right) celebrates the school's first berth in the state basketball tournament in 1979 with football coach Mick Wessel.

Ronnie Cookson answers questions from the media before the 1979 state championship game.

The bench coach and the floor coach of the Show-Me Kings. Coach
Ronnie Cookson sits next to point guard Jeff Limbaugh.

Six eleven Joe Kleine scored 35 points against Scott Central in the 1980 championship game, but Donnie McClinton and teammates celebrated their second consecutive state championship in a blowout victory.

Cookson and his team storm the court to celebrate their 94-52 victory over Slater in 1980.

The Show-Me Kings – the 1980 Scott County Central Braves.

Charleston's Lennies McFerren celebrates in 1980 the first of his many state championships.

Cape Central's Ronnie Jones holds the 1980 4A state championship trophy above his head. Cape Central, Charleston, and Scott Central all played in the same Christmas tournament won by Cookson's Braves.

1A: SCOTT COUNTY CENTRAL (26-6)

Front row, left to right: Jeff Turner, Charles Morris, Keith Masters, Terry Bell, Stanley Blissett, Steve Gipson, and David Gilliland. Second row, left to right: (standing) Robbie Coffee, Jerry Porter, Brian Coffee, Earnest Wheeler, Terry Blissett, Jay Cookson, Richard Sims, Glenn Pobst, Colie Taylor, and Coach Cookson.

SCHOOL PROFILE

SUPERINTENDENT: W. Ray Shoaf

PRINCIPAL: Jerry Crites

ATHLETIC DIRECTOR: Ron Cookson

HEAD COACH: Ron Cookson

ASSISTANT: Danny Farmer

CITY: Rural Area

COUNTY: Scott

SCHOOL NICKNAME: Braves

SCHOOL COLORS: Orange, Black and White

SCHOOL ENROLLMENT: 156

CONFERENCE NAME: Scott-Mississippi

ROSTER

Lt. No.	Dr. No.				
12	12	Charles Morris	Jr.	5-10	160	G
14	14	Stanley Blissett	Sr.	5-8	152	G
20	20	Terry Bell	Jr.	6-1	165	G
21	21	Jerry Porter	Fr.	5-11	160	F
22	22	Jay Cookson	Sr.	6-3	160	G
24	24	Richard Sims	Sr.	6-1	175	F
30	30	Keith Masters	Sr.	6-0	160	G
32	32	Jeff Turner	Sr.	6-0	175	G
34	34	Brian Coffee	Sr.	6-0	170	F
40	40	David Gilliland	Sr.	6-0	160	G
42	42	Glen Pobst	Jr.	6-1	170	F
44	44	Colie Taylor	Sr.	6-0	160	F
50	50	Earnest Wheeler	Jr.	6-1	170	F
52	52	Terry Blissett	So.	6-2	175	C
54	54	Donald Gipson	Jr.	5-10	170	F

Cookson's 1986 team became his sixth squad to win a state championship.

Scott Central's Ricky Sims shoots over Wellsville's Fred Johnson in the
1986 state championship game in Springfield.

A smiling Ronnie Cookson holds the state championship trophy after
an exciting three-overtime game against Wellsville.

Jerry Porter was the last of five Porter brothers to play at Scott County Central.

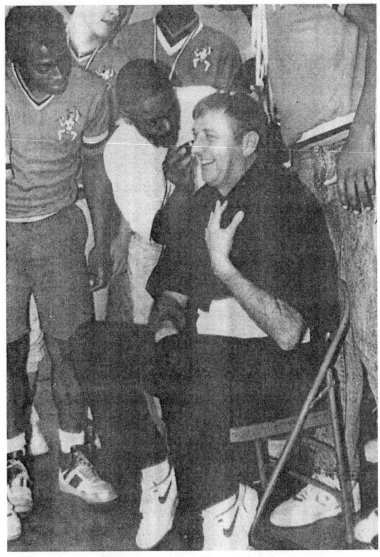

Cookson receives a haircut after winning his 500th game and tenth state championship game in 1990.

Marcus Timmons went 130-3 during his four year high school career at Scott Central and won four consecutive state championships. He became Cookson's first Division 1 athlete when he signed on to play at SIU-Carbondale. (Courtesy Southeast Missourian)

Cookson, near the end of his career, in 1994. The coach won twelve state championships during his twenty-five year coaching career, a Missouri state record.

CHAPTER SIX
Basketball Star at a Football School
1952-1978

"A school without football is in danger of deteriorating into a medieval study hall"

Vince Lombardi

B ill Bradshaw never played against Arnold Ryan's Puxico Indians, but he remembers watching them from the stands. He was a senior at Gideon High School in 1952 and was in attendance at Houck Field House the night Puxico blew out Shelbyville to win its second consecutive state title. Bradshaw found the Puxico style amazing, not so much that the players always seemed to throw the ball the length of the court, but that someone on the other end always caught it and scored so easily. Years later, he would be sitting in the stands at another state championship game completely dominated by one team. The only difference was that instead of a Cookson playing in the game, he would be coaching from the sidelines.

Bradshaw was born in Marmaduke, Arkansas in 1934. He was just a baby when the family moved a few miles to Piggott. When he was ten years old, his father went to work for a funeral home. A few years later, the business expanded with a site in Gideon and the family settled in Missouri.

Basketball in the 1940's was a low scoring, slow moving game. One referee was common for high school games and coaches couldn't address their teams during timeouts. The only time he could speak to his squad was before the game or at halftime. When he was in the eighth grade, Bradshaw recalls a game where Gideon's high school team was getting beat by eight or 10 points in the second half, a big margin in those days. The coach started bringing in the reserves. Seeing one substitute, the starters waved him off and told him to go back to the bench. The Gideon coach wasn't pleased. He stared at the players on the floor and pointed to the locker room. All five starters left the court and so did their coach. Substitute players finished the game and a school official had to fill in on the sidelines since there was no assistant. The starters did eventually return to the court– in street clothes – to watch the rest of the game from the stands. To Bradshaw, the lesson was clear. The head coach must always maintain control of the team.

A knee injury his senior season probably cost Bradshaw a college basketball career. Both Southeast Missouri State in Cape Girardeau and Arkansas State expressed interest, but the teenager lacked confidence because of the injury. A year after his high school graduation, he received his draft notice. The end of the Korean War came a few weeks later and Army officials indicated they would consider a deferment if Bradshaw was in college. After spending his freshman year in Cape, Bradshaw headed off to the campus of Arkansas State in Jonesboro where he would spend the next three years. The Army would have to wait.

By 1956, Bradshaw was a married man and a college graduate. He and his new bride, Alma, moved to New Madrid, where he took a job at the high school. The young teacher was a busy man. For the entire junior and senior high, he was the only coach. In addition to the junior and senior high basketball programs, he coached girls' volleyball and a new sport for the school – fast pitch boys' softball.

In the 1950's, most schools in the county took a long break in the fall for cotton-picking season. That meant school started in July, with a break starting in September and lasting sometimes until November, however long it took to bring in the crop. Fast pitch softball started at the beginning of the school year. That presented a problem for Bradshaw. New Madrid was one of the few schools in the county not to let out in the fall, preferring the more traditional school year. Bradshaw's contract didn't start until September. He had to recruit a team before he ever taught his first class. He succeeded in doing so and New Madrid had its first ever high school softball team.

His coaching career at his new school didn't last long. After spending one year at New Madrid, Bradshaw entered the Army in August of 1957. He spent two years in the military, spending the majority of his time training recruits at Fort Reilly, Kansas. In 1959, he moved back to Missouri, taking a job at Lilbourn. Bradshaw coached the junior high basketball team. Arnold Ryan was the coach of the high school squad.

Ryan had been coaching at Manila, Arkansas when the Missouri high school made him an offer – four thousand dollars a year - to come to Lilbourn. According to Bradshaw, Ryan refused their bid, holding out for a salary of six thousand. That word got back to people in the small Missouri community, with business people and farmers agreeing they would make up the difference. With the salary set, Lilbourn had its new head coach.

During his years at Lilbourn, Bradshaw learned a lot from the legendary coach. Ryan and Bradshaw both believed that basketball was not a democratic process. Players don't get to do as they wish on the court; they get to do what their coaches tell them. Team discipline was important and so was self-discipline. Players need to keep their composure during a game. When it comes time to yell at an official for a call, that was the coach's job. The player needed to stay focused on the task at hand. The Ryan work ethic also impressed Bradshaw. Not a minute was to be wasted on the court. Practice was work. Every shot needed to be taken with complete concentration. The former Puxico coach also had a way of making the game fun for his players. Bradshaw never remembered Ryan cutting a player on his teams. If a teenager wanted to come out for the squad and make the commitment, Ryan believed he deserved a jersey and a chance to play.

After leaving Lilbourn, Bradshaw went to an elementary school in New Madrid County as principal. He stayed there one year. In 1966, he got a new job offer, one that would take him farther north, to a small town tucked in the northwestern corner of Scott County. Bill, his wife Alma, and their two young sons, Jeff and Joe, moved there over the summer. And so it came to pass that one small piece of the Arnold Ryan legacy made its way to Chaffee, Missouri.

***

Bradshaw took a job as the grade school principal at Chaffee elementary school. One day, early in his tenure, he received a call from a high school student, an aspiring coach. The teenager wanted to know if Bradshaw would let him come over to the grade school in the afternoons and help sixth graders practice basketball. The new principal thought it a good idea and readily agreed. Day after day, the young coach would work his team. There was no formal schedule for the sixth graders. Games were scheduled on a strictly ad-hoc basis. Bradshaw wondered if the boys would ever play. Their coach had already turned down at least one request. One day, Bradshaw received a call from the new coach over at Advance. Carroll Cookson wanted to know if Chaffee was interested in playing in a sixth grade tournament. Bradshaw relayed the request and was once again turned down. By this time it was March, and it was dawning on the elementary school principal that his young coach wanted no part of an actual game. Bradshaw made up his mind he would take the team over to Advance to play. Without planning on it, Bradshaw was back coaching basketball. It would be a role he would enjoy for the next twelve years. Each year, he organized both fifth and sixth grade teams, practiced the kids after class, and worked the phones to schedule as many games as possible. To a generation of Chaffee High School athletes, he was the first person with "coach" in front of his name.

The next year, Bradshaw took his players over to Delta for a game. The two teams proved better at physical contact than shooting a basketball. It was one of those games that referees have a hard time calling with young players just learning the basics. Call too many fouls and players spend all game at the free throw line. Don't blow the whistle enough and players and coaches get frustrated. The referees chose the latter course, much to the chagrin of the Delta coach. After the Chaffee victory, he told Bradshaw, "I knew Chaffee played football. I just didn't think they did it on the basketball court."

A few years later, Bradshaw had perhaps his best team. His son Joe was a member of the squad. While it gave Bradshaw great satisfaction to coach his youngest boy, there were other reasons to be proud of the team. Monty Montgomery was one of the guards. The coach loved his hustle and intensity. "One day he ran so many killers (conditioning drill) he couldn't get his breath. He laid in the floor, cried and whined, gasping for breath, but I couldn't get him to quit."

Montgomery's dad, Morris, owned a motor home. For away games, the vehicle acted as the team bus. Players, cheerleaders and coach would all pile in to travel to games all over Southeast Missouri. In one tournament that year at Charleston, Chaffee beat Puxico and Charleston to make its way to the championship game against the local Catholic school. Bradshaw's team was winning 40-7 at halftime. "They wanted to quit right then. So I pulled the dogs off – no use rubbing their nose in it. We probably could have made 100, because they gave up before the half. We ended up beating them 60 something to 20 something. People were amazed. They said how do you get those kids to do that? They do it, I don't do it. They enjoy winning and they get out there and they pay the price. They work better than most high school teams do." Bradshaw's team went 19-1 that season. That group of players would be the class of '79 at Chaffee High School.

Their success continued in junior high school. In seventh grade, they lost one game. "Scott City. Tore me up all year until we finally got to play them again next year," remembers Montgomery. They got their revenge the following season. As eighth graders, the team went a perfect 13-0, winning the conference tournament. The fast break, full court press style of play that started under Bill Bradshaw continued under Terry Glenzy. In one memorable moment for the team, one of the players argued with his coach over the best way to get the ball up the court. The coach wanted him to pass it; the player wanted to dribble. To prove his point, Glenzy had the player start racing to the other end, dribbling all the way. The argument ended when a thrown basketball hit the player in the back of the head.

That same year, junior high football was introduced at Chaffee and the class of '79 was its first team. High school coach Charlie Vickery used the family business as a way to spread the word. "I think I signed up down at the Dairy Queen," recalls Montgomery. "They had a sign-up sheet in the summer down there. We were all excited." As 8th graders, they went undefeated on the football field as well. The school lacked practice facilities for the team. They scrimmaged on the baseball field and showered at the public swimming pool. The players quickly became known as the "Dirty Dozen." Team member Steven Whitaker describes how the nickname came about. "There was no hot water over there. When the season first started, it was warm enough you could take a cold shower. When the season ended, it was too cold."

Starting their high school careers in the fall of 1975, the class had rarely tasted defeat. Glenzy told them they had the talent to win three state titles; football, basketball and track. "We were going to conquer the world," remembers class of '79 member Whitaker. "We were going to be the class they all talked about." As sophomores, they joined together for the first time with the class below them on the junior varsity basketball team. One of the freshman players would soon make a name for himself.

The next summer, the tall, skinny, blond-headed teenager would win a state championship in tennis. But as good as he was with a racquet, it was not his best sport. His older teammates and teams around Southeast Missouri would soon find out that few players could shoot a basketball like Richard Wade Sanders.

***

The Sanders family has called Scott County home for nearly two centuries. The family can trace its history in America back to South Carolina in the 1700's. By the 1840's, many family members lived in Robertson County, Tennessee. When several brothers decided to migrate north, all but one decided on Williamson County, Illinois. Richmond Sanders and his wife Mary took a different path. They bought a forty-acre farm outside of Commerce, Missouri, the oldest town in Scott County. Richmond and Mary had nine children, including four sons who fought in the Civil War.[219] Three of their sons were named for U.S. Presidents: James K. Polk, Martin VanBuren, and Fillmore Sanders. [220] Fillmore, the youngest son born in 1852, also had nine children. His oldest son, Jesse Richmond married Alice Melbourne Loftin in 1906, and went on to have an even bigger family. One of their eleven kids was George Wade Sanders, born in 1926. When George was just a child, the family moved to Benton, the county seat.

By the time he was in high school, George stood six foot three and starred on both the basketball and softball teams. His junior season, the Benton Tigers basketball record was 19-3, with two of the losses coming against Chaffee. His high school yearbook notes that both of the defeats were played "without our center, George Sanders." That same year, Sanders was voted the best personality, most studious, and best athlete among his male peers. His favorite saying, the yearbook recorded, was "aw shucks." His senior yearbook noted his favorite song, "The Darktown Strutters' Ball." Written in 1917 by African-American composer Shelton Brooks, the lyrics begin this way:

"I'll be down to get you in a taxi, Honey. You better be ready about half past eight."

Perhaps the teenager could identify. His father ran a cab service from the county seat. Graduating high school in 1945, Sanders went immediately into the army. He worked as a dental technician during his two-year stint. An accomplished pitcher, he played fast-pitch softball all over post World War II Europe. Returning home from his military service, he married the former Nellie Francis Jackson in 1948. Two years later, he started work for the Frisco Railroad. Like many railroad families that eventually made their way to Chaffee, George and Francis lived in the Pemiscot County town of Hayti for several years in the 1950's. Because the state of Arkansas required three brakemen on every crew, Frisco would add an additional worker at Hayti for southbound trains. Working his way up to conductor, the Sanders family settled in Chaffee by the late 1950's. In January of 1962, they had their third child and first son. His first name was Richard. All his life, everyone has called him by his middle name, Wade. A second son and fourth child, Doug, was born two years later.

When Wade was 10 years old, his family moved to a new subdivision in town. It wasn't long before his dad put up a basketball goal in the driveway. Sanders would come home after school, pick up the ball and start shooting. He would shoot all afternoon. In the winter, the cold temperatures caused his fingernails to split from the skin. He wrapped his fingers in athletic tape and kept on going. Joe Bradshaw remembers going over to the Sanders house on winter days and shooting baskets. The young players worked out a system where they kept two balls inside the house and one on the court. The cold weather meant that eventually the ball would stop bouncing. The players traded it in for one of the warmer ones and the game would resume. After the sun went down, Wade and his younger brother Doug rigged together outdoor lighting so the games could continue well into the night. In his mind's eye, Wade had a vision of how to shoot the ball. He remembered watching Otto Porter of Scott County Central growing up and also listening to Braves games on the radio. Over and over, he would drive to the baseline and take a shot from his favorite spot on the court. Each time, he would hear the soundtrack in his head, "Porter drives, he stops and shoots….it's good!"

Sanders shot a basketball as if his hands were having an argument. As a right-handed shooter, the left hand would typically rest at the side of the ball. Wade though, supported the ball with his left hand in *front* of the basketball, directly opposite his shooting hand. As unconventional as Hank Aaron learning to hit a baseball cross-handed, Sanders shooting style was hard to duplicate, so was his success. One sportswriter, after seeing the Chaffee player pour in shot after shot from the baseline was immediately reminded of another blond-headed forward just beginning to make a name for himself. "Larry Bird, that's what we called him," said Mike Marsh, who was sports editor of *The Daily Standard* in the late 1970's. "I can still remember him sitting down on that baseline; boom! boom! boom! He had one of the purist shots I've ever seen."

As did the class before him, Sanders began playing organized basketball for Bill Bradshaw in grade school. "Teams couldn't believe Wade could shoot like he could in sixth grade," said his first basketball coach. "Just phenomenal shooting touch. He didn't develop that in the 10th grade or the 11th grade, he could shoot like that in the 6th grade." For his part, Sanders believes his early training under Bradshaw was critical to future success. "That's the best foundation I've ever seen for anyone training to be a basketball player." Bradshaw had an ability that all great teachers and coaches possess – the ability to motivate young kids. "He held you accountable for your actions," remembers Sanders. "He would admonish you, not embarrass you, he just had a great rapport with students. He didn't really want to be your friend; he wanted to be a counselor, a guide to you. I think he filled that really well. Wonderful man."

By his sophomore season, Sanders' talents were obvious to anyone who saw him play, including his new high school coach. Nick Walls was twenty-two years old and fresh out of Southeast Missouri State when he came to Chaffee in the fall of 1977. After watching Wade rack up high scoring performances early in the season on the JV team and seeing his varsity squad lose its first two games of the season, Walls made up his mind and promoted the sophomore. Sanders made an immediate impression. His first game up on varsity, he led the team in scoring with 17 points. The victory over University High was also the first win of Walls' coaching career. In his second game, Sanders again led the team in scoring, pouring in 22 points in a win over Woodland. But just when it looked like the young coach may turn around his first team, the bottom fell out. Chaffee lost its next ten games. Still, no team had a solution to stop its sophomore forward. He racked up 22 points in a game with Cape Girardeau Notre Dame, 27 against Scott Central, 30 against Illmo-Scott City. The team finally broke their losing streak in a game against Oran.

The Eagles thought they had a way to stop the one-man scoring machine by playing a box-in-one defense against Sanders. It backfired. Wade poured in 37 of his team's 69 points that night. Portageville tried the same defense the next game; Sanders answered with 32. The next time out, a victory over Meadow Heights, Wade scorched the nets for a career high 42 points. As the season neared its conclusion, the sophomore's scoring average stood at just over 25 points per game. Wade Sanders, son of a railroad conductor in a railroad town, had blossomed into a basketball star. But not everything came so easily that season to the sophomore sensation.

There were two problems; one was immediate and the second was looming. What bothered Sanders most about his first varsity season was the reception he received from certain teammates. He was a class or two younger than his fellow players. He was leading the team in scoring. It was his name in the headlines, game after game, week after week. He noticed it in huddles, in timeouts, on and off the court. Older players would make comments to him, some tried to intimidate him. Sanders believed certain players, not all of them, resented his success. The reaction the star player received from particular teammates was not lost on his coach. "He didn't play football, he wasn't in their clique," said Walls. "He just had an air about him. He had a lot of confidence and that just didn't meet well with them." The coach also added, "If I could score like that, I would be cocky too."

The second issue would begin to surface the following season, Sanders' junior year. Wade lived for basketball. The game he spent hours practicing on his driveway at home was his first love. His fellow starters the following season could not make the same statement. They all played and started in football. And in the fall of 1978, the Red Devils football team was convinced it was going to win a state title.

***

When Chaffee High School started its football program in 1921, Rufus Heeb scored the team's first touchdown. Nearly 30 years later, his nephew would have to sneak out of the house to play the game. Don Heeb didn't play football at Chaffee his freshman season. When he decided to go out as a sophomore, he didn't tell his mom when practice started. She also didn't see the paperwork needed for a student to play the sport. The teenager signed everything himself. When Heeb was a junior, a new coach took over the football program. Bob Goodwin had played college basketball; first for Henry Iba at Oklahoma A&M (now Oklahoma State) and later at Southeast Missouri State. Goodwin coached both basketball and football. While he knew hoops well, he didn't know as much about football. His first season as coach, the Red Devils didn't win a game. While the team improved greatly Heeb's senior season, it was his last basketball game that stands out in his memory. Playing in the regional tournament at Oran, Heeb was fouled while shooting the basketball. With less than a minute to go, Chaffee trailed by one. He missed both free throws. The Red Devils lost the game by a single point. Returning to Chaffee after the defeat, Heeb never forgot what his high school coach told him. "I remember walking home. He stopped the car and said get in, and I'll give you a ride home. We talked and talked and I was crying. He said if that's the worst thing that ever happens in your life, you're going to be the luckiest person in the world."

Heeb's family was in Chaffee from its beginning. His grandfather, John W. Heeb owned land that was sold to the original developers of the town. His father worked for the Frisco Railroad. A class behind Bob Kielhofner, Heeb's matriculation through the school system was identical; Catholic school through eighth grade and then on to Chaffee High School. His Catholic roots come from his mother's side of the family. Her maiden name was Amrhein and like many German-Catholics in northern Scott County, the family history can be traced back to Europe's Alsace-Lorraine region located on the France-Germany border. Growing up, Heeb played a lot of sandlot football and baseball. On summer afternoons, the local priest, Father Walter Craig, would interrupt the games. "He would drive by in the car and stop where we were playing and say, 'hey, come get in the car, get in the backseat, you're going to confession.'" It wasn't long before the young ballplayers would always be looking over their shoulders. "Anytime after that, we'd get nervous when we'd see that car and we would take off because we didn't want to go to confession."

When he got to high school, he discovered another powerful and influential person in the community. "Oscar T. Honey was the band director down there. And Oscar probably had more clout than the football coach does, which is unbelievable in a small town." Even after he started playing football, Heeb continued to play in the marching band at home football games – wearing his jersey and shoulder pads. "I had to march down with my football uniform on, play the trombone and after the national anthem, gave it to a manager who put it in a case and put it under the bench, and I got in a huddle for the game."

Recruited by Southeast Missouri State to play football, the 1954 Chaffee graduate lettered in three sports his freshman year in college: football, basketball and track. His sophomore year, the football team under coach Kenny Knox went undefeated. By 1958, Heeb had graduated from college and taken his first coaching job at the now defunct McBride High School in St. Louis. In 1966, he became the head football coach at Vianney. He would remain there until he retired. Heeb's legacy can still be seen on NFL football fields on Sundays. Trent Green starred for the Vianney Golden Griffins in the 1980's. When Green returned home to play for the Rams for a few seasons, Heeb found himself in football heaven. "It was the best job I ever had in my life," said the coach who kept statistics for the Rams. "Sat in the press box, got two meals, they feed the press good. I got free parking and got paid 30 bucks a game. I couldn't believe that." The coach's legacy at Vianney lives on in other ways as well. Football teams at the school now play their home games at Don Heeb Field.

When Heeb decided to retire, one of the first people he called was his coach at Chaffee High School. Fifty years after playing for Bob Goodwin, he'll always appreciate what his coach did for him. "I thanked him for his influence. Basically, that's why I got into coaching was because of him." The advice Goodwin imparted after the bitter basketball loss stayed with him. "When my first son was born, seeing that take place, I thought, boy, I am lucky."

After Heeb graduated from Chaffee in 1954, Bob Goodwin's football teams got even better. In 1956, the Red Devils went a perfect 9-0, to this day, the only undefeated season in school history. The first game of the 1956 season, Chaffee defeated Sikeston, snapping the Bulldogs 25 game winning streak. In 1958, Chaffee won the "Little Six" conference championship for the fifth season in a row. Goodwin, who came to Chaffee with a basketball pedigree, left with a football legacy. He would be coaching at Cape Central High School the following season. Terry Glenzy was a junior on Goodwin's last football team. He remembers the coach as a strict disciplinarian who focused on the fundamentals.

"He didn't do anything fancy. We just spent a lot of time blocking and tackling." *The Signal*, the Chaffee paper, once published a list of Goodwin's rules for his players. Similar to Arnold Ryan, Goodwin did not tolerate any smoking, drinking or swearing. He had curfews on his players every night of the week. He closed his list of rules by encouraging his athletes "to attend Church every Sunday somewhere. It is good for us all and really good athletes should and do lead good religious lives." [221]

Under new coach John Stolt, Chaffee claimed its sixth consecutive conference championship in the fall of 1959, Glenzy's senior season. The split end would take his football talents to Southeast Missouri State where a knee injury cut short his career in his sophomore season. Joining the staff at Chaffee High School in the fall of 1967, Glenzy saw and coached many of the school's best athletes over the years. [222] One of the first and one of the best was Charlie Vickery. A three-sport star in high school, Vickery's played football, basketball and baseball. His favorite sport, and his best according to Glenzy, was basketball. His senior season, a team in the Scott-Mississippi conference won twenty games, averaged 83 points a contest, and set a school record for most 100 point games. It was not Scott County Central. It was the Chaffee Red Devils, led by their sharp-shooting guard, Charlie Vickery.

Like so many others in town, Vickery's father worked on the railroad. When Charlie was twelve, his parents purchased the Dairy Queen in downtown Chaffee. Both he and his younger brother Jim had to run the business over the years, which opened every spring and shutdown every fall. His first taste of organized sports was baseball at the age of eight. "Could not wait. Couldn't wait to get to the minor leagues." He would have to wait until high school to play any organized football.

As a football player, Vickery developed into an all-state quarterback. It didn't start out that way. His freshman season, his coach decided to play him at an end position. Due to the small squad, the freshmen were expected to participate in all the drills and scrimmages. Getting into his stance on the offensive line, the 120-pound freshman had the responsibility of double-teaming an upper classmen defensive tackle. The freshman grabbed his jersey. "Course I wasn't strong enough to hold him, but I slowed him down just a little bit." The coaching staff wasn't pleased by their performance of their defensive tackle and let him hear about it after the play was over. Lining up on the next play, the upperclassman had a word of warning for Vickery. "He said, if you ever do that again, I'm going to kill you. Last time I ever held anybody."

After high school, like Glenzy and Heeb and so many other Chaffee students of the 1950's and '60's, Vickery went to Southeast Missouri State to get his education and continue his athletic pursuits. His football career ended early. Playing in a freshman game against Murray State, Vickery broke his sternum. The quarterback had thrown his last pass ("I didn't play that no more.") He also played two years of junior varsity basketball and was a four-year letterman on the baseball team. Graduating in 1974, he took his dream job: head football coach at Chaffee High School. "I would have done anything to go back there. That's what I really wanted to do." Before football practice began, Vickery helped coach a group of 15 year-old baseball players over the summer. They went on to win the Missouri Junior Babe Ruth state championship. That group formed the core of two state champion baseball teams at Chaffee High School.[223] One of the players on the team was Mark Whitaker., He was among those dressing out in helmet and shoulder pads when two-a-day football practices rolled around in the brutal heat and humidity of August. Returning for his junior year, he would be a starting running back when the team opened its season. He scored the Red Devils first touchdown of the year on a 61-yard pass. But the pleasure of that moment has long been forgotten. On Friday night, September 13th, in Vickery's first game of his coaching career, tragedy struck on the football field at Chaffee.

It's a memory seared into the mind of the coach. His team had the ball and was driving down the field. Vickery called an option play and the quarterback pitched the ball to running back Whitaker. One defender hit the junior in the shoulder and spun him around. A second player made the tackle. Whitaker didn't get up. By the time Vickery rushed to his side, he was already unconscious. An ambulance took him to the Chaffee Hospital. By 2 a.m. Saturday morning, Whitaker was on his way to a hospital in Memphis. On Saturday night, residents of Chaffee turned out for a prayer service at the high school gym.[224] The following night, Whitaker died in the hospital at Memphis, the victim of a massive blood clot at the base of the brain. After absorbing the hit on the football field, the sixteen-year old never regained consciousness. The sudden death dealt a blow to the small tight-knit community and its 22-year old football coach. "That's what was so good about a place like Chaffee, everybody was so close, you know everybody," said Vickery. In his short time back at Chaffee, the coach had spent a lot of time with Whitaker in the classroom and on the football field. One game into his first season as coach, one of his players was dead. "I was real close (to Whitaker and his classmates)," Vickery remembers. "Does that affect your career? Absolutely. I mean I think that makes you take in perspective a whole bunch of things." The football field at Chaffee is named in Whitaker's honor. In addition, every year the school recognizes one senior male athlete for citizenship, leadership and scholarship. It's called the Mark Whitaker Award.

It was three years before Vickery had a winning team at his alma mater. In 1976, the Red Devils finished 8-2 and won the conference championship, the first for the school since its glory days of the 1950's. Terry Glenzy was a senior on that team and was the defensive coordinator seventeen years later when Chaffee allowed just 54 points.[225] The following season, the Red Devils suffered through a losing season but won four of its last five games. Vickery knew the upcoming1978 football season would be a special one at Chaffee. The team would return the starting quarterback and several key players, including perhaps the most talented lineman in school history. Tony Dalton was 6'3", 245 pounds, and a legitimate Division I recruit. He started as both an offensive and defensive tackle. By the fall, he was generating so much interest by college football teams that Oklahoma coach Barry Switzer would pay a visit to Chaffee.

Vickery would not be the coach. Head coaching positions at the three largest schools in Southeast Missouri, Cape Girardeau Central, Poplar Bluff and Sikeston, all became open.[226] Vickery applied only at Sikeston. He was offered the job. He weighed his options for a couple of days and phoned Sikeston officials on a Friday morning telling them he was turning down the job. He continued to wrestle with the choice he had made, unsure it was the right one. That afternoon, he was teaching a P.E. class at the grade school and ran into Principal Bill Bradshaw. The counselor to young Chaffee athletes asked if he had made his decision. Vickery told him he had turned it down. He also admitted he thought it was a mistake. Bradshaw agreed and told the coach to make another call. Vickery told him he wouldn't do it. Bradshaw persisted and told him if he wouldn't pick up the phone, the principal would make the call for him. The argument convinced the football coach that Sikeston was where he needed to be. He made the call from Bradshaw's office and left Chaffee that afternoon to meet with Sikeston school officials. The Bulldogs had a new head coach.

Vickery coached his last game at Sikeston in the fall of 2003. In his twenty-six year tenure, Vickery became the all-time leader in wins at the school, racking up 156 career victories. Second on the list at Sikeston is Bill Sapp, who coached the Bulldogs from 1952 to 1968 and won 135 games. In his seventeen-year career, Sapp only lost 17 games.[227] Both men got their start coaching football in Chaffee. Sapp started his career at Chaffee in the fall of 1947.[228] One of the players on his team was Vickery's father. While Vickery spent the overwhelming majority of his head-coaching career at Sikeston, he cherishes many memories of growing up and getting his start at Chaffee. "You could ride your bike anywhere in town," remembers Vickery, "it was a great place to grow up." Vickery has also hung onto something else, a special keepsake he's had ever since 1974 - a football picture of Mark Whitaker.

***

Vickery's departure meant assistant coach Mick Wessel was now the man in charge of the football team. Like Vickery and Glenzy, Wessel had grown up in Chaffee and played football in high school. His father was the principal. Male athletes at the high school could choose among five sports: football, basketball, baseball, track and tennis. But to both Wessel and Glenzy, football was their real passion. The two men, and their philosophies, would dominate their high school's sport teams for decades. All high school male athletes were encouraged to play football at Chaffee. Few, if any, were encouraged to play basketball. Glenzy was fond of saying, "Basketball is what you do to kill time between football and track." He was only half-joking. In fairness to the two Chaffee coaches, there are only so many good athletes in a high school of about 200 students (a male population of about half that). They wanted the most talented ones to play the sports they coached (football and track at that time). Neither coached the baseball team, and it didn't stop that program from winning three state titles in nine seasons. The timing of the basketball season made it an enemy. Winter months were for weight lifting training – training that would pay off in track events like the shot put and the discus (three track athletes won a combined nine state titles in these events over a nine year period – all three also starred in football). And of course, that weight lifting training would also pay off in next year's football season. If an athlete wanted to play basketball, it was not discouraged. But if he decided to just dedicate himself to weight lifting during the winter, this was even better. Quite naturally, this produced tension over the years between the basketball coach and the rest of the athletic department (which primarily consisted of Wessel and Glenzy). With Vickery's departure to Sikeston, the goal and the chant were the same: "To State in 78." For the Chaffee Red Devils, football practice couldn't start fast enough.

Nick Walls knew Chaffee was a football school when he took the job. The young coach had just graduated from college when Chaffee offered him a teaching position. He was paid an additional six hundred dollars to coach the basketball team. He quickly accepted. Basketball was in his blood. His father Troy Walls had coached against Arnold Ryan's Puxico team in the infamous game at Greenway, Arkansas. Nick wasn't born yet when that game was played, but he does remember hearing stories about that night. "There was an article in the paper, 'Troy Walls wanted dead or alive for stalling the ball against Puxico, Missouri.'" The younger Walls opened his coaching career against Puxico native and Scott County Central coach Ronnie Cookson. The Red Devils lost his coaching debut by 24 points, 41 points less than his father lost his first game against Ryan's Puxico Indians twenty six years earlier. It was Troy Walls' second game against Puxico where he decided to employ delay tactics against Arnold Ryan. Ironically, in the biggest game of his coaching career, the younger Walls would also go into a stall against a quicker, full-court pressing opponent.

Arriving in Chaffee in the fall of 1977, Walls recognized football was the focus. He sought ways to connect with his coaching peers. "The reason I connected with Mick (Wessel) and Terry (Glenzy) is because I went and scouted (football teams) for them," remembers the coach. "That made me accepted. They saw I wasn't coming in here and trying to push basketball over football." With basketball taking a back seat, it meant that Walls had to wait until football season ended until full-scale practice could begin. When he coached his first game against Scott Central in the Oran Tournament that year, his team had only been together a few weeks. Walls didn't complain; he was doing what he loved. "It's not the norm to be head coach at 22, but I walked into a situation where they needed someone to do a lot of work for six hundred bucks. I was just chomping at the bit to coach. That's all I knew. That's all I wanted to do."

The short, wiry coach was all raw nerves and energy on the sidelines. A spectator never had any doubt how Walls felt at any moment in the game. Monty Montgomery remembers his father's business partner used to attend Chaffee's basketball games just to watch the antics of the head coach. "He'd say that's the craziest man I've ever seen, come down the sidelines, pulling his ties out before the end of the game. After five minutes, his shirt would be hanging out."

Walls grew up in St. Louis. His father didn't coach basketball anymore after leaving Bragg City. Troy Walls took a job in school administration in the St. Louis County School District. After graduating from Pattonville High School, Nick played junior college basketball for two seasons and then transferred to Southeast Missouri State. His last two years in college, he didn't play basketball but another sport. "Wasn't good enough to play (basketball) there, played on the golf team." He did his student teaching at Chaffee before joining the faculty. He brought with him a love for the game of basketball and a distinctive presence on the sidelines. "I was a very hyper coach – always had intensity."

As his team wound up his first season with a record of 7-15, Walls was optimistic about what his second season would bring. With nearly every starter returning, he was confident they would succeed. "I knew that we could be good. I knew that we had to get the football out of them. I knew we wouldn't be real good early, but I knew we could be real good late." Walls would have to wait to start practice. Even his star player, Wade Sanders, joined the football team that fall. For Sanders older teammates, it would be their senior season. The class of 1979, the class that was "going to conquer the world," had one last chance.

CHAPTER 7
Winter of '79
1978-1979

"It is the third year of the new Ice Age."

Southeast Missourian, February 27th, 1979

D epression possible. That was the front-page headline of the *Southeast Missourian* on November 17th, 1978, as government officials grew increasingly concerned about the deteriorating shape of the U.S. economy. It would not be the grimmest news of the month or even the week. By the weekend, Americans were reacting in horror to the stories coming out of the South American nation of Guyana. More than 900 people died in a mass suicide, following the instructions of their cult leader, Jim Jones. As winter approached, Americans worried about the spread of Legionnaire's Disease, read about the spectacular Lufthansa heist at Kennedy Airport, and contemplated the possibility of dollar a gallon gasoline. In the far off country of Iran, people were demanding more political freedoms from the Shah, the country's absolute ruler. They would soon get change but not freedom in a revolution that saw dozens of Americans held hostage for more than a year. The death of artist Norman Rockwell that fall seemed the perfect metaphor for the time; gone was an age of American innocence and optimism.

In the Bootheel of Missouri, change was making its way, but some people apparently had to be convinced it was for the best. An opinion piece in the local paper featured the headline, "Advantages of Cable TV." The winter of 1979 saw record breaking weather in Southeast Missouri and the beginnings of a basketball dynasty in the state. The blizzard and a basketball game were not mutually exclusive events. As we'll find out, Mother Nature played havoc with both drivers on the road and players on the court. A memorable headline that winter read in part: "New yardstick." It referred to the weather. It could have just as easily described a team and a coach in Scott County.

Ron Cook knew he had a special group of seventh graders the year he started coaching junior high basketball at Scott County Central in the fall of 1974. They were one game from a perfect season when they lost in the conference championship finals. One player stood out from the rest; Melvin Porter, younger brother of Otto. "He was head and shoulders above everyone in size," remembers Cook. "Melvin would have been a very good football player. Very strong, low center of gravity." The style of play that Melvin and his teammates would play in high school started in junior high. "We started pressing right away," said their coach. When they weren't playing basketball, they talked about it constantly in class with their junior high health teacher. The teacher even talked about them winning the state title. Ronnie Cookson liked to plant the seed early.

While Porter and his teammates raced through a near perfect season, Cook's eighth grade team didn't win a game all year. One night, he was sick and didn't coach the team. High school coach Cookson took his place. After the game, the two talked on the phone. "Did the 8th grade win tonight?" asked Cook. "Yeah, we sure did," said Cookson. "Great," came the reply from Cook, while in truth, the news made him feel even worse. Cookson didn't let him linger too long. "Hell no, Ron. No one could win with that bunch."

When Melvin Porter's class – the class of 1980 – entered high school in the fall of 1976, the talented freshmen class and "that bunch" of sophomores joined together on the junior varsity team. Their first game was against Puxico in a junior varsity tournament at Bell City. It was primarily a game of Puxico's sophomores against the Scott Central freshmen. When the box score appeared in the newspaper the next day, names that would be familiar to area high school basketball fans a few years later were there: Porter, Limbaugh, Jones, and Timmons. What was different was the outcome and score of the game. Puxico routed Scott Central 66 to 28. The thirty-eight point loss would be their worst loss in high school. The players never forgot what their coach told them afterwards in the locker room. Cookson told his troops that Puxico was the team Scott Central would play in the regional finals their junior year. "You got 40 points to makeup" was a mantra that Cookson repeated over the next few seasons to remind and motivate his team. To reinforce his disappointment in his young players, Cookson had a surprise in store when the bus returned to Scott County Central. "I never will forget that night," remembers Melvin Porter. "We come back to the school and we thought we were going home. And he – Cookson- told us go in there and get your tennis shoes on." As punishment for the embarrassing loss, the players had to run conditioning drills while their coach yelled at them. "He said they were good, but they ain't that good," recalls Porter.

By the fall of '78, two starters' spots seemed ensured. Both Melvin Porter and point guard Jeff Limbaugh had played on the varsity the previous season as sophomores. They were joined by three classmates who spent their entire sophomore seasons on a junior varsity squad that went 23-2: Donnie McClinton, a 6' 2" forward who would emerge as perhaps the most talented of the five, Anthony Jones, a matchstick thin 6'2" center, and Mayfield Timmons, a 5'9" guard with great leaping ability. All three of them had come a long way since their days of playing junior high ball for Ron Cook. In seventh and eighth grade, Timmons and Jones rarely played. "Mayfield and Anthony were the tenth, eleventh or twelfth man on the team," remembers Cook. Both of them kept at it and steadily improved every year. By their sophomore season, Timmons was the leading scorer on the junior varsity team.

It was around this time McClinton began to emerge as well. Teammate Limbaugh chronicles the change. "Donnie is a success story. The freshman year on the B team, he played like seven seconds. Ronnie (Cookson) knew that he was going to be a ball player. Our freshman year, he made me work with Donnie after practice. I thought what in the world, that's the stupidest thing, Donnie don't even play." Limbaugh remembers asking his coach what he saw in McClinton. "He always told me, if Donnie's hands ever materialize, he'll make something. And that's what he had me do with Donnie after practice. That's all we did, I threw him the ball." Eventually, Limbaugh finally saw the talent his coach had already spotted. "The light switch went on. I can remember the summer between our freshman and sophomore year, we'd play ball every night at the gym. You could just tell he was going to be a ballplayer." The Scott Central lineup was set. Limbaugh, McClinton, Porter, Jones and Timmons would play more than sixty games together over the next two seasons. Rarely would they walk off the court on the losing side.

Elsewhere in the Bootheel that fall, other schools experienced coaching and administrative changes. With Charlie Vickery's departure to Sikeston, Mick Wessel became head football coach at Chaffee. That same fall Jim Davis joined the Chaffee faculty. The Puxico native was just out of college and in his first year of teaching and coaching. Five years after defeating Advance and stopping the Hornets thirty game winning streak with a last second shot, Davis performed his student teaching under Carroll Cookson. The following school year, he started his career. Coming to Chaffee from basketball rich Puxico was a new experience for Davis. "Chaffee was a baseball town, but it was a football school," said the school's new baseball coach.

High school principal Clarence "Gus" Wessel hired Davis. Wessel was known throughout the area as a standout baseball catcher who played semi-pro ball for several years. Terry Glenzy played baseball with Wessel on the Chaffee Red Wings, the town's amateur team. He recalls a doubleheader in July when the team traveled to St. Louis. Wessel, well into his fifties, caught both games. One of the pitchers Wessel frequently caught was Lloyd "Lefty" Fisher from Puxico. Fisher stories are legendary in Southeast Missouri baseball circles because of a pitching duel against Robin Roberts and a barnstorming all-star major league baseball team. The Fisher-Roberts match-up in Sikeston in October of 1949 went ten innings before the "Harry Walker's All-Stars" managed to score a run and win the game 1-0.[229] It was the baseball connection that helped Davis get his job. "A lot of people here in Puxico have a lot of respect for Gus Wessel," said the coach. One of those people from Puxico who knew Wessel was Carroll Cookson. The Advance coach spoke to the Chaffee principal and recommended his former student teacher for the opening.

Advance had several significant changes that same school year. After thirteen years as the head basketball coach, Cookson had resigned from the position and was now the high school principal. Their new basketball coach was Jim Keeling. Overseeing the entire Advance School District was a new superintendent, Bill Bradshaw. After twelve years at Chaffee, the Bradshaws moved to Advance in the summer of 1978.

The move meant Joe Bradshaw would play his senior season with a new team. Basketball practice started in June. Unlike Chaffee, there was no football program at his new school. Much like Scott Central, it was all basketball, all the time. The newest member of the Advance student body grasped the difference immediately. "At Advance, you were absolutely, positively expected to win. The players expected to win, the fans expected you to win, the student body expected you to win, the coach expected you to win. There was never that expectation at Chaffee." All summer long, he practiced with his new teammates, typically four nights a week. Friday nights in the summer time meant freedom when he lived in Chaffee, it meant basketball in Advance at the high school gym. "I can still remember the smell, just the smell of the heat being trapped in there. But at nine o'clock at night, you'd be in there and of course, by that time you've lost ten pounds just by sweating." The Friday night practice was more like an exhibition than a scrimmage. That's because the high school team wouldn't play against each other, but rather former Advance greats. Bradshaw remembers some of his opponents. "I've played against Steve Cookson. I've played against Richard Hitt. I've played against Terry Wills." The games would attract a crowd from townspeople, wanting a glimpse of the future, and remembering the glories of seasons past. The newest addition to the Advance Hornets that season remembered something else; the high school team rarely won those games. "They usually whipped us. They were good players, but it made you a whole lot better."

By the time school started in the fall, the practice schedule changed to six days a week. The only day off was Saturday. When they weren't practicing or playing former Advance players, the team was playing unofficial scrimmages with other schools, games that never showed up on calendars or the newspaper. Bradshaw remembers playing Scott County Central and several other teams before the season tipped off. In one scrimmage, he hyper-extended his left knee and tore cartilage. He kept playing. Two days before school started, he tore ligaments in his wrist. The doctor told him he would miss six to eight weeks of practice. He didn't miss a day. The senior forward became swept up in the hoops hysteria of his new surroundings. "It was God, country, family, basketball and I'm not sure it went in that order," said Bradshaw of his new school.

When the season did finally get underway, Advance and Scott Central met for the only time in mid-December. The Braves entered the game undefeated and averaged more than 95 points a game in their first seven contests, twice scoring more than 100 points. Advance entered the match-up 7-1. On the Hornets home court, Advance took control early and led by nine points at halftime. The Braves cut the lead to three at one point in the second half, but Advance never trailed. It won the game 79-70. The contest would be the Braves only loss as they headed into the Christmas Tournament in Cape Girardeau the following week. Scott Central scored 116 points in its first round match-up against Meadow Heights, a new tournament record. Chaffee also won its first round game. In the second round of the sixteen-team tournament, the Scott Central Braves met Chaffee for the first time that season. Over the next few months, the two squads would come to know each other's every move.

Basketball practice started late that fall for Chaffee. Compared to other area teams, practice always started late. But this year, the school's football team made the state playoffs for the first time. With a regular season record of 7-2, the goal of "To State in 78" had been achieved. But the talented Red Devil team wanted more and gave every indication that it had the ability to win a state title. In the first round of playoff football, Chaffee traveled to Ash Grove, a town in Southwest Missouri. The Red Devil defense set the tone early. Defensive end Jim Fowler remembers the signature play of the game. It involved his teammate, all-state defensive back Monty Montgomery. "They had a long, lanky kid (who) went up for a pass and he (Montgomery) damn near cut him in two." The Chaffee defense had eight interceptions on the day with Montgomery picking off three of them. The Red Devils won the game 51-3.

Basketball coach Nick Walls spent the weekend scouting for the football team. He watched Chaffee's next opponent, the Cass-Midway Vikings. He reported back Monday to coach Mick Wessel. What Walls saw was an unusual defense. Cass-Midway played a "radar" defense where all eleven players stand up. The defensive alignment by the Vikings was just one of many frustrations for the Chaffee players. Playing in front of their home crowd on Mark Whitaker Field, just one game away from a state championship contest, it all fell apart. On Chaffee's second possession, Cass-Midway recovered a fumble and scored to put them up 7-0. It was 21-8 at half. The Red Devils never solved the radar defense and Cass-Midway won the game 40-14. Terry Glenzy calls it the most disappointing loss of his football career. "That was the game for us where nothing went right," recalls the longtime Red Devil defensive coordinator. "That was a (Chaffee) team that should have won state. There was no doubt about that."

The next week, Cass-Midway won the state title that so many Chaffee players were confident would go to them.

The game marked the end of football for several Red Devils seniors. The talents of one player, High School All-American tackle Tony Dalton sparked a recruiting battle between the University of Mississippi ("Ole Miss") and the University of Oklahoma (OU). Coach Barry Switzer had become enamored with Dalton the previous summer, when the Chaffee player attended a football camp at Oklahoma. That fall, Switzer and his assistants came calling at Chaffee High School. Terry Glenzy remembers Switzer walking into the coaches' office. "We had an old chair that had been broken. Just had it sitting on the floor and Switzer came in and sat in it." The OU head coach spent a couple of hours talking to the coaches about their talented lineman. Glenzy recalls the attention lavished upon Dalton to convince him to play for the Sooners. "They were hot and heavy after him. They had the Selmon brothers (Lee Roy and Dewey) – the All-Americans who played out there – they were calling Tony at night and recruiting him." Mick Wessel remembers Oklahoma as the only school that recruited Tony that spoke to him without the presence of either his mother or the head coach. The OU coaches told the Chaffee lineman, "When you come to Oklahoma, we'll take care of you," said Wessel.

Dalton's decision shocked the Oklahoma coaching staff. "They called and wanted to know why in the hell are you going to Ole Miss?" said Glenzy. What Switzer and his staff may not have realized is that the Rebels had an inside connection to the Missouri Bootheel town; David Lee was the Quarterback coach at Ole Miss. "David Lee's grandfather was from Chaffee. David's daddy was raised in Chaffee." Dalton didn't make his decision formal until well into the winter of '79. Until then, there was plenty of basketball to be played.

***

When Chaffee and Scott Central met for the first time that season on the basketball court, the two schools had much in common; the same county, the same conference, nearly identical student populations separated by less than 20 miles. There were also distinct differences. Chaffee put five starters on the floor that had just played their last football game the previous month. Tall in those days for a small school – their front line was 6'5", 6'4", 6'3" – the all white team played a physical style and relied upon the shooting talents of their junior forward, Wade Sanders. Scott County Central put four black starters on the court and no one stood over 6'2". They were extremely quick and played the distinctive Cookson style of ball: a furious pace, full-court press and fast break at every opportunity. Anyone was a threat to score for the Braves. Chaffee athletes who played baseball in the spring remember going down to Scott Central for games and thinking the Braves would have to forfeit. They didn't have enough players on the field. They were all in the gym shooting baskets. Finally, enough players would put on a uniform and a game would be played. It rarely was close with the ten run rule frequently invoked. Basketball season was usually the time for Scott Central to return the favor.

There were other, more subtle distinctions as well. The Chaffee players noticed that often times the shoes a Scott Central player wore to the game would be the same ones in which he played the game. Once the ballgame was over, most Chaffee athletes returned to a typical middle class home life. Sanders father worked on the railroad; Monty Montgomery's dad owned his own business; Jim Fowler's father worked construction and his mother was a beautician; Charles Felker's dad was a farmer while his mother taught school. Life was different for Scott Central athletes. "None of the five kids who started had a father at home," recalls Melvin Porter. "That father figure that Cookson played was very important." While their coach is often reluctant to discuss the home life of his players, a story he once related to Mike Eisenbath of the *St. Louis Post-Dispatch* provides a vivid example of the conditions. In the early 1980's, Cookson found out one of his players was struggling in a subject at school. He discovered the family home had exactly one functioning light bulb. He bought the player a light bulb so he could have extra time to study at night. "He got an A on the test," Cookson told the paper.[230] As his assistant coach Ron Cook described it, "We could not begin to imagine their living conditions."

On the basketball court, none of that mattered. Once the warm-ups finished and the buzzer sounded for the tip-off, Scott Central engaged its opponents in a 32 minute track meet to the finish line. Rarely could an opponent keep up. On this night, with one team essentially already in mid-season form and the other one just starting to get in basketball shape, it was a fait accompli. The Braves scored early and often en route to a 92-60 victory. Their Christmas Tournament run lasted only one game longer. In the semi-finals, Scott Central lost to the Notre Dame Bulldogs. In the 1970's, one thing proved as difficult for Ronnie Cookson as winning a state championship; beating Ed Arnzen's team from Cape Girardeau.

***

Arnzen didn't start playing organized basketball until his junior year in high school. That's because Leopold High School didn't have a gymnasium until then. Once the team did begin playing, they weren't very good. "I think we won maybe two ballgames my junior year and two ballgames my senior year," remembers the 1961 Leopold graduate. After getting his college degree from Southeast Missouri State, Arnzen began his coaching career at Century High School in Ullin, Illinois. He took a position as the assistant basketball coach and the head track coach. "I could not even identify the events in track. I started the program and had to get a book to find out what they had in it." After two years at the Illinois school, Arnzen left to continue his education and get his master's degree. Returning to Cape Girardeau, he taught fourth grade and P.E. while also attending classes at Southeast Missouri State. "The longest year of my life," remembers the coach. In the fall of 1968, he accepted a position at Cape Girardeau Notre Dame High School. After two years duty as an assistant, he became the head basketball coach in the fall of 1970, the same year that Ronnie Cookson started at Scott County Central. The two men's teams would meet on the basketball court every year for the next nine seasons. Off the court, the two coaches developed a friendship. After a Friday night game one year, the pair went goose hunting the next day. Arnzen remembers Cookson describing to him his approach to bow hunting. The Scott Central coach would sit in a deer stand while bringing members of his team to fan out across the woods in search of game. It was this off the court relationship with his players that impressed Arnzen. "How many coaches have that kind of rapport with their kids?"

Scott Central and Notre Dame met for a second time in the 1978-79 season one month after their Christmas Tournament match-up. The junior dominated Braves team had lost only two games all season – to Advance and Notre Dame. On this night, they would lose their third. Arnzen always prepared his teams well for Scott Central, particularly focusing on the Braves' ability to generate great momentum from easy fast break buckets and the need to block out on the boards. "His kids would rebound so well...even on free throws that his kids were shooting, they would get the offensive rebound if you didn't do a good job of blocking out." With solid rebounding, smart ball handling, and selective use of timeouts to block runs by his opponent, Arnzen's Bulldog teams experienced great success against Scott Central. No team dominated Ronnie Cookson like Notre Dame did in the 1970's. Cookson's squads only defeated Arnzen's teams twice in the decade and one of those games was in 1976, Scott Central's first state championship team. In the 1978 regular season match-up on Scott Central's home court, the Braves led by 12 points going into the fourth quarter. Notre Dame outscored Scott Central 29-9 in the final frame to rally for victory. Back in Cape Girardeau for the 1979 game, Arnzen's team followed much the same formula. Down by 8 points at the end of the third quarter, Notre Dame outscored Scott Central by 13 in the final quarter to win again. The game marked the final match-up between Cookson and Arnzen. The following season, Arnzen would be at his college alma mater, as the assistant men's basketball coach. He ended his high school coaching career with a nine and two record against Ronnie Cookson.[231]

***

Losing to Notre Dame twice in a month's time, Jeff Limbaugh has vivid memories of the post game locker room conversation. Cookson's "thing for trash cans" emerged again in a legendary tirade. "He came in, in one of those modes where he doesn't say anything and you don't dare breath," recalls Limbaugh. Scott Central had ordered soft drinks for the players after the game and during the middle of Cookson's explosion, someone opened the door to the locker room and slid them in. Teammate Melvin Porter remembers what their coach did next. "He had a soda in his hand. He took that soda and he threw it and when he threw it, the soda splashed on Jeff Limbaugh's face. Jeff took his tongue and he licked it. He said 'man that was good.' That kind of broke the ice." When the team entered regional play the following month, Scott Central still had only three losses. Along the way, Cookson's team had picked up twenty-two victories.

Sandwiched in between the two losses to Notre Dame, Scott Central faced Chaffee two more times. The rapidly improving Red Devil team made it to the conference tournament championship game against the Braves, only to lose 71-53. Wade Sanders scored 34 of his team's points that night. This was another Cookson trademark: let the star player have his points and shut everyone else down. "One thing Ronnie is amazing about – I've seen him do it year after year after year – was if you had a team with one stud player – you're going to lose, if that's all you had, " said Mike Marsh, who covered both teams as a sportswriter during that era. During the second match-up – the two teams third contest against each other that season – Chaffee tried a different approach with a more balanced scoring attack. All three frontline Chaffee players, Jim Fowler, Charles Felker and Sanders, scored in double figures but Scott Central still won the game handily 81-67. After that ballgame, Nick Walls conceded, "we've finally realized that they're just better than we are. Those guys are just so much quicker than we are. They're just a good team."[232] Still, Chaffee could take some solace in the fact that in each loss, the margin of victory shrank; from thirty-two points to eighteen and now fourteen. Playing and practicing in only their second full month of action, the Red Devils were getting better and gaining confidence. According to their coach, another key factor was that Sander's teammates began to appreciate his role. "Those guys were smart. They knew they had to have Wade to score."

Sanders role in Chaffee's offense was underscored by another game that season – a loss to Illmo-Scott City. During their first meeting, Chaffee won easily by 19 points. Sanders scored 25 that night but in the rematch, he managed only four points as Rams triangle and two defense frustrated him all night long. Illmo-Scott City[233] won the game 58-37. It was Sander's lowest output of his career and the only game all season he didn't score in double digits. Following that loss, Chaffee won six of its next seven games and entered regional play with a record of 16-7.

While Sanders has fond memories of battling against Illmo-Scott City, the rival school just eight miles down the road from Chaffee, he also recalls an off the court conversation with their coach. On a Saturday morning, the coach placed a call to the Sanders' residence. "(He) beat around the bush for a few minutes before he asked if I would consider moving to Scott City." The Rams were unsuccessful in their recruitment of Chaffee's star player, but the Sanders family did consider moving before Wade's senior season. George Sanders had played at nearby Benton, which was now a part of Kelly High School, another conference rival. He wanted his son to play for a more basketball focused school. Wade's uncle, Forrest Jackson, was superintendent of schools at Kelly. "Dad was sharp enough to know Kelly was bigger, I'd get more exposure and my chance for college would have been greater," remembers the Chaffee All-State forward. The Sanders went so far as to look at a house in the Kelly School District but eventually decided against it. If Wade had his choice, the school he would have preferred playing for would have been one in Stoddard County with a great basketball tradition. "Advance. It was just a great basketball school. That would have been the one school if I could have played for a team without football, it would have been Advance."

While Wade never got that opportunity, his good friend Joe Bradshaw did. Playing only one year at the school, Bradshaw remembers how his teammates took the game seriously, not only in games but also on the practice court. "We had a fight every day," said the Advance forward. The intensity of the practice sessions was something Bradshaw wasn't accustomed to seeing at Chaffee. To illustrate the point, he recalls one practice where he went up for a rebound against Parks Long, the Advance Center who stood about 6'3" and outweighed Bradshaw by at least fifty pounds. "He hit me with an elbow going up and he just splattered my nose. He was my best friend on the team," said the 6'1" Bradshaw. "Later I said, man, why did you do that? He said, 'my ball, man.' That's the way it went." Contentious on the court during practice and divided in cliques away from the game, the Advance team wasn't an especially tight knit group. But Bradshaw had no doubts as how his teammates would respond during a ballgame. "Not close off the court, but in a game, I have no doubt those guys would have died for me or for anyone else. It was the strangest bunch of guys I ever played with. But boy, they could play and they loved it."

Adding extra tension to the season was the coaching change due to Carroll Cookson's resignation the previous year. Cookson remained at the school as principal and cast a long shadow over the program. It was not an easy situation for the new coach. "Jim Keeling was following a legend," said Bradshaw. Team manager Brad Fowler remembers how Keeling would scrimmage with his team, blurring the line between player and coach. It was something Cookson never did.[234] Even modest changes to the style of play came under heavy scrutiny. One thing Keeling brought with him to Advance was more of an emphasis on a more traditional style fast break: getting the rebound, kicking it out to one side and then quickly getting the ball into the hands of a second player who filled the middle of the court. "I think people began to ask – where's the long pass? Where's the long pass?" Bradshaw said, referring to the style that Cookson brought with him from Puxico playing under Arnold Ryan. But one thing didn't change. The Hornets continued their winning ways under their new coach. They won seven of their first eight games under Keeling, including the victory over Scott Central. Their next game, a loss against Notre Dame, was one of the more memorable games that season, according to Bradshaw. He remembers going after a loose ball and crashing head first into one end of the Notre Dame bench. He expected concern, or at least empathy, from the rival players. What he got instead was an earful. "I remember their players leaning over and saying things like 'get up you pussy!' and cussing me like nobody's business." Bradshaw quickly got up, fired off a few expletives of his own in their direction and ran back down court.

That same season, a season of many firsts for Bradshaw, he also got introduced to the Advance-Puxico rivalry, one that extended at least as far back to Grady Smith's defection from Advance to the rival Indians nearly thirty years before. The two teams both claimed two state basketball championships over the years and both towns were fiercely proud of their schools' basketball traditions. To an outsider experiencing it for the first time as a senior, the event made a lasting impression. "I had never seen anything like it. Chaffee and Scott City in football I guess was probably pretty close to it," said Bradshaw. "When we went there, I remember going into the locker room and a line of our parents formed two lines for us to walk into the locker room between them and people were yelling stuff at us as we walked in. It was the darndest thing I had ever seen. During the game itself, we nearly had a fight or two." On this night, Bradshaw and his teammates prevailed. Advance went on to post a 17-7 regular season mark under their new coach. Puxico also had a talented team that season and entered regional play at 19-6.

When regional action got underway in late February Puxico and Scott County Central were pitted together at one site; Advance and Chaffee at another location. The winners of the two regionals would meet in the first round of state tournament the following week at Bloomfield. All four clubs won their first three games. The regional finals were set. Both games would be played on the same night. The Friday night action between Puxico and Scott Central would get underway at Bloomfield.

The game between Chaffee and Advance would tip off at the gym in Zalma.

Puxico, Scott Central, Advance and Chaffee. To three of those schools, state tournament basketball was familiar territory. All of them had been there before; all of the schools had championship hardware on display in trophy cases. But what was familiar territory for three schools would be new ground for one. The last time Chaffee had made it as far as a regional final took place seventeen years before. Ironically, the opponent in 1962 was the same one as 1979, the Advance Hornets.

The '62 Red Devils went 21-3 that season. Two of the three losses were to Advance, the second defeat ending their season. Seven years before that, Chaffee entered the post-season on a roll, racking up 15 consecutive victories. One of the games in that streak was a 100-80 victory over Lincoln of Sikeston, the town's all black school. One year after Brown vs. Board of Education, the walls of segregation were just beginning to crumble on Missouri basketball courts. But Advance snapped the winning streak and the Devils' season with a victory in the sub-regionals at Oran.

On the night of Friday, February 23, 1979, a standing room only crowd in Zalma, Missouri watched the Red Devils and the Hornets battle it out for the right to advance to the state tournament. Principal and former coach Carroll Cookson was there to see the team he had coached for many years. Advance Superintendent Bill Bradshaw and his wife Alma arrived to watch their son Joe play and see many friends from their former hometown. Chaffee football coach Mick Wessel, who guided the Red Devils to the state playoffs in football for the first time ever, looked on to see if his basketball counterpart could do the same.

It started as a blowout. To the delight of Chaffee fans and the disappointment of Advance faithful, the Red Devils were on fire. Joe Bradshaw had the unfortunate assignment of guarding his buddy from Chaffee, Wade Sanders, for much of the night. "He was my friend, but I stood on his feet, I held his shorts, I held him, I tugged him, I did everything but stick a knife in him." It didn't work. "He hit everything he threw up, I couldn't stop him." When Advance did stop Sanders, a foul often resulted. Wade went to the free throw line twenty three times that night, making seventeen of them.

Chaffee led 19-8 after the first quarter, extending the lead by five points in the second quarter, and led 42-26 at halftime. Nick Walls heard afterwards that the Advance coach had been fired at halftime that night. It simply was inconceivable to Advance fans they could lose twice in the same season to Chaffee. But in fact, Jim Keeling had turned in his resignation earlier that month.[235] Coaching in the shadow of Carroll Cookson proved difficult. "Naturally, there was a lot of banter back and forth because he didn't do this like Cookson did and he didn't do that," said Superintendent Bill Bradshaw. "A lot of people criticized him." Bradshaw also tried to talk the young coach out of his decision. "I said, Jim, you're doing this premature, don't do it, wait until the season is over and get a good objective look at it. He said no, I don't want to come back." Keeling wasn't coming back, but he wasn't giving up either. Team manager Brad Fowler remembers the team always saying a prayer before each game. On this night, with a state tournament berth on the line, Keeling asked senior Charles Wiggins to lead a *second* team prayer at halftime. [236] If 1979 were to turnout like the last time the two teams met in the regional finals, his prayers would be answered.

***

The 1962 Chaffee Red Devils entered the regional finals with only two losses. One of the defeats was a 46-45 loss at the hands of the Advance Hornets. On February 24, 1962, the two teams met again. The Hornets were coming off a third place finish in the state tournament the previous year and entered the contest with a record of 24-4. The Red Devils led by their 6'6" center, Steve Cunningham, were 20-2. The regional tournament at Scott City had followed form. Advance was seeded first with Chaffee right behind them in the number two position. The winner would play the Bloomfield regional winner in the first round of state play. The Puxico Indians, with a guard named Ronnie Cookson, were the number one seed of that regional.

When the championship game tipped off at Scott City, Chaffee came out firing on all cylinders. Cunningham, who earlier in the year had scored 47 points in a game and was averaging close to 30 points a contest, could do no wrong. Of his seventeen field goal attempts that night, he missed only three times.[237] The Chaffee center had a scholarship waiting for him at the end of the season. He played college basketball at Western Kentucky. In the 1965-66 season, four Hilltopper players would make the all-conference team. Cunningham was one of them. So too was teammate and future NBA player Clem Haskins who eventually coached in the collegiate ranks as well. Wayne Chapman, father of future University of Kentucky star Rex Chapman, played on the same club.

Back at Scott City, the Red Devils led by six points at the end of the first quarter. With three and a half minutes to go in the second quarter, Chaffee extended the lead to 12 points. Advance refused to quit. The Hornets gradually narrowed the lead. With just over three minutes to go into the game, the score was tied at 47. With a minute left, Advance guard Fred Ritter was fouled while driving to the bucket. His shot counted and his free throw put Advance up by a single point, 54-53. Chaffee missed a shot on its next trip down the court and Advance went into a stall. Forced to foul, the Red Devils caught a break when the Hornets player missed his free throw. With one last chance to take the lead, Chaffee missed its shot and was forced to foul again. Two late free throws made the final score 56-53. Advance lost to Richland in the first round of state tournament action two nights later. Richland had upset Puxico in the regional finals at Bloomfield, bringing an end to Ronnie Cookson's high school career.

The following night, Sunday, February 25th, 1962, disaster struck in downtown Chaffee. Sometime around 7:30 that evening, flames began engulfing the Chaffee Hotel. Situated at the main downtown intersection, the site had twice previously seen buildings end in ruin. The Hotel Astoria was built shortly after the Frisco came to town. It was destroyed in a blaze in December of 1913. The location was nothing but a fenced in hole in the ground for thirteen years. A new two-story building was constructed in 1926 and was named the Byrd Hotel. It lasted until 1957 when a tornado proved its demise. The Chaffee Hotel was the third attempt to put lodging on the downtown site. It would be the last. Firemen from Cape Girardeau, Jackson, Scott City, Sikeston and Oran all helped battle the blaze along with the Chaffee volunteer fire department. They would spend over four hours attempting to get it under control. It caused an estimated $250,000 in damage.[238] Never again would Chaffee have a hotel. It's said that history doesn't repeat, but it does rhyme. Seventeen years later, a ballgame and a blizzard would put the theory to the test.

***

In February of 1962, many of the players on the court at Zalma were most likely just a year old or even younger. The Red Devils players probably didn't know their predecessors had blown a big lead under identical circumstances: a regional championship game against Advance with the chance of playing a Ronnie Cookson team in the first round of state play. Ignorance was bliss.

Sometime in either the second or third quarter, memories and game accounts are not clear. Keeling received a technical foul. It occurred when Chaffee had the ball and Wade Sanders was shooting. After the referee called a foul on the play, the Advance coach said something he shouldn't have and was slapped with the technical. Sanders stood at the free throw line all by himself. Thanks to the combination of player and bench fouls, he would have four shots. He made all four. Each time the ball would go through the net, the crowd got just a little louder. By the time he sank the fourth one, a crescendo of cheers had turned into a full-throated roar. The Chaffee player had never heard a crowd so loud. He thought the roof was going to come off the Zalma gym. The rout was on. "Hand us the trophy," thought Sanders.

By the end of the third quarter, Chaffee led 57 to 41. Advance hadn't made a dent in Chaffee's halftime lead. While the 16 point margin provided comfort, there was also some concern. Monty Montgomery, the team's point guard and best ball handler had fouled out. Junior reserve guard David Dannenmueller took his place. In a desperate, fourth quarter move, Advance renewed full court pressure. Earlier attempts at doing so had proved futile. Joe Bradshaw knew the reason why. "You take Monty Montgomery off the floor and we handled them because they couldn't handle the ball. They couldn't have handled our quickness or our pressure. But he single-handedly beat our pressure all night. " This time the pressure worked. Chaffee started turning the ball over and the Hornets chipped away at the lead. At the same time the press started paying off, an Advance player who was barely expected to contribute that night started heating up. Eddie Dunivan had only scored two points the night before in a victory over Bunker. That's because he was violently ill and played less than a minute. Teammate Bradshaw recalls the circumstances. "He had a bad case of the flu. I remember we were going up to the game (against Bunker) and he was riding in the car in front of us and he stuck his head out the window and smiled at us." Seconds later, he threw up. "He was sick as a dog," said Bradshaw. Before the Chaffee game that night, the Advance coach had told a reporter that Dunivan was "starting as a psychological ploy." [239]

In the fourth quarter, Dunivan was still in the ballgame. He saved his best for last. With five minutes to go in the game, the lead was 18 points. With full court pressure and Dunivan hitting nearly everything he threw at the basket, Advance pounded away, refusing to give in. The senior guard wouldn't let his teammates quit. "Eddie was tons of intensity, he was tough, aggressive," remembers Bradshaw who also recalled his teammate's streakiness. "Eddie would come out and miss five in a row, hit five in a row, miss five in a row, hit five in a row. But (he) never quit playing hard." With Dunivan pouring in 21 fourth quarter points, the lead evaporated. Standing over on the Chaffee sidelines, Nick Walls was worried that his beleaguered Red Devils would collapse under the Dunivan onslaught and the Advance pressure. He'll never forget what Chaffee fans were screaming at him. "Don't you know how to hold the ball? Don't you know how to hold the ball? I was thinking to myself; no, I don't."

With just under a minute to go in the game, Bradshaw was fouled. He went to the free throw line to shoot a one-and-one. If he made both, Advance would tie the game. As the senior stood waiting for the referee to hand him the ball, his friends from Chaffee took their spots on the court as well. Bradshaw had been their teammate for years, now he had the chance to help end their season and send Advance into state tournament play against either Scott Central or Puxico, teams that the Hornets had already beaten earlier in the season. He missed the front end of the one-and-one. But hope wasn't lost. A teammate got the rebound and he was fouled. He made one of two free throws and Advance trailed Chaffee by a single point. Slowly, haltingly, the game ground down to its final seconds. At this point, it was a battle of attrition. In a game that featured 57 fouls, three Chaffee starters could only sit on the bench and watch. Two Advance players had fouled out as well. Chaffee clung to its one point lead when with four seconds to go when Advance fouled David Dannenmueller. The back-up guard had been the target of the Hornets full court fourth quarter harassment. Their efforts had largely succeeded. Now Dannenmueller had his chance to strike back in the game's most critical moments. He walked to the free throw line and shot twice. He calmly sank both shots, putting Chaffee up three and the contest out of reach.[240] Chaffee had won the game 77-74.

Red Devil fans exploded in applause and stormed the court. One of the first people out to greet coach Nick Walls was football coach Mick Wessel. Returning to the locker room, Dannenmueller started hyperventilating. The reserve guard had scored nine points, all in the fourth quarter. The pressure packed performance had finally overwhelmed him. Amidst the bustle of the gym, Joe Bradshaw tried to escape the fans of his former hometown and quickly exit. He felt a tug on the back of his jersey. "I remember slinging away from them and turning around with my fist clenched. It was Terry Glenzy and I felt so badly about that." Glenzy, Bradshaw's junior high coach, stopped to tell his former player he was proud of his performance that night. As the rest of the Advance team and its fans walked off the court and out of the gym, Chaffee fans continued to yell, part in celebration, part in sophomoric taunting. In the midst of the clapping and cheering, Bill and Alma Bradshaw began their descent out of the stands, their path taking them directly in front of fans from their former hometown. Alma was crying on her husband's shoulder as they walked out of the gym.

Nick Walls has two distinct memories after the victory that sent Chaffee into state tournament basketball play for the first time in its history. The first one still sends chills up his spine. Returning to town with his players on a school bus, an anonymous voice came over the CB radio. "They said we will never get that bus back to Chaffee, Missouri. They were waiting for us. I remember that like it was yesterday." The trip home from Zalma would take them directly through Advance. Whoever made the threat didn't follow through. The school bus returned to Chaffee without incident. The second recollection of the evening is also vivid, but on a much lighter note. Chaffee's opponent in the first round of state play would be the winner of the Scott Central-Puxico game. The radio dial on the school bus was tuned to the play by play as the game was winding down.

***

The Puxico Indians had undergone several coaching changes since the days of Arnold Ryan. Jim Davis had three different head coaches in his four seasons at the school in the early 1970's. His freshman year the coach was Gene Wilfong. He had succeeded Grady Smith, another star from the 1950's championship teams. Later, Carroll Cookson tried his hand at coaching Puxico, marking the third former Ryan player who returned to his alma mater. Davis's coach his senior season was Pete Townsend. He was still at the helm in 1979 when Puxico met Scott Central.

It had been twenty years since Puxico had made the state tournament and twenty-seven years since Ryan led Puxico to their last state title against Shelbyville. Still, the legacy of the legendary coach loomed large. Townsend heard about it often. He remembers a frequent lament. "The boys don't have the dedication that the Arnold Ryan boys had." Complicating matters for Townsend, "Lot of my players, their fathers played for Arnold Ryan. That made a difference," said the coach. "They always brought up the Arnold Ryan teams." Jim Davis heard the same thing, not from the parents, but from students. Several years after he graduated, Davis returned to his alma mater to take a job in the school system. "When I first came here, I had a kid tell me, 'you don't realize how much pressure there is to put that jersey on.' I said what do you mean? He said, 'well, we're always being compared to the teams of the fifties.'"

The Puxico squads of the fifties played a fast paced fast break style of basketball. So did Townsend's teams. The former Fisk standout played junior college basketball at Southern Baptist in Walnut Ridge, Arkansas. He left the campus in the spring of 1962. Ronnie and Carroll Cookson arrived that fall. After finishing up his college basketball career and getting his degree at Southeast Missouri State, Townsend took his first coaching job. Three moves and nine years later, Townsend started at Puxico. Being in the same conference as Advance and with a regular season game scheduled every year against Scott Central, Townsend saw a lot of the Cookson Clan. Earlier in the year Scott Central had defeated Puxico by fifteen points. Still, the season had played out just as Ronnie Cookson had predicted more than two years after the ballgame at the Bell City B-Team tournament. His team would be playing Puxico in the regional final.

The first half gave every indication it could be a blowout. Scott Central led by 11 points, 45-34 at halftime. Then, according to Cookson, "we just kind of went berserk there in the second half."[241] Puxico rallied in the third quarter while managing also to shut down the Braves. Scott

Central only scored six points in the third quarter. The lead was one as the fourth quarter tipped off. Puxico continued its surge. Halfway through the final frame, the Indians led by four. The game was played in front of a full house at the Bloomfield gym in the middle of Stoddard County. Racing through the northern end of the county and heading for home was the Chaffee team bus. The players and their coach were celebrating a victory, listening to a radio broadcast, and pulling for an underdog. Nick Walls left no doubt which team he wanted to win. "We were listening to it and we were screaming for Puxico that night."

With ninety seconds to go, the game was tied. In the last minute, four different players would go to the free throw line to put their team ahead. It appeared that the contest would come down to fouls and free shots. Over on the Puxico sideline, coach Pete Townsend must have had a sense of déjà vu. He had seen this game before.

***

In 1969, Townsend was the coach of the Delta Bobcats. The Cape County School made it the regional final against the Matthews Pirates. Jim Hart's Matthews club was attempting to become the first team in the Bootheel to repeat as state champions since the Puxico Indians of the early 1950's. By halftime, up by nine points, Matthews seemed firmly in control of the game. But the Delta defense took control of the contest in the third quarter. With a little over three minutes to go in the ballgame, Delta led Matthews by nine points. A Matthews' rally cut the lead to four. With time winding down, the Pirates began to foul. In a span of less than thirty seconds, Delta had three one-and-one opportunities. If the Bobcats converted all the opportunities, they could push the lead back to ten points. Instead, each time a Delta player went to the line, he missed his first shot. Seizing the opportunity, Matthews rallied to take the lead and won the game 65-61. Townsend remembers the missed free throws as the turning point. "My best free shooters were shooting because I wanted them to have the ball. That's the way it goes."

Ten years later, Townsend was at Puxico. One of his Delta players, Ron Cook, was an assistant coach for Ronnie Cookson. Back in Bloomfield, the game was tied at 62. Puxico missed a shot and a chance to take the lead. Scott Central had the ball when one of their players was fouled. He went to the free throw line and missed the attempt. A Puxico player rebounded the ball and he was fouled. He missed his free throw.

Now Scott Central had the ball and the clock on their side. Less than thirty seconds remained. The Braves never got a shot off. They turned the ball over. Back it went to Puxico. With eleven seconds remaining in the game, a second Puxico player was fouled and went to the free throw line to shoot a front end of a one and one. He missed it. But the Indians caught a break when one of their players grabbed the rebound. With nine seconds left, he was fouled. In a span of thirty seconds, three separate Puxico players had the opportunity to send the Indians back into state tournament play for the first time since 1959. All three failed.

When the final missed free throw came off the glass, the Braves kicked the ball out and made a mad dash to the other end of the court. With just a few seconds left, the ball was in Mayfield Timmons hands. He was somewhere around the free throw line when he let the shot go. Melvin Porter had fouled out of the game and watched Timmons' shot from the bench. "I watched the ball go up and I said it was short. I knew it was short when it left his hand." Porter was right. The line drive shot was short. It hit the front of the rim. But instead of bouncing straight back, the ball went straight up in the air and back through the goal. Porter couldn't believe what he was seeing. "It was so loud in there. To this day I believe the momentum from the crowd forced that ball in."

Timmons shot went in with one second left on the clock. Scott Central had won the game by two points – or had it? The referee was waving his arms as if the bucket wasn't allowed. On the Scott Central bench, Cookson blew up. "What the hell you mean it wasn't good?" he barked. The coach recalled the referee's reply. "He said, 'coach, Puxico has called their sixth timeout (only 5 per half were allowed). You're up two and you're going to go down and shoot a free throw and get the ball out of bounds on the side. And if you don't win this damn game, you don't deserve to win. My advice to you is get your ass back on the bench.'" Cookson took the advice. Donnie McClinton made a free throw and Scott Central survived in a 65-62 victory. The Braves players were so excited they ran immediately into the locker room. They had to be retrieved to come back out to the court to receive their regional championship trophy. For the second time in his coaching career, Pete Townsend lost an opportunity to make it to the state tournament. Each time, his club's free throw shooting had failed him. "That just drained me. It took everything out of me that year." Townsend didn't coach another high school game for eight years.

***

The first round of state tournament play was scheduled for Monday, three days away. Chaffee and Scott Central would meet for the fourth time that season at the gym in Bloomfield. The players didn't know it at the time, but they would get extra rest that weekend. That's because a major winter storm was just around the corner. But what many remember as an isolated event, others saw as a worrisome trend. The earth was getting colder. A new Ice Age was dawning.

Somewhere along in the 1970's, perhaps sooner, the media began covering stories on global climate change. Probably the most popular article, or at least the one most cited, appeared on the pages of *Newsweek* magazine in the spring of 1975. Under the heading of "The Cooling World," the story begins this way: "There are ominous signs that the earth's weather patterns have begun to change dramatically and that these changes may portend a drastic decline in food production – with serious political implications for just about every nation in the world. The drop in food output could begin quite soon, perhaps only ten years from now."[242] Citing a two-week loss of the growing season in England and a rash of tornadoes across the United States, reporter Peter Gwynne also added this:

> *"The central fact is that after three quarters of a century of extraordinary mild conditions, the earth's climate seems to be cooling down. Meteorologists disagree about the cause and extent of the cooling trend, as well as over its specific impact on local weather conditions. But they are almost unanimous in their view that the trend will reduce agricultural productivity for the rest of the century. If the climactic change is as profound as some of the pessimists fear, the resulting famines could be catastrophic."[243]*

A little more than three years later, in November of 78, the *Southeast Missourian* warned its readers of dry conditions and a possible drought. Less than 19 inches of rain had fallen on the area in the first eight months of the year and the arid conditions promised to cause problems for area farmers in the coming winter. The paper concluded the editorial by saying, "what is needed…is a series of soaking rains….and then several snowfalls that will soak into the ground through the winter months." The editors would get much more than they bargained for in the winter of '79.

The day after the regional championships, Saturday, February 24th, 1979, promised poor weather conditions but nothing out of the ordinary. Snow was expected but accumulation would only be a few inches; or so everyone thought. It began with a rainstorm on Saturday night. Thunder and lightning accompanied the rain that continued through the early morning hours of Sunday. Some time overnight, the temperature began dropping. It plunged into the teens. Rain became snow. It snowed all of Sunday morning. It continued to snow Sunday afternoon. The snowfall was accompanied by wind gusts of up to 50 miles an hour. When it finally ended, the region was blanketed with accumulations up to 24 inches. The two feet of snow and high winds produced drifts ten feet tall.[244] It caught everyone by surprise. An estimated six thousand people were stranded by the storm in Southeast Missouri and Southern Illinois, with many people spending the night in gymnasiums and makeshift shelters.[245] In Scott County, nearly 350 people spent Sunday night at the National Guard armory in Sikeston while hundreds of others flocked to the county courthouse in Benton. Missouri Governor Joe Teasdale sent 250 National Guard troops to the region while helicopters airlifted passengers stuck along Interstate 55.[246] It was the blizzard of the century. On Monday, the *Southeast Missourian* missed publishing for the first time in its nearly 75-year history. A day later, the paper's executive editor John L. Blue described conditions for readers and for history this way:

"Researchers and reporters, delving into the weather records hereafter will use this as their reference point – and what a point it is. Never, at least in recorded city history, has there been anything like it. Cape Girardeau is paralyzed. Nothing moves but emergency vehicles and a few with four-wheel drives authorized by police. All others are subject to arrest. Grocery stores, doing a rush of walk-in business, are running out of bread, milk, and other staples. Businesses are shut down. There are no burials – the bodies are being held until

the weather moderates. Everywhere there are snowdrifts, man-made or nature-made. The man-made ones are a canyon down the streets, allowing one-way traffic for police and other emergency vehicles. The nature made ones are drifts six and eight feet high. Cars are buried."[247]

Blue then describes what he believed was a weather trend in the late 1970's, one that dated back to around the time of the Newsweek article of a few years before. "It is the third year of the new Ice Age. Zero temperatures and below have been common each of these three winters. Snowfall is far above what normally has been in the memory of anyone now alive. Last winter there was a 15 inch snowfall, but it was peanuts to what is outside right now."

What was outside right now would take time to clear. There would be no basketball Monday night at Bloomfield. Chaffee and Scott Central would have to wait to play another day. Fortunately, for everyone, conditions improved rapidly. The mercury climbed into the thirties on Monday. The snow began to melt. National Guard Troops and local farmers began clearing roads. With quarterfinal play scheduled for Wednesday night in Flat River, there was little time to lose. The game was rescheduled for Tuesday afternoon. But the weather was not done wreaking havoc.

Chaffee players arrived at the gym in four-wheel drive trucks. Along the way, Wade Sanders glanced out the window to see one of the few vehicles out that day; a snowmobile passing by on the side of the road. Getting there was just half the battle. Once inside, the players and fans soon discovered the heat at the Bloomfield gym was not working. It was chilly inside when the ballgame tipped off. For the Scott Central players, it was positively ice cold.

When the game was ready to tip-off, a melee broke out on the Scott Central bench. Coach Ronnie Cookson remembers the scramble. "The biggest fight of the whole game was who was going to get the five starters warm-ups to cover up on the bench." The cool conditions made a big impression on the Scott Central coach and his players. Invariably, it's one of the first things they will mention when discussing that day. On the other side, Chaffee players' memories of the lack of heat are far less vivid. What they recall is how they started the game.

Scott Central counted on its full court press to generate turnovers and points. But with point guard Monty Montgomery breaking the pressure and pounding the ball inside to 6'5" center Jim Fowler, Braves players found themselves on their heels. By the end of the first quarter, Chaffee had an eight-point lead. Cookson began worrying the elements may influence the outcome. "Donnie McClinton nearly froze to death," said the coach of his star forward. "His hands were so cold, he couldn't even catch the ball."

In the second quarter, the Red Devils stretched the lead to thirteen points. Nothing was working for the Braves. Cookson thought he knew the reason why his opponent was playing so well. "Chaffee played football and was used to playing in the cold weather." Midway through the second quarter with a double-digit lead, the Chaffee coach made a tactical decision. Fowler, who scored 16 of his team's 33 first half points, remembers the turning point. "We went into this four corner stall, and we were beating them. Once we did that, it was a dogfight after that." It was a dogfight that would go down to the game's final seconds. Scott Central came storming back. The slower Chaffee team was no match for the quicker Braves lineup when it came to dribbling and passing the ball. "The thing about Scott Central was you didn't have time to think about putting anything in action," recalls Wade Sanders, "because the moment you stopped to think about it, they stole the ball." Stealing the ball practically every time down the court, the Braves took off on one of their patented runs that buried many opponents. "At some point during (a) game, it may be the first quarter, second, third or fourth – but some point during that game, they were going to have their four to five minute run," said Cookson. In a four minute run to end the second quarter, Scott Central outscored Chaffee 16-2, turning a 31-18 deficit into a 34-33 halftime lead.

The halftime pause broke the Braves momentum. In the third quarter, they could only stretch the lead to four points. But the jump ball at the beginning of the fourth quarter marked progress for Chaffee. Never had it played the Braves so close this late into the game. "I just kept telling those guys, if you can get in the fourth quarter and you got a chance guys, you never know what might happen," remembers Walls. Scott Central wasn't letting up though. With five minutes to go, the Braves increased their lead to ten and once again it looked like Scott

Central would walk off in a route. Nick Walls decided to mix it up. Instead of their usual one-three-one zone defense, the Red Devils went to man-to-man. Normally, this would be suicide against the quicker and faster Braves lineup. But there was nothing normal about a game played in a gym with no heat two days after the worst blizzard of the 20th century. The move seemed to confuse the Braves who had difficulty scoring the rest of the game. Scott Central led 65-60 when back to back three point plays put Chaffee up by one. The Red Devils were in uncharted territory – a lead against Scott Central in the final minutes of a game.

Advance senior Joe Bradshaw made the drive over to the Bloomfield gym that day with his father. "I remember sitting up there in the stands thinking how in the world could we have beaten one of these teams and played with the other one?" wondered the former Chaffee player. "That was the state championship game right there." To Bradshaw, the game represented the best of two very different styles of play, the physical Red Devils against the fast break Braves. "It was the hammer against the velvet glove. It was a wonderful game to watch."

It's at this point, with Chaffee winning 66-65, that memories get hazy and written game summaries produce conflicting accounts. The two teams traded buckets before a Melvin Porter rebound and put back had the Braves in the lead 69-68. With less than a minute to go, Chaffee had the ball. "As soon as the ball crossed mid-court, Walls began calling for a timeout. Then he began screaming for a timeout. Then he literally jumped up and down trying to draw the attention of his team." [248] The coach never got his time out. Instead, someone – it's not clear who – took a shot for Chaffee. He missed. A second Chaffee player rebounded the ball. He missed as well. Scott Central rebounded the ball with a one-point lead. Jeff Limbaugh of Scott Central was fouled and he made one of two free throws to put the Braves up by two points, 70-68. [249] Chaffee had one last chance. They worked the ball down the court and it made its way to forward Charles Felker. With less than ten seconds to go on the clock and standing about 15 feet from the basket, he lifted a shot toward the goal. The ball hit the rim. It bounced straight up in the air, and just as Mayfield Timmons attempt had done against Puxico, Felker's shot got a friendly bounce. It went through the cylinder. Chaffee had tied the game. But just as Red Devils fans burst into jubilation, a referee blew his whistle. When the ball bounced in the air, it had briefly touched a guide wire hanging overhead to support the goal. Once the ball touched the wire, it was ruled out of play. No bucket. Scott Central ball.

Sitting near the top of the Bloomfield gym, Joe Bradshaw had a near eye level view of the play. "Charles (Felker) always shot a real flat ball, shot it hard and shot it flat, shot like a football player. It hit the back iron and went straight up and it just nicked that wire and it came back down." From Bradshaw's perspective, the wire didn't alter the fate of the ball. "It was exactly the right call, but it wouldn't have changed anything. If it doesn't hit the guide wire, it still goes in. It didn't change the direction of the ball." Proper call or not, Walls argued with the referees. "Yes, violently. That's just how I was." Once order was restored and play resumed, Scott Central took the ball out underneath the Chaffee goal, still clinging to a two-point lead. It's what happened next that Ronnie Cookson remembers more than the ill-fated bucket that would have tied the game. "That wasn't the biggest deal. The biggest deal was with about four seconds to go, (a) Chaffee player stole the ball on the sidelines." On the inbounds play, Chaffee applied full-court pressure. A poor pass sent the ball directly to Chaffee guard Anthony Austin. "He was standing right inside on the front on the press. There was no one between him and the goal," remembers Cookson. A lay-up would tie the game.

***

When Bill Bradshaw moved to Chaffee, one of the jobs he took on over the summer was as a scout for the Cincinnati Reds. Bradshaw's position was known as a "bird dog." Bird dog scouts couldn't sign athletes to contracts. Full-time scouts for the club had to perform that function. The only way for a bird dog to get paid for his work was if one of his recommendations ever signed with the club. Bradshaw received other perks as well. When the Reds would play the Cardinals in St. Louis, he would receive four complimentary tickets to each game. Acting in his scouting capacity, Bradshaw hosted a Cincinnati tryout camp every year at the baseball field at Chaffee. When the Reds first began experimenting with the camps, one of the first athletes they signed was their future first baseman Dan Driessen. That whetted their appetite. When the Reds Midwest Scouting Supervisor Chet Montgomery asked Bradshaw to host one in Chaffee, the grade school principal readily agreed.

On those summer days years ago, baseball players from around the area, as far away as St. Louis, would come with their bats and gloves to spend the day at Harmon Field in Chaffee. The mornings were spent doing drills while the afternoon was reserved for an actual game. Many years, so many players would show up, the less talented ones were cut before the game even began.

For the Reds' scouts of the 1970's, speed and arm strength mattered most. Hitters were timed going from home to first and from first to third base. Fielders had to make the throw from the outfield to home plate. The Reds rated arms from zero to sixty. Thirty-five, or slightly above average, was needed to merit further attention. "Anytime you threw a ball from the outfield and it hopped, you were out of the running. It had to skip," remembers Bradshaw. "That was the Cincinnati philosophy." For pitchers, only one thing mattered - how fast could he throw? Radar guns were not nearly as prevalent then. Bradshaw and scouting supervisor Montgomery used a stopwatch instead and made an educated guess of how fast the young arms were throwing the ball. An 85 mile-per-hour fastball would catch a scout's eye. One of the few who ever cracked that magic number, Bradshaw remembers, was Anthony Austin. The 6'2" slender lefthander was nicknamed "Moose" and was a standout player on the Chaffee baseball team. He also started as safety on the football team and doubled as the quarterback his senior season. Basketball was his third sport. He started as a guard opposite Monty Montgomery. In a cold gym in the middle of the winter of 1979 with four seconds to go in a basketball game, all eyes were on him.

***

Austin deflected the inbound pass. The ball rolled over his head. Frantically searching for it, he turned around and grabbed the basketball, and started making his way to the bucket. His lay-up would tie the game and send it to overtime. He never made it. Once again, a whistle blew. In his rush to grab the ball and make the shot, Austin had traveled. In a span of less than five seconds, Chaffee had two opportunities to tie the game. Both attempts failed. They wouldn't get a third chance. This time, Scott Central successfully put the ball in play and Chaffee was forced to foul. A last second free throw made the final score 71-68.

The game ended the Red Devils run and coach Nick Walls' career at Chaffee. A twenty-victory season and a first round state appearance were not good enough for certain members of the Chaffee School Board. When it came time to renew his contract, the board deadlocked 3-3. The impasse meant Walls fate would be in the hands of the new school board, elected in the spring. The coach didn't want to wait around. The next year, he would coach at Gainesville, a small town in Southwest Missouri. For Walls, now retired from coaching, the 1979 season marked his first and only chance at a state title. "For 95% to 98% of coaches, you might get one shot. Maybe. I never got that close again." That ballgame and that team still cross his mind. "When I think of stuff in my past, that game will be the foremost thing I think about; to get that close with those boys."

Walls also remembers his conversation with the opposing coach afterwards. "I think Cookson knew right then he beat the second best team in the state. That's what he told me. He said you guys were awesome. I told him, I said if I had your wisdom, you would have never beat us. He didn't comment on that."

A town and school that celebrated two high school baseball championships in the '70's and lived for football Friday nights took the best team in the state to the wire, and lost by a guide wire. Just a few months earlier, hundreds of Chaffee fans made the 270 mile drive across the state to watch a playoff football game. The following weekend on their home field, with a berth in the state final at stake, more than a thousand fans took in the action. With two feet of snow starting to melt outside, the Chaffee basketball season ended with a total of maybe 300 people in the stands.

For the class of 1979, both their high school football and basketball careers were now over. A business owner today in Cape Girardeau, Monty Montgomery still reflects on a season full of what ifs. "The basketball season doesn't disappoint me because we weren't supposed to be there," he said. "But the football season? There aren't too many weeks that pass that I don't get disappointed thinking about the football season."

***

Ronnie Cookson's Braves lived to play another day. One year before the miracle on ice at the 1980 Winter Olympics, Scott County Central survived a miracle attempt in near icy conditions. Cookson's team had escaped Bootheel basketball and all that was left between them and a state championship were three teams not used to the Braves style of ball. Think of a race car driver coming out of a turn and in the lead.

All that was left between Scott Central and the finish line was a long straightaway.

Donnie McClinton believes the Chaffee game served as a turning point in the Braves march to the state championship. Afterwards, one player's actions served to inspire his teammates. "Melvin Porter - he sang a song on the bus. I can't remember the song, but it got everybody fired up," remembers McClinton. "We had a team meeting afterwards when we got back to school. We said hey, we're going to have to get away from these close ballgames, we don't want nothing like that to happen again."

The Braves served notice the following night that close ballgames were over. Scott Central met Clopton in Flat River for the quarterfinal round match-up. It marked the second year in a row that Dale Miller's Clopton Hawks had met a team from the Bootheel on this floor in this round. In 1978, Miller's team beat Richland on the way to a third place finish in state. That Richland team had defeated Advance by one point in the first round of state play at Bloomfield, ending Carroll Cookson's thirteen-year run as coach at the school.

Playing Scott Central for the first time in his coaching career, Miller would later write that his halftime speech that evening was very simple. His team already trailed the Braves by thirty-three points. Scott Central maintained that margin in the second half, winning the game 102-69. The Braves point total set a class 1A state record for tournament play. For the second time in four years, Scott Central was bound for Columbia. Their semifinal opponent was the Harrisburg Bulldogs

"Shout it loud. Sound the bell. Bootheel basketball is alive and well," announced the *Columbia Daily Tribune* after the game. "Continuing the run-and-gun tradition that has set Southeast Missouri basketball apart from the rest of the state, the Scott County Central Braves sprinted past Harrisburg 92-60 in the first semifinal game of the class 1A state tournament. 'Shoot, holler and foller,' Scott Central coach Ron Cookson said afterwards with a chuckle. 'That's the way we play.'"[250]

The way the Braves played left their opponents bewildered and confused. The following night, meeting Sparta in the championship game on the Hearnes Center floor, Scott Central led 7-0 two minutes into the game. The lead was fourteen points by halftime. The final margin was twenty-four. Led by Donnie McClinton's 30 points, the Braves defeated

Sparta 75-51. Appropriately enough, it was a free throw by McClinton with 1:57 to go in the game that allowed the Braves to set another state record: the most points scored by one team in four state tournament games. Scott Central racked up 340 points in their four game run to the state title. The previous record for was 333 set by Carroll Cookson's 1972 Advance Hornets.

After the game, Ronnie Cookson sent signals to his team and the media that only one state tournament title by this junior dominated Braves lineup would not be acceptable. Jeff Limbaugh will never forget Cookson's speech to the team immediately after the game. "We had three seniors. He walked up, he shook their hand, he give'em a hug and he said 'boys we've had the time of our life. You three seniors – you take you a shower, the bus leaves at 10:00 in the morning. If you're not here to get on the bus, you'll stay in Columbia.' And he gives them another hug, shook their hands and he turned around and looked at us juniors and said, 'boys, you just won the state tournament, congratulations. I want you to take a shower, get your clothes on, we're going to McDonalds to have supper and we're going back to the motel and we're going to bed.' And we did. Not a celebration one."

Outside the locker room, addressing members of the media, Cookson attempted to downplay his team's performance. "They're lucky and they're weak," he said.[251] "They just wanted a week off school and a chance to eat steak."

Not many people were ready to accept the Scott Central coach's attempt to poor mouth his team. Sparta coach Randy Teague was among those not buying his act. "If he says they're weak, I'd hate to see them when they're strong. I'm at a loss for words. Those eight players I saw out there could play for MU (University of Missouri)."[252]

When the team returned the next day to Scott Central, the school and the towns of Haywood City, Morley, and Vanduser welcomed them home. "It was the biggest dadgum parade of your life," remember Jeff Limbaugh. According to the Braves guard, once the parade finished and the Braves were ready to depart the bus, Cookson had one last message for his team. "We got to the school parking lot and he (Cookson) stood up in the front of the bus and said, 'Hey Limbaugh, tell everybody they got one week – bring your gym shorts." The players' reward for winning the state championship was one week off from practice. Barely back home from a 250 mile bus ride, Cookson's thoughts had already turned to next year. Basketball season never ended at Scott County Central.

CHAPTER 8
The Show-Me Kings
1979-1980

"After they won state, I never will forget, even as brothers, we were kind of competitive. I said the only thing I can say is we are going to do it twice."

Melvin Porter's challenge to his brother Otto.

In 1980, residents of Chaffee gathered to celebrate the town's sesquicentennial. The 75th anniversary of the town's founding by the Frisco was a bittersweet moment. Just months after the celebration, the Frisco was sold to the Burlington Northern Railroad. While trains still stopped in the town daily for railroad crews, the roundhouse, which once had employed hundreds, had long since disappeared. So had passenger train service. The last passenger train made its stop in town in 1965. The town's only hotel burned down in 1962. The local bowling alley burned down in the early 1970's. Burned out or boarded up, the former thriving businesses had plenty of company in downtown. In the early 1960's, 113 local advertisers bought space in "The Mogul," the Chaffee High School yearbook. By 1980, the number had dropped to thirty-six.

The late 1970's and early 1980's were a time of economic contraction, but this was no recessionary advertising cutback. Many of those companies simply disappeared over the two-decade period. Modern technology played a role. Chaffee residents no longer had a need for an ice and coal company. Wal-Mart is a typical villain in stories of how small town life changed in America. It surely played a role as well. The first Wal-Mart outside of the state of Arkansas was in Sikeston. The store in Cape Girardeau opened in the early 1970's. But there were far greater trends at work than one discount chain. Interstate 55 was completed by 1972, and Chaffee was eight miles from the nearest on-ramp. The consolidation of travel over interstate roads produced a virtuous cycle for towns and cities along the routes. Additional traffic meant more businesses and more jobs for these areas, which in turn generated even more traffic. But the virtuous cycle for those towns also meant a vicious cycle for the isolated communities not privy to an exit ramp. Less traffic made the communities less desirable for business. Fewer jobs and opportunities followed. The widespread popularity of the automobile allowed people to commute longer distances to work. People shopped where they worked, and increasingly for residents of Chaffee, that place was Cape Girardeau, a fifteen-minute drive.

By the early 1980's, the shoe factory in town had shut down production and Kielhofner Clothing had shut its doors, marking the end of a seven-decade period where the Essner and Kielhofner families ran businesses in northern Scott County. Around the same time, Slaughters, a favorite restaurant of locals for more than six decades, went out of business. The town which once had seven or eight grocery stores eventually saw that number dwindle to one. While the wheels were coming off the local economy, teen pregnancy took its toll at the high school. When the class of 1982 entered high school in the fall of 1978, the roll call included two girls who already had children, the first one giving birth in seventh grade. By the time graduation came, half of the girls in the class were married, pregnant, or already raising a child.

Basketball coach Nick Walls left Chaffee in the summer of 1979 and the talented class of seniors he coached was gone as well. Football coach Mick Wessel found himself in charge of two sports. With Wade Sanders back for his senior year, the Red Devils season played out much like the one before, but without the drama. There would be no blizzards, no barnburner regional finals, no controversial calls over a basketball hitting a cable. There also would be no escaping Scott County Central. The student population at Chaffee High School pushed it into the 2A bracket. The Braves would play the year in the same classification. Regardless of school population, there was one team in 1980 that dominated high school basketball like few others ever have. When it was all said and done, one team could claim the title as Missouri state champs. Ronnie Cookson watched them play every day at the gym south of Morley.

***

With all five starters returning from a state championship season, even their coach could relax a little bit. Guard Jeff Limbaugh recalls the atmosphere of his final year at Scott Central. "My senior year, he didn't even have to coach. He said that's what he did my freshman, sophomore, and junior year. He'll tell you that the most relaxed year of his coaching life was my senior year because he knew we was going to play the same way every night. We practiced the same way every day – wide open." This was no accident but rather a Carroll and Ronnie trademark: push the players as hard as possible at a young age. By the time their final years roll around, the work ethic has been instilled, the desire is in place, and the talent has taken hold. At that point, the coach can give the players some leeway. Advance's Richie Walker agrees with Limbaugh's assessment.

"Once you got to the level where they could turn you loose, which would be your junior or senior year, in our case, it was our senior year, they more or less turned you loose. You would scrimmage in practice and you more or less learned from the scrimmage."

According to his assistant coach, Ronnie Cookson believed playing the game was the best way to teach the game. "He was a scrimmage coach," remembers Ron Cook. "By what I mean by scrimmage coach, he didn't just turn the clock on. He would stop and teach and coach from that point, and then continue." He also learned a valuable lesson from the Scott Central mentor. "What I learned the most from him was discipline of the players and to push for their potential. And sometimes you have to push pretty hard."

At Scott Central, the push was on from the beginning of practice. It started early and ended late. It began during seventh hour P.E. class. During the final hour of the school day, the players would get all the preliminaries out of the way: stretching, shooting, lay-up drills, etc. When the bell rang to let school out, the real practice began. "He (Cookson) put 80 minutes on the clock and we'd start scrimmaging," said Limbaugh. "And when that 80 minutes was over, he'd put another 80 back on there. We would just scrimmage until we couldn't go no more." The scrimmage sessions wouldn't involve just current players. "My sophomore, junior and senior year, we scrimmaged Otto Porter about every day. Otto, Ricky (Thomas), that bunch that won the state tournament in 76. Christmas break, when they was all home, we scrimmaged them every day."

Limbaugh believes playing against the older players was a key to their development. "You take a 16 or 17 year old playing against a 21, 22 year old man that's still in shape, you learn how to play," said the Braves point guard. "It was an unwritten rule that when you went to Scott Central and played basketball, for the next four or five years you scrimmaged against the high school teams."

Cookson had other unwritten rules as well. A parent wanted to stop in and see how his son was progressing? Forget about it. A teacher wanted to watch her student perform after hours? Not going to happen. Practice was closed. Cookson did allow one person to come in and watch if he wanted: the school's superintendent. Otherwise, it was just players, coaches, and invited scrimmage guests. The gym was his domain. Even when high school concerts were scheduled, the coach wouldn't relinquish control. He would tell the band director that the team would set down and arrange the chairs rather than calling off practice early. Cookson himself could be found sitting on the gym stage during practice, often drinking a Coke, watching and waiting for the moment to blow his whistle, make his point, or get out his paddle. The Braves senior point guard knew the routine. "He'd blow the whistle, and holler 'Limbaugh!' And when he hollered Limbaugh, you had to come a running." Once the player ran over to where Cookson was sitting, he heard the dreaded request from the coach – go get his paddle. "Into his office you would run and go get the paddle and come back out and him still sitting on the stage drinking a Coke, you'd hand him the paddle and bend over and he'd bust your butt now, man I'm telling you." Before practice could resume, the coach had one last request. "He'd give you the paddle and make you take it back and put it in his office." The players accepted the punishment, knowing that it was part of the price to be paid in order to play basketball at Scott County Central. The way their coach conducted himself off the court also made it easier to handle. Limbaugh puts Cookson's behavior in perspective. "The thing about him was that he could holler at you, he could scream at you, he could paddle you, but the minute ball practice was over, he was your friend. He was the coach during basketball practice, but he was your daddy after that."

He was your daddy after that. For many Scott Central players through the years, Cookson was the dominating adult male presence. Forward Donnie McClinton remembers a time early in his basketball career the team was running wind sprints. During a break from running, McClinton leaned over and put his arm on a teammate's shoulder. "Cookson looks at me and yells at me and says, 'Get up off of him, he's not your leaning post!'" The Braves forward knows why the incident is still vivid in his mind. "I never had a man screaming at me, and so that was kind of an eye opener for me."

McClinton's family is from Mississippi. In the early 1950's, they saw better opportunities in Southeast Missouri and moved north. Donnie's father was a farmer with a big family. "I have seven sisters and five brothers. I'm the next to the youngest," said McClinton. Donnie was born in 1962 after the family moved to Missouri. They first located in Oran but later settled in Haywood City. Similar to teammate Melvin Porter, Donnie lost his father at a young age. "I think his dad had a heart attack and mine got shot. I was six years old and he got shot." The strength shown by his mother following the loss helped McClinton develop an inner resolve. "My mom, she's always been strong hearted, there was always a meal on the table. She always did her best and I thank her for that. Part of that kind of helps strengthen you not to give up."

On the basketball court, McClinton had ample opportunities to give up. All through junior high and into his freshman season, he saw little playing time. But McClinton knew no other way. "I stuck with it and I stuck with it because I wanted to be a part of it. All my friends played, and we played from sunup to sundown there in Haywood City. I wouldn't know what to do with myself if I couldn't have played." His passion for the game started at a young age. "I can remember getting off the bus when I was 8,9,10 years old. You run home and you get your chores done. We didn't have concrete to play on and we'd go right to the court." There on the dirt court in Haywood City, McClinton learned to play the game that would ultimately be his ticket out. Future teammates Melvin Porter and Mayfield Timmons also got their start on the same court.

McClinton saw plenty of playing time on the playground, but he didn't see much action his first year in high school. "When I was a freshman, I was so far down on the bench, nobody knew who I was." His sophomore year, he began to play more often, but it's the one night he didn't play at all that stands out in his mind. The Sunday before a game against Lilbourn, McClinton missed practice. He knew he wouldn't start but kept expecting Cookson to put him in. "Coach kept walking right by me all game long -never would put me in," remembers McClinton. "I learned from that mistake." He renewed his commitment to the game his junior season. "I worked out pretty hard that summer and I came in there with fire in eyes and I was ready to play." McClinton credits a simple exercise with helping to develop his game. The team had a drill where players would jump back and forth over a wooden bench. "That helped with the timing, with your coordination, with your rebounding skills. It did a lot of things for you." Along with Melvin Porter, McClinton was a first team all-state performer his junior season. "Once Donnie started believing in himself," said Porter, "he was unstoppable."

His senior season, Scott Central opponents, no matter how tall or how talented, would find out just how difficult it was to stop the Braves 6'2" forward. "He was just a big player in a little body," recalls teammate Limbaugh. "To this day, there's not a high school kid that you could consider as strong a rebounder as he was." Mike Marsh was sports editor at *The Daily Standard* in Sikeston when the Braves were bidding for back-to-back state championships. Like Limbaugh, he was amazed at McClinton's rebounding prowess. "We used to talk about how you used to see a hand go up and the ball go in on an offensive rebound. You wouldn't know who it was, but you would write down Donnie because you knew it was him."

Early in the season, the talented and confident Braves had developed a bit of a swagger. Limbaugh remembers a game against Oak Ridge where McClinton's performance gave their head coach heartburn. "Donnie come down the floor and took the ball behind his back to make a lay-up." Showing off was not part of the Cookson playbook. "I didn't know if Ronnie was going to let him play the rest of the year or not," remembers the Scott Central guard. Cookson immediately called timeout. McClinton recalls the first words out of his coach's mouth. "'What in the world is going on here now?' But that kind of set the tone for the year — it really did."

Through their first seven games, the Braves were undefeated. Twice Scott Central broke the hundred-point barrier. In no game had Cookson's team scored less than 93 points. Just as they did four years earlier, Scott Central entered the Christmas Tournament with a perfect record and a number one seed. By the 1979-80 season, Ronnie Cookson had achieved many successes; his teams dominated their conference, he had two state championships, matching his brother's output, and with all five starters back from a 30-3 squad the previous year, he was all but assured of his eighth winning season in ten tries at Scott Central. The one thing he had yet to do was win the annual Christmas Tournament in Cape Girardeau. Held every year since 1945, it was the crown jewel of Southeast Missouri's winter sports calendar. Fans from all over the area would pack Houck Field House for four days of high school hoops.

Scott Central started the tournament with a rematch against Oak Ridge. The Braves won by 53 points. Their second game, against conference rival Kelly, they narrowly missed hitting the century mark, but still won easily, 98-71. Cookson's team had made it to the tournament semi-finals. If Scott Central could survive its game with Clearwater, Cookson would have his team in the finals for the first time since Otto Porter met Ricky Frazier. Charleston was to face Cape Girardeau Central in the other semi-final match-up. Charleston had changed coaches in the intervening years but had not stopped its winning ways. If one program and coach could challenge Ronnie Cookson's Braves as kings of Bootheel basketball, it was coach Lennies McFerren and his Charleston Bluejays.

***

McFerren grew up in Howardville, a Bootheel community in New Madrid County. Howardville was established shortly after World War Two by Travis B. Howard. He came north from Memphis and bought 110 acres of land south of the town of New Madrid along Highway 61. It was on this land that the village of Howardville was established.[253] Baseball fans will recognize the name of Travis' son, Elston Howard, the former New York Yankees great. In the mid 1960's, there were still several all-black high schools in the Missouri Bootheel.[254] One of those schools was the Howardville Hawks. Their starting point guard was Lennies McFerren. In his junior and senior years, the Hawks made it to the first round of state play, only to be knocked out. In 1965, Howardville lost to Advance. The following season, the Hawks went into overtime against Oran, only to lose 66-60. In that game, the senior McFerren played against Oran freshman Fred Johnson who drew the charge that ended the Howardville guard's high school career.

Two years after Lennies graduated in 1966, Howardville played in one of the most memorable championship games in Missouri history.

Bradleyville needed four overtimes to defeat the Hawks, a win that also established a state record winning streak of 64 games. This streak was later equaled by Glasgow in 1975, but Carroll Cookson's Advance Hornets made sure that a new record wasn't set in the state semi-finals. The 1968 season marked the last one for Howardville as it merged with Lilbourn the following school year.

After high school, McFerren spent a couple of years in the army during the Vietnam War. He was working at the Wrigley Chewing Gum factory in Chicago when he came home one weekend and played a game of pickup basketball at the Lilbourn gym. Seeing McFerren play, Lilbourn coach Ted Mauk took an interest in the guard and asked him if he would be interested in playing college ball. McFerren quickly answered yes. Mauk asked him where he wanted to go. McFerren didn't care. "Anything that got me out of the chewing gum factory at Wrigley," he remembers. The coach got McFerren a try-out at Three Rivers Community College in Poplar Bluff. He enrolled there in the fall of 1970. He hurt his wrist his first season and didn't play. Three Rivers new head coach, Gene Bess, talked McFerren into staying two more years. Bess, who was at Oran before coming to Three Rivers, was coaching the Eagles in 1966 when they knocked McFerren's Howardville team out of the state tournament. McFerren credits Bess for the coaching philosophy he would later take to Charleston. "Everything that I put into the game of basketball came from Three Rivers; defensively, the philosophy, the discipline, all of that came from coach Bess."

McFerren later played two years at Southeast Missouri State and in 1975 joined the Charleston coaching staff as an assistant to Mitch Haskins. The new assistant had a front row seat to the 1975 Christmas Tournament final between Scott Central and Charleston, a one-point victory for the Bluejays and the only loss that year for Cookson's state championship team. When Haskins and his star player, Ricky Frazier, left for St. Louis University following the 1977 season[255], McFerren was promoted. For integrated Southeast Missouri high schools, the appointment was a rarity: a black head basketball coach. It took some time for people to get accustomed to it. McFerren still chuckles at how in his early days, the Charleston bench was a source of confusion for referees. Before each game, the officials would walk over to speak with the coach about his team, find out the captains, and so forth. Invariably, the referees would start talking to a Charleston assistant coach – a white assistant coach. "He would have to turn around and say, 'I'm not the coach, he's the coach,'" remembers McFerren.

In those first seasons, McFerren knew that certain referee's calls might not go his way. The coach and his team never let it deter them. "It helped us more than it hurt us. We didn't sit back and say ok, we're not going to win this game because we're not going to get the calls. We said we're just going to outplay whoever we're going to play." McFerren is especially grateful for the players on his first squads. "They just said, hey, we're not going to let him fail," said their coach. "It was all the players' doing. If they didn't do that, I wouldn't have lasted that long." If there are two things in life that are colorblind, it's money and winning. McFerren didn't make a lot of money as a high school basketball coach, but victories he accumulated in abundance. He won seven state championships at Charleston before departing for New Madrid County Central in the early 1990's. With that program McFerren did something that Arnold Ryan, Carroll Cookson and Ronnie Cookson had all done before him – win his first state championship at the school in his sixth season as coach.

McFerren has fond memories of his battles with Ronnie Cookson. The two coaches met many times at the Christmas Tournament. He'll never forget one game that was nearly over with Charleston firmly in control. From the opposing bench, Cookson made a request to his Charleston counterpart. "He looked down there and he said, 'Mac, call timeout because I don't have anymore and I need to chew them out.'" McFerren complied. The puzzled Charleston players walked off the court to conference with their head coach. "He said to call timeout," explained McFerren, pointing to the Scott Central coach. "That's one of the things that stand out because we have so much respect for each other. I miss that. I really do."

While their results were similar, their styles were not. The up-tempo track meet style of the Braves was nowhere to be found on the courts at Charleston. While Cookson's teams honed their fast break with endless scrimmages, Charleston players would go days in practice without ever shooting a basketball. The emphasis was on conditioning and constant defensive drills. During pre-season practice, four days could be spent on one end of the court. On the fifth day, McFerren would let his players scrimmage. "When they got a ball in their hands and they actually got to play offense; that was just like seeing Santa Claus." Like Cookson though, McFerren demanded much of his players. Their work ethic made them winners. "Any one of the players that I had in my life, they have a special place in my heart, for a very simple reason. They did some things that I asked them to do that I don't know if I could have done it because it was so tough."

***

One game separated McFerren and Cookson from squaring off in December of 1979. One of the teams survived to make it to the finals of the Christmas Tournament; the other one did not. Not surprisingly, Cape Central found itself in a defensive struggle with Charleston. McFerren's team led 13-10 at the end of the first quarter and extended the lead to 19-12 at the beginning of the second. But a defensive switch by Cape Central stymied Charleston the rest of the game. The Tigers 1-3-1 zone defense and the inside scoring of Ronnie Jones propelled them to a two point lead by the end of the third quarter. Charleston managed to tie the game and thought it had taken the lead when forward Jewell Crawford hit a shot from the corner. But before Crawford had taken the shot, a whistle blew. A Charleston player had signaled for timeout. Neither team converted opportunities at the end of the game. When the buzzer sounded at the end of the fourth quarter, the two schools were tied at 51. Charleston managed only one bucket in the overtime session. Cape Central advanced to the finals with a 57-53 victory.

After the game, McFerren voiced his frustrations. "Our ball club isn't as physical a team as Central and the officials let it be a physical game. There was a lot of holding and pushing going on underneath. I really don't want to say anything bad about the officiating on this game but I will say this. I've been very disappointed with the officiating in the tournament. It hasn't been up to par."[256] McFerren and his team had to settle for a chance at third place in the tournament. They would play the loser of the Scott Central-Clearwater game.[257]

Cookson's team entered the Clearwater game with a 9-0 record and averaged almost 98 points a game. In their quarterfinal victory against Kelly, Donnie McClinton scored a tournament record 41 points as four Braves players hit for double digits. Just when everyone assumed Scott Central would once again be off to the races, the team promptly hit a brick wall in the form of the Clearwater Tigers. Refusing to back off its own fast break style of play and handling the Scott Central press with relative ease, Clearwater led by one point at the first quarter mark. It was the first time all year Cookson's team trailed in a contest. With McClinton leading the way in the second quarter, Scott Central rallied to take a 35-29 halftime lead. They extended the lead to eight points at the beginning of the final period, but Clearwater refused to concede defeat. With just over four minutes to go, the Braves led by only two points.

Scott Central point guard Jeff Limbaugh played in over sixty games his junior and senior seasons. The game against Clearwater still stands out in his mind. "We played a bunch of white boys from Clearwater that was salty," remembers Limbaugh. His accent and emphasis made the adjective sound like two words: saul-TEE. "They had a good ball club. We really struggled with them." Just when it looked like Clearwater may tie the game, Limbaugh and his teammates pulled off a play that would have made Arnold Ryan proud. "(Melvin) Porter…pulled down a rebound and hit Jeff Limbaugh with a snowbird pass to make the lead four."[258] The "snowbird" play, where one defender takes off running toward his team's goal once the shot goes up while his teammate rebounds the ball and fires it the length of the court, was a play perfected under Ryan at Puxico. The four point lead would be the closest Clearwater got to the Braves the rest of the game. Scott Central survived, winning 72-63. "You know, coaches don't want their ball clubs to be real smooth yet this time of year," Cookson remarked after the game. "We want to be able to peak at state tournament play, but we are just too rough and unsettled right now."[259]

Once again, a single game separated a Cookson team from a Christmas Tournament championship. In the 1975 tournament, Cookson's teams had come up one point short against 3A Charleston in the finals. Now his 2A Braves had another opportunity against an even larger school, the 4A Cape Girardeau Central Tigers. The theme of this contest would be revisited later in the season: the smaller, quicker Scott Central team facing a taller team dominated by an all-state center.

***

In 1967, psychologist Stanley Milgram conducted an experiment that became known as the "small world phenomenon." He conducted a series of tests that later demonstrated how everyone in the world can be reached through a short chain of social acquaintances. Milgram's experiment is commonly referred to today as "six degrees of separation." The psychologist also pointed out that not all links in the chain of six people were equal. In his book, *The Tipping Point,* author Malcolm Gladwell explains why some were more equal than others.

> **"Six degrees of separation doesn't mean that everyone is linked to everyone else in just six steps. It means that a very small number of people are linked to everyone else in a few steps, and the rest of us are linked to the world through those special few."**[260]

Gladwell called these people "connectors." In the six degrees of Bootheel basketball, Oran's Fred Johnson is a connector. Johnson was on the court the night of Lennies McFerren's last high school basketball game. He had the ball in his hand at the free throw line at the state championship game in 1969 when the referee's whistle blew, ending Oran's shot at a state championship. Johnson followed his high school coach to Poplar Bluff and helped Gene Bess lay the foundation for a phenomenally successful junior college program. Later, he did his student teaching at Scott County Central the year before the Braves finally won their first state title. After graduating from college, Johnson took a job in Cape Girardeau. He also served as director of a local recreational center. He coached a basketball team of 8th and 9th graders. One of his players was Ronnie Jones. Now a senior at Cape Central, the 6'4" center would be playing alongside Steve Stipanovich and Jon Sundvold a year later at the University of Missouri and take part in three of the Tigers four consecutive Big 8 titles under Norm Stewart.

Jones career didn't start out so promising. "He (Jones) came to me a bitter kid, a bitter kid, mad at the world," remembers Johnson. "The first day he was so rude. I put him against the wall and I told him he ever come in there with that kind of attitude, I would kick his butt." Gradually, his attitude improved. Jones became a gym rat. Each day, Johnson would arrive at the rec center only to find the future basketball star on the court. "Every day I would go down and that son-of-a-buck would be there waiting. He just kept playing. I'd be on his butt. I'd tell him 'you can't play, you're a chump, you can't do this.' And that son-of-a-buck would go and he would work harder and harder." Jones had a lot to learn. A profile near the end of his senior season described his talents as an incoming freshman at Cape Central. "When he came over from junior high at the close of his freshman season, about all Jones could do was jump and rebound. His shooting touch was something close to a jackhammer and he had trouble dribbling the ball three times without kicking it away."[261]

By the time he was a junior he was an all-state performer. His Tigers lost in the state quarterfinals that season to Vashon by two points. Cape Central had led at one point in the game by eight. When the two teams met the following year in the regular season, Jones had revenge on his mind. "He told me he was waiting for this game all year. He said he owed us this one," said Vashon coach Floyd Irons after the game.[262] Jones broke two school records during the contest. He became the all-time scoring leader at Cape Central while his 48-point effort was also a single game school record. Jones scored 48 of his team's 69 points that night.

Back at Houck Field House in December of 1979, Jones and his teammates were about to discover a single star and a surrounding cast were no match for the Scott Central system. Covering the game that night for *The Daily Standard*, sportswriter Mike Marsh knew the secret to the Braves' success. "Teamwork. 100%," said Marsh. "They didn't have the best players," he emphasized, "(but) they were so fast and when I say team, that's capital T-E-A-M." In each of the Braves first three tournament games, Donnie McClinton had led them in scoring. On this night, the Braves would demonstrate why their offense was so difficult to stop.

"Anthony Jones, the string-bean forward of the Braves, turned out to be the hero of the night for Scott Central as he hit everything he put up in the first half. While the Tiger defense concentrated on Melvin Porter and Don McClinton, Jones ran free, scoring most of his team high 22 tallies in the first half."[263]

By halftime, the Braves led by 12 points, 40-28. In the third quarter, Scott Central stretched the lead to 16 and then almost let it slip away. Cape Central started pressing their rivals. The tactic worked. Six straight times down the court Scott Central turned the ball over. With a four-point lead and the ball with just over a minute to go, Cookson's team resorted to a ploy that had saved Arnold Ryan's Puxico team in a state championship game played in the very same gym. The run-and-gun freewheeling Braves went into a four-corner stall. Cape Central fouled McClinton with twenty-nine seconds left. He missed his free throw. The Tigers failed to capitalize and Scott Central regained possession. Forced to foul again, this time Porter went to the free throw line. The Braves senior never felt comfortable that night. He remembers why. "That day we were playing the championship, I was getting my uniform ready and I left it on the ironing board and I left the iron on top of it. So my uniform got scorched." He had to tell his coach he needed a different jersey. "It just bothered me," Porter recalls. Distracted by a different jersey or perhaps frustrated by a Cape Central defense, the Braves forward had only scored four points on the night. But now nearing the game's final moments, he had the chance to put it away at the free throw line. He missed the shot. Cape Central quickly scored and the lead was down to two points with ten seconds left. As time wound down, the Tigers had Porter trapped in a corner on the press. Just when it looked Cape Central may foul again, Porter spotted an open teammate down the court. He threw the long pass and Scott Central scored at the buzzer. The Braves held on for a 66-62 victory.

For the coach's wife, the thrilling second half action was more than she could stand. "When a game gets close, I go hide in the bathroom," confessed Dee Cookson. "I didn't know who won until someone came and got me."[264] At the beginning of tournament play, Dee's husband told a reporter, "at one time or another, we've won every tournament we've entered. Except one."[265] At the end of his first decade of coaching, Cookson finally had that elusive trophy.

***

Winning the Christmas Tournament for the first time, the Braves still had one score to settle. Scott Central had already avenged its loss to Advance the previous year, defeating the Hornets by twenty-five points. Their only other two losses during their state championship run both came against Notre Dame. The Bulldogs were the first opponent of the new year. There would be no fourth quarter comebacks and post-game tirades on this night. Scott Central won easily, 99-67, as Cookson's team ran its record to 12-0. "This is the first time we've got them in four years," said the Scott Central coach afterwards. "I think this makes it only three times in 10 years that we beat them."[266] In their next six games, the Braves scored 100 or more points four times. After recording Cookson's 200th career victory in the conference tournament championship game and running their record to 18-0, Scott Central's output dropped off to 86. It was still enough to beat Chaffee by 29 points.

Although three starters had graduated, coach Mick Wessel's team still had all-state forward Wade Sanders. It also had his brother, sophomore Doug Sanders. The two represented a contrast in styles. The taller and slower Wade relied on his deadly accurate outside shooting touch, particularly from the baseline. Doug was quicker and could jump much higher. A track star in the spring, his leaping ability would win him three state championships in the high jump. After graduation, he continued his education at the University of Missouri where he became somewhat of a social legend. One time, while dating a girl, he and a buddy walked over to her sorority house. When they arrived, they discovered she wasn't there and they prepared to turn back around and walk back home. But just as they walked out, another guy walked in with his car parked out front and his keys still inside the vehicle. Doug and his friend decided to go for a joyride. When they finished, they parked the car on the front lawn of the sorority. They laughed about it all the way home until they discovered a cop waiting for them. "You must be Doug Sanders," said the officer. Sanders had returned the car but left his checkbook on the seat. Fortunately for Doug, the person didn't want to press charges. His junior year in college, Sanders competed in a BOMC (Big Man on Campus) contest, an annual sorority fundraiser. He finished second. An aspiring journalism student by the name of Brad Pitt came in third.

While not nearly as dominant an economic force it had once been, the railroad still meant a great deal to Chaffee in the 1970's, especially when one's father was a conductor. George Sanders would often call from St. Louis letting the family know he would be on the next train home. A few hours later, Doug would hop on his bicycle to greet his father downtown. One summer, he spent a week with his sister in St. Louis. When it came time to take him home, she dropped him off at the Frisco depot. Doug rode in the caboose back to Chaffee with his dad. By the time he was a teenager, he was a self-described train nerd. He organized

groups that drove out to Rockview, the small community just north
of Chaffee. At Rockview, the Frisco tracks crossed those of the Cotton
Belt. Every night, at exactly 9:15 p.m., the "Blue Streak Merchandiser"
whistled its arrival and departure simultaneously. "And it really was a
blue streak," remembers Sanders. "I don't know how it got to do that
because it was going 80 miles an hour. It was short, it was filled with
auto parts, and it was going from St. Louis to Dallas."

Growing up in the Calvary Baptist Church, he always knew when
the Frisco departed town. "It seemed like every deacon in the church
worked on the railroad and you always knew when somebody was gone
because they were out on a train run." Like generations before him,
Sanders quickly identified a religious rift in the community. He still
remembers a joke he heard as a child. A Catholic Nun asks three young
children what they want to do when they grow up. The first boy says
he wants to be a doctor while the second says he dreams of becoming a
lawyer. The third child, a girl, tells the Nun she wants to be a prostitute.
The Nun promptly faints. As the Priest revives her, he also reminds her
of the words that caused her to pass out. "Oh, a prostitute," says the Nun.
"I thought she said a *Protestant*." Sanders also remembers who told him
the joke – his Sunday School teacher.

It was possible in the small town of three thousand people for
Catholic and Protestant school children to live separate, parallel lives.
"We knew everybody," recalls Sanders. "We thought we knew everybody.
The one difference was we didn't know the Catholic kids." With many
Catholic school kids attending St. Ambrose Elementary, the children
in public schools would often not come across their counterparts from
September to May. "We knew they went to St. Ambrose," said Sanders.
"It was almost like they didn't exist." The one time of the year they
would cross paths would be in the summer. "You'd see them out playing
baseball."

Summertime in the seventies meant playing baseball at night and
hanging out at the swimming pool during the day. The public pool, a
depression era project of the Roosevelt Administration, acted as a magnet
that attracted kids from other small towns in the area and occasionally
even an out-of-state guest. "We knew every good looking granddaughter
that was coming from out of state to stay with Grandma over the
summer."

After baseball season ended and school resumed in the fall, the youngest Sanders child couldn't wait until he got to the fifth grade. "In the fifth grade, it was a big deal to be on the (basketball team) coached by the principal, Bill Bradshaw." While he couldn't play organized basketball until his fifth grade year, Doug got involved two years earlier as the manager for his brother Wade's first team. He began to realize his brother's ability on the basketball court. "We started noticing pretty quickly he had this weird shot but it worked for him."

Two years apart in school, Doug's sophomore season represented the first time in his life he had the chance to be his brother's teammate. It also marked the first time in his career he played in a varsity basketball game against the Scott Central Braves and coach Ronnie Cookson. "There was just an aura about them with Cookson." Sanders remembers the few times anyone from Chaffee saw Cookson and his team off the court. It usually occurred during a tournament and the Scott Central coach would walk in with his team during the game before they were scheduled to play and take a seat in the stands. "When they walked in," recalls Sanders, "you would point and whisper. There was nobody there that didn't know who Ron Cookson was or didn't know his team." Once the Braves took the court, he watched with awe and wonder at the players' talents but also Cookson's behavior on the bench. "When you watched them in games — how amazing it was how he dressed down his players." Growing up in an all white town, part of the fascination was the racial angle. "There was a part of it being from Chaffee that was hard to understand because you were around no one of color." That lack of exposure also fed racist stereotypes. "People would always make up stories that he had to have Jeff Limbaugh on that team because they had to have a white guy. That was the Chaffee version because that was all we could think." Sanders always noticed something else about Cookson's clubs: that no matter the skin color or the talent level, everyone was treated the same. "There was no star treatment," said Sanders. "They could be up thirty points and someone kind of lagging it on (defense). A lot of coaches would be laughing or whatever. He was as angry being up by thirty in a meaningless game as he would be when he was down by two." One final item that Sanders remembers is something that many people around the Bootheel and around the state from this era could also claim about Cookson's teams. "I don't know if I ever saw Scott Central lose a game."

With a record of 19-0 after their victory over Chaffee, Cookson's team looked unbeatable. Two additional victories by margins of 41 and 24 points did nothing to dampen the enthusiasm for his first undefeated team. A regularly scheduled game against Bell City looked to be nothing out of the ordinary. Earlier in the season, Scott Central had beaten them by 36 points. The Braves had a 35 game winning streak dating back to the previous season. Just when it looked like Scott Central was invincible, Bell City proved their rival was mortal. The Cubs defeated the Braves 61-59. "We spent all week getting ready for this game," explained Bell City coach Carl Ritter. How did they do it? "We played a control game and shut down the middle."[267] The 59 points represented Scott Central's lowest output of the season. In fact, only four times all year would the Braves score less than 86 points. All-state forward Donnie McClinton was held to eight points against Bell City. Melvin Porter led Scott Central with 21 points. "We had gotten a bit cocky," admitted Porter. "When you're beating people however you want it, it's hard not to." The Scott Central player remembers the scene in the locker room after the game. "There was about four or five of us – we were in tears. One of our goals was to go undefeated that year. We were just dumbfounded. We didn't know what to do or what to think. We were just shocked." One of the Braves starting five, Mayfield Timmons, was so upset by the defeat he didn't show up at school the following morning. Cookson had to go to his house to convince him to go to class.[268] But as the one point loss to Charleston five years earlier served as a wakeup call in Cookson's first championship run, the defeat at Bell City became a turning point in their drive for back to back state titles. "The good thing about it was it got us mentally ready," said Porter.

There is a lingering debate about that night. It concerns the role of Scott Central player Jeff Limbaugh. Due to a leg injury, the Braves guard only played the last few minutes of the game. "I had a seven inch crack on the inside of my bone. I had to stay off it for three weeks to get it to heal." While rehabilitating, he couldn't run in practice. Cookson devised a way for him to stay in shape. "Ronnie made me ride a (stationary) bicycle 10 miles every night," recalls Limbaugh. "After practice was over, he would take me home and I would get on that bicycle. I remember he would sit up there and tighten that screw to tighten the front tires, and he'd make me ride it ten miles. When the speedometer would roll over

10 miles he'd go home." With blowout victories over Oran and Kelly in their two previous games before Bell City, the Braves demonstrated their ability to win without their point guard. But the two-point loss against Bell City showed why they needed their floor general. "They had that zone packed in on us real tight," remembers McClinton. "I played on the inside and we just couldn't get that ball on the inside."

This brings us back to the source of the debate on the night of February 11, 1980. "The debate is – I could have played that night at Bell City," confessed Limbaugh, who believes he knows the reason why he didn't see action earlier in the game. "I think he (Cookson) wanted to lose. I honestly think he wanted to lose." While his coach disagrees with that opinion, Limbaugh, like teammate Porter, thinks the Bell City loss got them ready for state tournament play. As the Scott Central player saw it, his coach had his eye on the prize. An undefeated season didn't mean as much. "How many people talk about (a single loss) vs. how many people talk about the state champions?' said Limbaugh. "Honestly, I think that's his mentality."

His coach would always struggle to describe his role. But years later, Cookson put into words what part Limbaugh played on his team. "He didn't make the pass that led to the bucket, but he made the pass that made the pass that led to the bucket," his coach would say. Limbaugh can trace his family's roots to the northern part of the county. His grandfather, Jack Limbaugh, owned the Grain and Seed Company in Chaffee. He was a young child when his parents divorced. He settled in Morley with his mother. From his seventh grade season on, he was a constant presence in a Scott Central starting lineup. His coach recognized his skills at an early age. Limbaugh described his responsibilities. "I was basically the captain, the team leader. For whatever it's worth, Ronnie taught me from the very beginning to call the shots. And so when we hit the floor, he basically had me take care of everything. If one of us made a mistake, I got chewed out for it."

He started playing varsity basketball his sophomore season but also scrimmaged with his junior varsity teammates. He remembers the practices and the aftermath. "You cannot believe how hard it was on us kids in high school. There was literally days after ball practice that I would drive home in my car and my mother would have to come out to the car and get me and help me get into the house. That's how bad it was." Asked to describe the daily routine, Limbaugh put it this way. "In laymen's terms, I puked every day, I puked every day." He did so because he loved the game and had a coach who kept him and everyone else motivated. "I wouldn't say brainwashed, but he had our minds set at winning. When you take five kids that are all six feet tall and play like they're all seven footers, you've got be some kind of philosopher to be able to do that." Cookson gave Limbaugh and teammate Melvin Porter keys to the gym. The players had year round access to the facility. "We all worked on the farm. We worked till dark in the summer, eight o'clock at night, then we played ball until 11:00 p.m. Every night, every night, EVERY night. We didn't do nothing else. That's why we was so good."

During basketball season, Limbaugh got to tag along with his coach on scouting trips. When Cookson wanted to see an upcoming opponent play, he would slip out after practice with his point guard at his side. "Nobody would know we was gone," remembers Limbaugh. They would arrive at the gym. The Scott Central coach would usually spot a colleague to chat with. As they sat down to watch the game, Cookson would converse with the coach while drinking a soda and eating a bag of popcorn. Limbaugh would be furiously scribbling notes with his pencil and paper. After seeing one half, the two would get up to leave. "We'd get out and he could tell you every player and I swear he never even looked at the floor." Limbaugh was stunned by his coach's recall. "He could tell you every player, their name, their number, whether they was left handed or right handed, if they shot good. And I'd sit there during the entire first half with a pencil and paper and trying to write everything down and couldn't do it. But he was that good. It's simply amazing some of the things he could do with a basketball team."

Cookson's basketball team now had a record of 21-1. There would be no undefeated season but another shot at a state championship was right around the corner. The Braves had four regular season games left. They won all four easily, never scoring less than 88 points. Regional action started in late February with Scott Central a heavy favorite to return to Columbia. The Richland Rebels had the unfortunate task of being the Braves first opponent in post-season play. Limbaugh recalls Cookson's conversation with Richland coach Danny Rowland right before the game. "He said 'Danny, you know, this is the (regionals), I'm leaving'em in for 32 minutes.' I was standing right there when he told him. Danny said, 'I understand – keep'em in shape.'" Regardless of the time of the year or the opponent, when the Scott Central starting five took the court, they knew only one way to play. "We played for blood," said Limbaugh.

It was 35-5 at the end of the first quarter. By halftime, the lead was 60 points, 76-16. In a game reminiscent of the Puxico Indians blowout of Greenville, Cookson's squad had exceeded the Arnold Ryan team's first half output. Puxico had led 71-5 in their first round sub-regional game in 1951. Scott Central let up slightly in the second half, "only" scoring 48 points. The final was 126-46. In a season full of lopsided wins, this would be the biggest one. "Ronnie's philosophy is really simple, it's I'm always on offense. It's just that sometimes they give the other team the ball," said sportswriter Mike Marsh. "That's how you score 100 points every game was if you think that way." The Braves had scored 100 points for the seventh time in the season, the 12th time in the last two years. The blowout victories caught the attention of the media, the fans, and opposing coaches who suspected Scott Central was trying to run up the score. Former Advance player Richie Walker, who played for both Carroll and Ronnie, believes both brothers had a purpose behind all those points. "I've heard a lot of people say the Cooksons run the score up on you. They would," said Walker. "If you had a good team, they're gonna beat you as bad as they could because they're gonna have to play you again sometime. They knew that. It was structured; it wasn't to embarrass; it was to make a point." Or, in this case, 126 of them. The point total created a buzz that followed the Braves the rest of the year. "I've heard one guy said there were some people who came from way down in Florida up to the state tournament because they wanted to see this team that was scoring all these points," recalls Braves forward Donnie McClinton.

Melvin Porter remembers the Richland game as the culmination of years of hard work with the bitter defeat at Bell City still burning in their memories. "The intensity level was just mind blowing," said Porter. "Everybody was just on the same sheet of music. It was like poetry in motion. It was amazing." Playing basketball under the same coach with the same style with the same group of guys for so many years, Jeff Limbaugh knew his teammates every move. The slightest noise or movement was all he needed. "I knew where Melvin was going to be every time. I could sit there and throw the ball behind my back, blindfolded. I knew where he was going to be. I could tell by the grunt that he made, I could tell by the noise that he made. I could tell by the way Donnie rebounded the ball, if he slapped it hard. I could tell if he rebounded the ball on this side, which way it was coming out. It was just one of those deals." So comfortable were the Braves starting five they could execute their fast-break offense multiple times without ever dribbling the basketball. "I've had people tell me that we made as many as five trips down the court consecutively back to back without ever bouncing the ball," said Limbaugh. Remembers sportswriter Marsh, "You could turn out the lights and they could still run a fast break on you. They just knew where the other guy was going to be."

There were so many nights on basketball courts across the Bootheel when Cookson's teams put it all together, it was hard to tell whether it was basketball or ballet: the fluid movements, the graceful athleticism, quickness – the ability to explode to the ball or the bucket at just the right moment. It all looked just so easy, *too easy*. Opposing fans and coaches would walk out the gym those nights convinced of the team's greatness, but not necessarily the coach's ability. Any coach can win at Scott Central, they would say. But they didn't see the practices and scrimmages that would start at the end of school and end well after the sun went down, the relentless coach who was never satisfied, the year round dedication to the game, the running, the discipline, more running. There was also something else beyond their view: Cookson's devotion to his players after they walked off the court. Anyone who needed a ride home after practice got one from Cookson. He was coach, disciplinarian, and a father figure to his athletes, especially to those who lacked a male role model at home.

In public, the Braves put on a show on the court while Cookson did his act from the sidelines. Most high school gyms hold between several hundred and a few thousand people. A dominant Scott Central team would always attract a large crowd. Fans could clap their hands and stomp their feet, cheerleaders could chant and yell, referees' whistles could blow; nothing, absolutely nothing would be louder in those gyms than a screaming 6' 2" Ronnie Cookson storming the sidelines. He was Bobby Knight with a bowl cut, pleading, demanding, inciting his players to push themselves to new levels. "You would think he was insane," remembers Doug Sanders. "So overdone, but you got the point and everyone in the whole damn gym knew. It became a distraction.

(Opposing) players, during the game, would be looking at the other bench for the yelling because it was interesting."

Sanders and his Chaffee teammates got their second look at Cookson's team during the regional finals. The Red Devils entered the game with a 17-6 record. It had been another banner year for Doug's brother Wade. The senior forward averaged more than 26 points and 11 rebounds his final season. During the regional semi-finals against Kelly, Wade scored 23 points in Chaffee's victory. After defeating Richland, Scott Central raced past Puxico 86-52 in the other semi-final game. The 1979-80 season also marked a reunion on the basketball courts of the Bootheel. Carroll Cookson had returned to coaching at his alma mater. His younger brother now led the all time series between the two, seven victories to three.

Playing Scott Central for the sixth time in two seasons, the Chaffee team was at a distinct disadvantage. The Braves had all five starters back and had been part of a program that hadn't changed coaches or philosophies their entire careers. Chaffee returned only two starters, Wade and Anthony Austin. The two were playing for their third basketball coach in four years. Outgunned, coach Mick Wessel had his team try to do what others had attempted against the Braves; lessen the pace of the game and force the Braves into slowing down and running an offense. Their efforts succeeded on one front. Scott Central only scored 65 points in the contest. Outside of the loss to Bell City, it would prove to be the Braves lowest point total all year. But even when their offense couldn't find its highest gear, Cookson's team found a way to win. Scott Central won by 14 points, holding Chaffee to 51.

The game brought an end to the career of Chaffee's only all-state basketball player in the school's history. Wade Sanders had one of his worst shooting nights, only scoring nine points. He remembers being distracted that evening. "We beat Kelly (in the semi-finals) and boy, they couldn't take it. They come over in droves and they booed us," remembers Sanders. "I don't know what it was. I just didn't seem to be in the game. I was paying more attention to the crowd." Wade's father had grown up in Benton and starred in basketball for the Benton Tigers, one of the schools that consolidated to create Kelly High School. After Wade's junior season, George Sanders had considered moving the family to the Kelly School District where Wade's uncle was the superintendent.

Kelly fans didn't know it, but they were directing their wrath at a player who almost starred for them his final year in school. "They packed the stands," recalls Sanders. "They sat with Scott Central and just booed the piss out of us."

Practicing for an all-star game in the spring, Sanders hurt his knee. He didn't know it at the time, but he had torn his ACL. He dreamed of playing college basketball, but in tryouts at two different junior colleges, his knee gave out. "After that, it was like; you're going to have to get the knee fixed." Sanders ultimately did undergo surgery but not until the fall. "Back then, they didn't do arthroscopic surgery." His junior year in high school only ten of the forty players in Missouri who received all-state honors were juniors. Four of those ten juniors were Ronnie Jones, Donnie McClinton, Melvin Porter and Wade Sanders. All four would repeat as seniors. All but Wade would go on to play college basketball. Sanders' knee injury and slow recovery cut short any plans of continuing his career. Largely because of his efforts, the school that saw basketball as an afterthought had become a winning program, albeit briefly. During Wade's final two seasons, Chaffee won thirty-seven games, celebrated a regional championship, and had back-to-back winning seasons. None of those achievements has been repeated. "Larry Bird, that's the way I remember him," said Mike Marsh. "Just sitting there on that baseline and popping jumpers."

Wade's younger brother Doug had two years left at Chaffee. There would be football games in the fall, basketball season in the winter months, track meets in the spring, and mad dashes out to Rockview in the summertime to catch the "Blue Streak Merchandiser." His love for trains continued right to the end of his father's career. Returning home to Chaffee for a fall weekend in 1988, the trip coincided with his dad's last run on the train. After nearly four decades of riding the rails, George Sanders was retiring. When he departed the caboose for the last time, he had a surprise visitor. Just as he had done as a kid, Doug was waiting on his father as he exited the train. George's retirement didn't last long. He soon contracted cancer and became ill. Living in Texas, Doug drove home to see his dad one last time. He never made it. He called home to his mother from Little Rock, Arkansas and was told his father had passed away. George Sanders died in 1994 at the age of 67.

***

Beating Chaffee and back in the state tournament, Ronnie Cookson's team had rarely been challenged. Their record stood at 28-1, the only blemish being the two point loss at Bell City. Only twice during their 28 victories had the winning margin been in single digits. Cookson and the rest of the Bootheel knew his team was special. Just how dominant his team had become could only be appreciated in hindsight. The victory over Chaffee did have something in common with the win over the Red Devils in the first round of state play the previous year. Both contests marked the closest games Scott Central would play in the entire post-season.

State tournament play opened with North Pemiscot. Returning to its running ways, Scott Central scored early and often en route to a 97-74 victory. It was 14-1 after the first three minutes. In the second quarter, the Braves only outscored North Pemiscot by three points. Cookson thought he knew the reason why. "We ran out of gas there at the end of the first half. We're a little out of shape."[269] That news may have been a shock to the team. Scott Central had just played its 30th game of the season. Conditioning drills and scrimmages were conducted year round. Led by Donnie McClinton's 35 points, four Braves players reached double figures.

When Cookson and his players arrived in Flat River two nights later to compete in quarterfinal play he told reporters, "We're going to bring home two trophies. But I don't know which ones."[270] The choice of the word trophies – plural – was no mistake. That's because both the boys and the girls teams at Scott Central were playing that night. In only the program's second season, the Scott Central girls would go on to finish third in the state. Like their male counterparts, they would become a dominating force. From 1982 to 1993, the Scott Central girls program won seven state championships. While Cookson didn't coach the girls during their championship runs (the ubiquitous Fred Johnson and former Charleston player Danny Farmer coached the teams during that timeframe), he did help get the program off the ground. "The girls were playing volleyball and they wanted to play basketball," remembers the coach. Along with Marvin Ohmes, he helped coach the squad in its first few seasons. He points with pride to the accomplishments of the 1980 girls team. "First time any girls school south of the Missouri River had ever won a game in the final four."

The girls team made its way to the final four that night thanks to a hard fought six point victory over Crystal City. The boys game was never that close. The Braves blitzed Bismarck early with their familiar full-court press and fast break game. By halftime, Scott Central led by 25 points, 42-17. With McClinton and Porter combining for 46 points, the game was never in doubt. With the 85-44 victory, Scott Central was returning to Columbia and the Hearnes Center for the second consecutive year and the third time in Cookson's career.

"2A Money is on the Scott Central boys," heralded the headline of the *Columbia Daily-Tribune* the day the team arrived in town. Ronnie Cookson's squads had always liked to fly under the radar, preferring the underdog role. The Scott Central coach loved to talk down his teams. This year, no one would believe him.

> *"The word has been out for some time.*
> *Don't take a chance investing in gold Krugerrands or grain futures. Put every last buck you can scrape together on the Scott County Central basketball team. It's an investment without risk.*
> *'If you've got any money to bet, put it all on Scott Central right now,' advised one coach at midseason. 'There isn't anybody who can play within 20 points of them.'"*[271]

Despite the hype and the attention, Cookson did try to joke his way into lowering expectations. "We're not as fast as we were last year," the coach tried to tell the paper with a straight face. "They've all grown since last year; they've gotten fat."[272]

On the verge of back-to-back state titles, Braves forward Melvin Porter was seeing a dream unfold before his eyes. It had been four years since the first Porter and the first Scott Central team had won a championship. He'll never forget the conversation he had with Otto afterwards. "I said the only thing I can say is we are going to do it twice. That makes me better than you," said Melvin who also recalls his brother's reply. "He said that ain't going to happen."

Melvin was the third Porter brother to play at Scott Central. Otto and Johnny had worn the uniform before him. Growing up, he was always following his older siblings. When Larry Mosley was dating (and would later marry) one of Melvin's sisters, he would take the Porter brothers out to the dirt court in Haywood City. "It would start at 3:00 or 4:00 in the afternoon and it would be 10:30 or 11:00 at night before you got done playing." Playing against the older competition made Porter better. "Larry is probably about 10 maybe 12 years older than us. He was one of those guys that when he scored, he would talk trash to you. You just learned to play. It got to be like a life or death situation with him in the ballgame. That's where it all started."

Mosley or Fred Johnson would sometimes stop by the Porter house to pick up Otto and drive to Oran to play. Melvin got to tag along just in case they needed an extra player. The outdoor basketball court at Oran where they played made an impression on Melvin. The players could actually dribble the ball. The court surface was concrete. "For us, to go up there and play on concrete courts, that was big. We were big time."

Melvin grew up in a large family that would soon lose its father. His dad passed away when he was in the fifth grade. Growing up, he was aware of, but never bound by the impoverished conditions. "We were poor kids. We were poor in one sense and rich in other ways. Poor in that we didn't have the money to be at the mall, doing this or doing that. The rich part of it was that we always had access to a basketball. It was simple. Even if your regular rim was broke, you take a bike rim, tear the spokes out of it and nail it up, you was good to go. There was always a way to play ball."

Playing basketball was important to all of the Porter brothers. But more important to their mother was family discipline. "We'd get off the bus everyday. All the other kids would go here and go there, and after my father died, my mom would say you better get off that bus right here, you better be home. And she went through great extremes to make sure we stayed busy." The Porter kids had to go to work, often finding employment from an area farmer. Basketball season provided relief. "We couldn't hardly wait for ball season to get here. That was our break from work."

What the Porter children never got a break from was attending church services. Melvin found that out one Sunday morning. After staying out late Saturday night, the teenaged Porter made up his mind he would be sleeping in and not going to church. When his mother came into his room to wake him up, he informed her of his decision. She didn't yell or scream at Melvin, but she did get her point across. "She said that's fine. She told me there was two suitcases in the closet. She said just be gone by the time we get back." The calm but pointed response caused Melvin to immediately rethink his position. He began to appreciate all his mother did for him. "It just made me think a little bit. For the first time, I thought I got it made right here at home. I'm going to college in a few months. Why do I want to mess that up? It didn't take me long to get up and get ready to go to church."

On this March weekend in 1980, Porter would once again be staying up late. The state championship game at the Hearnes Center in Columbia wasn't scheduled to tip-off until 9:45 P.M. Saturday night. The Braves secured the right to play in the game with a convincing 86-63 victory over Wellsville. "Just shocked by them didn't we?" commented Cookson after the game. "Got by on the skin of our teeth." The furious pace of the Braves made an impression on the Hearnes Center crowd.

> *"Scott Central ran so hard for so long even the officials looked a bit haggard by game's end. 'That one official got so winded he couldn't even blow his whistle,' said Cookson, who gave the refs guff despite the lopsided score. 'But you know I'm just teasing.'"*[273]

The coach took time in his post-game remarks to pay tribute to two players, one of them his own, the other from the opposing team. Scott Central reserve Mike Montgomery was always the first person off the bench for Cookson's team. The 6'1" senior was a perfect six for six from the floor. He joined three other players in double figures for the Braves. "It's a shame Mike Montgomery plays for Scott Central because he'd be starting for anybody else in the state," said his coach. "He's not really a sixth man, he's another starter."[274]

Sophomore Bill Roundtree led Wellsville in scoring with 19 points. Cookson was impressed. "Quote me on this," the Scott Central coach insisted. "That Roundtree is the best sophomore I've ever seen."[275] The star guard would ultimately set a state record for most career points in Missouri high school history. Another player from the same school would later break it. As we'll find out, Cookson and Scott Central hadn't seen the last of record scorers from Wellsville.

In the other semi-final game on Friday, Slater defeated Willow Springs 54-45. Slater, the community that made headlines across the state during the railroad strike of 1922, was back in the news for a basketball team and a star player. A lot had changed in the nearly six-decade interim. It's a story other small-town railroad communities like Chaffee would recognize.

In the early 1920's, the thriving railroad town had a population of nearly four thousand people. With roundhouse operations for the Chicago & Alton Railroad, the trains employed close to a thousand workers. But the switch from steam to diesel engines would ultimately be the doom of many roundhouses. The one in Slater, like the one in Chaffee, was long gone by 1980. With it, a large chunk of the population had disappeared as well. When the Slater Wildcats arrived in Columbia, the total number of residents in the town roughly 100 miles east of Kansas City had dwindled to less than 2,500. Despite its small size, the town could boast of two famous residents over the years. The first one is actor Steve McQueen who spent part of his troubled youth with family members in Slater. The second one is Joe Kleine. His senior season in high school, Kleine stood 6'11", weighed 240 pounds and starred as the center for the Slater basketball team. If Ronnie Cookson's Scott Central Braves were going to repeat as state champions, they had to figure out a way to go over or around the Wildcats behemoth. "Maybe we'll stack one guy on top of another," Cookson told reporters. "Or maybe we'll give everybody tennis rackets and see how that works."[276]

***

It was only fitting that Kleine would play a Scott Central team for a state championship. Along with his three brothers, he grew up on Porter Street in Slater. By the time he was in fourth grade, a coach recognized his potential. Joe's father was skeptical. "I didn't really believe it then," said Robert Kleine, Jr.[277] Over the next several years, Joe would turn his father and many others into believers. "Probably from about the seventh grade, he got very serious about basketball," remembers John Merk. The Slater coach was an assistant in 1980 and would later become the head coach at the school before finishing his career in Fayette. "He was one of those kids, that all summer long, he'd be going around with a jump rope to work on his foot speed and his coordination and he'd be constantly playing."

Kleine was pushing six feet by the time he was in junior high. By the time he was a sophomore, he was 6'8" and still growing. That season, he was honored as an all-state basketball player for the first time. He received the same recognition as both a junior and senior. It was between his junior and senior years that college coaches began to notice the talented center. He played on an AAU team in the Kansas City area. "As soon as they saw him play before his senior year, then all of a sudden, the college coaches started to get on the hotline, writing him letters," remembers Merk. Kleine would promptly take the letters and stuff them in a drawer. But soon his dad began to take an interest in the process. "I had about 200 letters in a drawer," said Kleine. "My dad, being an ex-marine and an accountant, right away, everything had to get filed."

By the time practice rolled around at the beginning of his senior year, there wasn't a college team in the country that didn't know him. Merk recalls the scene at Wildcats practice. "They (college programs) usually had a representative at almost every one of our practices, one way or another. Assistant coaches would come to practice, a head coach would even show up at practice, so they were in constant contact." Some of the head coaches who made the trip to the rural Missouri town were among the nation's elite. When the Slater team opened their basketball season Kleine's senior year, Arkansas's Eddie Sutton, Kansas coach Ted Owens, and Notre Dame's Digger Phelps were all in attendance. A game that same night for the Missouri Tigers prevented Norm Stewart from coming to the gym.[278] Kleine didn't disappoint the crowd. He scored 34 points and grabbed 29 rebounds as Slater easily defeated the Marshall Owls, 88-65.

The following week, Kleine made up his mind. He announced he would be playing basketball in the fall for Digger Phelps' team at Notre Dame. The allure of the school was overwhelming for both him and his family. "I consider myself a strong Catholic," said Kleine. "When they came calling (at his home) it was a big deal. The priest, grandmother, my parents, all my brothers were there, it was just a different deal. Nobody told me this is the way you got to go," he said but then quickly added: "they didn't have to say anything." Kleine's early commitment meant other college teams would no longer be monitoring his progress in practice. But Notre Dame officials continued to show up at the gym in Slater. "We would see them on a fairly regular basis throughout the season," recalls Merk. "But after that early signing period, the rest of the coaches backed off."

According to the Slater assistant, Kleine's decision helped the entire team focus the rest of the season. "It was quite intense," said Merk. "Just thinking about his teammates and what kind of circus it could turn into, he (Kleine) didn't want that to be a distraction or a detriment." With the decision out of the way in early December, the team could focus on the goal they had set for themselves that season, a trip to Columbia and a chance to play for a state title. "We had very high expectations, there was no doubt about that," said Merk. "We wanted to get to the final four."

Slater had its first real challenge their sixth game of the season. The Wildcats encountered Glasgow in the championship game of the Brunswick tournament. Kleine was forced to the bench after receiving his fourth foul in the game with five and a half minutes to go in the third quarter. Reinserted into the lineup in the fourth quarter, he fouled out with his team winning by six points. Glasgow rallied in the game's final ninety seconds to pull out a 67-66 victory. Meeting for a second time later in the season, Kleine poured in 44 points. It wasn't enough as Glasgow, a school thirteen miles away, beat Slater 72-64. The Yellowjackets, losers to Carroll Cookson's 1975 Advance team and to Ronnie Cookson's 1976 team, played a style similar to the Bootheel schools. "They had a very quick, aggressive, pressing team and we just did not handle their press very well," said Merk who remembers the Glasgow strategy. "Try to get out, try to run, try to make Joe (Kleine) run between the free throw lines and never get involved." It was a style of play that Slater would see one more time at the end of their season

The Glasgow game marked the last regular season loss for Kleine and his teammates. In January, the Slater center celebrated his eighteenth birthday by scoring 40 points in a victory over Concordia. The Wildcats later defeated Concordia a second time in a game that propelled them to the state tournament. Slater had now won twelve straight. Kleine was just warming up. Opening state play on the Central Missouri campus at Warrensburg, he pumped home 42 of his team's 73 points and grabbed 30 rebounds in a victory over Butler. Two nights later, in the quarterfinal round in the same building, he took seventeen shots at the goal. He missed only once. Slater crushed Smithville 73-39 in a game coach Jim Thomas called "our best performance of the season." His best player scored 36 points and added 23 rebounds. His team was headed to the Hearnes Center.

By the time Joe Kleine arrived in Columbia for the final four, his reputation preceded him "I think he's probably a better shooter than (Steve) Stipanovich," said coach Thomas, referring to the University of Missouri and former DeSmet High School star. "At least that's what the coaches I've talked to have told me. He's not quite as quick as Stipanovich, but he's definitely stronger. The kid has huge shoulders on him."[279] The Slater Wildcats, riding on the shoulders of their all-state performer, knocked off Willow Springs in the semi-finals. Kleine scored 23 and pulled down 11 rebounds. He was 30 points away from a state tournament scoring record and one game away from being a state champion. The only thing that stood in his path was Ronnie Cookson's team from the Bootheel.

Kleine's height and talent would take him first to the University of Notre Dame and later the University of Arkansas. While at Arkansas, he led the Razorbacks to three straight NCAA appearances and in his senior year, was the top scorer in the Southwest Conference. He was a member of the gold medal winning basketball team at the 1984 Olympics. The next year, the Sacramento Kings made him their number one draft-pick, the sixth overall selection. He played fifteen seasons in the NBA, once grabbing twenty rebounds in a single game. While in the professional ranks, he called Charles Barkley, Larry Bird, Michael Jordan, and Shaquille O'Neal teammates over the years. He has a championship ring from his one season with Chicago. Between college and pros, he had more than a thousand games left in his career, but only one game left in high school. On March 8, 1980, Joe Kleine's Slater Wildcats took on the Scott County Central Braves for the 2A state championship. The 6'11" Kleine would be pitted against a team with no starter taller than 6'2". He didn't stand a chance. David was about to slay Goliath.

***

When Kleine and his Slater teammates took to the floor for warm-ups, some fans in the Hearnes Center began to taunt the big center. Earlier in the day, the University of Missouri had upset Notre Dame — Kleine's college choice — in an NCAA tournament game. If the fans behavior bothered him at all, Kleine didn't let it show. Once the championship game tipped off, the crew from Slater proceeded to dominate Scott Central in the first quarter. When the buzzer sounded after the first eight minutes, Slater led 20-16. Twice, Melvin Porter had tested Kleine inside. On both occasions, the 6'11" center blocked his shot. Kleine had also been key to breaking the vaunted Scott Central press. Each time, Slater would inbound the ball to their big target, the Braves would swarm him with a double team, but Kleine, while holding the ball above his head, would simply dump it off to a wide-open teammate. The Braves looked a little jittery at the beginning of the game. Cookson's crew had seven turnovers in the first quarter. Slater, using Kleine to break the press, only had four.

In the early part of the second quarter, the pace continued to favor Slater. After Kleine hit two throws, the Wildcats led 26-20 with a little over seven minutes to go in the half. It would be their biggest lead of the game. Soon, it would be their last lead of the game. Cookson knew the explosive nature of his team. His players were fast, in phenomenal shape and played a harassing, full-court pressure defense that never let up. The inevitable run was right around the corner. "At some point during that game, they were going to have their four to five minute run and during that four to five minute run, they were going to score about 40 points and it's all over. All of a sudden — 'whoop!' - and I'd look up and we'd be up by forty." The coach could be accused of engaging in a little bit of hyperbole, but only slightly. It took Cookson two more quarters before he could look up at the scoreboard and see a 40-point lead.

In a span of four possessions, Scott Central scored three buckets to tie the game. After McClinton scored to even the contest at 26, he stole the inbound pass and made the lay-up. The Braves had their first lead of the game. Around this time, Scott Central made a change in their press. The double-teaming of Kleine had proved futile. It was Carroll Cookson, sitting in the stands that night at the Hearnes Center, who came up with an idea and offered his brother some advice; instead of pressuring the Slater center, why not back off Kleine and force him into dribbling the ball or making a bad pass? The strategy worked brilliantly. A black and white videotape copy of the game that night provides the evidence.

After a Jeff Limbaugh bucket put the Braves up 30-26, Slater inbounds the basketball to their star center. Instead of encountering two Scott Central defenders, Kleine only sees one. Everyone else has fallen back and is guarding a Slater player. Left alone at one end of the court, Kleine fires the ball to the other end. A teammate catches his pass but misses the shot. Kleine, hustling all the way, races down and grabs the rebound. The ball is knocked out of his hands and in the ensuing scramble it goes out of bounds. Scott Central basketball. With their next possession, Kleine walks with the ball. The next time down, he is fouled but misses the free throw. After an Anthony Jones bucket puts Scott Central up by six points, Kleine is again the recipient of the inbound pass. Once more isolated in the backcourt, he throws a full-court pass. His Slater teammate catches the ball but steps out of bounds. Meanwhile, Scott Central is showing no signs of letting up. A Melvin Porter shot puts them up by eight. A Donnie McClinton bucket extends the lead to 10 points. With a little more than three minutes left in the half, a Slater player is fouled and goes to the free throw line. As the players lineup along the lane, Kleine settles into his slot. He is bent over, head down, hands on his knees. For a full seven seconds, he doesn't look up. Joe Kleine is tired. Slater is beaten.

From that point, it only got worse, or better, depending on one's perspective. With less than a minute to go in the second quarter, McClinton takes a shot and misses. Rebounding the ball on the weak side is backup Scott Central guard Hubert Ray. The 5'10" Braves player goes straight over the top of the 6'11" Kleine to convert the bucket. The lead is now 16 points. At halftime, the Braves led 46-30. In the third quarter, Kleine went up for a shot only to find it swatted away by the Scott Central center, 6'2" Anthony Jones. Just as he had done in the Christmas Tournament final against Cape Central, the 140-pound senior had a stellar effort against Slater. He led the Braves with 26 points. His block of Kleine's shot earned him a standing ovation from his teammates. Mike Marsh of *The Daily Standard* described the Braves approach to handling Slater's star player.

"The defensive job on Kleine reminded me of bear beating, a medieval game where a full grown bear was chained and then harassed by a pack of hunting dogs. The dogs are much smaller but their constant motion wore the bear down, allowing the pack to move in for the kill."[280]

The symbol that the kill was complete came with 4:26 left in the game. Scott Central led 81-43 and Slater called for a timeout. Cookson "jumped to his feet and raised his arms in the sign of victory. The team ran to his side and gave the 'We're number one' sign to an ecstatic group of fans."[281] Sitting on the Braves bench was senior guard Jeff Limbaugh. He recalls the moment when the celebration began. "We won the state tournament our junior year, he would not let us hold our finger up and say we were number one," said Limbaugh. "My senior year, with (a few minutes left) to go in the ballgame, we was all sitting over there, he leaned down the bench and said, 'Hey Limbaugh,' I said what's that? He said, 'You wanna know something? You're number one buddy; tell everybody." When the final buzzer sounded, Scott Central had its biggest lead. The Braves won 94-52. Joe Kleine scored 35 for Slater, setting a 2A record for the most points in a four game state tournament run. However, his teammates only scored 17. Besides Kleine, only two other players put up points for Slater. By contrast, Scott Central had four players in double figures with eight different players contributing to the point total. "You can stop one. You can stop two and maybe you can stop three. But you can't stop five," said Cookson after the game. "They wouldn't be 62-4 (over two seasons) if there was any jealousy on this team."[282]

Sitting among the Hearnes Center crowd that night was Bill Bradshaw. The Advance superintendent, who seemingly was present for every state championship game for more than four decades, was instantly reminded of another blowout. "I saw another game like that one time in the finals of the state championship, in 1952, when Shelbyville and Puxico played." Playing future University of Missouri star Norm Stewart, Arnold Ryan's team won that game by 48 points. Twenty-eight years later, Ronnie Cookson's squad defeated a club with future NBA first round draft pick Joe Kleine by 42.

In the opposing locker room, a coach and his star player paid their respects. "We tried to run with them," remarked Slater coach Jim Thomas. "That was a mistake." Kleine agreed with his coach. "You just can't keep up with them. Nobody can."[283] Slater only lost three games that year: two close games to a Glasgow team that went on to win the 1A state championship and a decidedly lopsided contest to the 2A winner. A quarter-century later, assistant coach John Merk puts the Braves team in perspective. "In the last 30 years, they've got to be in the top five that I've seen. And that's regardless of class of school or size of school." Merk added that his dream high school match-up would pit the 1979 DeSmet team from St. Louis (with center Steve Stipanovich) up against the 1980 Scott Central Braves.

The team that nobody could keep up with had completed an incredible two-year run. The five Braves starters, denied the opportunity to celebrate after winning their junior year, finally got the chance to enjoy the moment. "I've never let'em say nothing all year long. I've always told them they were nothing; they weren't any good. But I told'em I'd turn'em loose tonight after the game if they won," admitted their coach.[284] Jeff Limbaugh remembers seeing a different Ronnie Cookson that night. "We seen a side of him we had never seen before in our life. We seen the grumpy old man turn into Santa Claus. He was really cuttin' a rug," said the Braves guard. "It wasn't McDonald's that night – we partied."

The Columbia media always enjoyed talking to the ever quotable Cookson. Two days after the Slater victory, writer Mark Kiszla had this description of the Braves coach.

> *"Scott County Central Coach Ron Cookson isn't much of a sophisticate. His suit appears to have been purchased in somebody's bargain basement. It looks like he got his haircut on somebody's back porch. His drawl and cornball wit are straight backwoods.*
> *...During his team's quest for the Class 2A state championship...over the weekend, Cookson never appeared uptight and seldom even got serious. Often, he seemed more like a man making a guest appearance on Hee-Haw instead of an important visit to the state tournament...*
> *Minutes before Saturday night's championship against Slater, Cookson's assistant coach, Marvin Ohmes, inquired of one of Cookson's observer: 'Well, have you figured him out yet?'*
> *'Yeah,' the guy answered. 'He's nuts.'*
> *Ohmes laughed manically. 'You mean to tell me it took you all this time to figure that out. You shouldn't have gone to all that trouble. I could've told you that a long time ago.'"*[285]

Commenting on the article, assistant coach Ron Cook said, "That kind of humbled Ronnie." One week after the Braves won the 2A state championship, Cookson had another reason to smile. Two more teams from Southeast Missouri got the opportunity to celebrate at the Hearnes Center. Charleston, won its second state championship in five seasons in 3A. The title was the first of coach Lennies McFerren's career. In the 4A championship game, Cape Central, led by Ronnie Jones' 23 points, edged Hickman Mills by two points for the title. Cape, Charleston, and Scott Central. All state champions. All had played in the same Christmas Tournament back in December; a tournament won by Ronnie Cookson's club. The Scott County Central Braves could rightfully make a claim to being Missouri state champions.

The starting five of Jones, Limbaugh, McClinton, Porter and Timmons had one game left together. In the spring, the Rotary Club sponsored an annual all-star contest of players from around Southeast Missouri. Played at Houck Field House in Cape Girardeau, squads were divided into two teams – the North and the South. All five Scott Central starters were invited to participate on the South team. Players from both Charleston and Cape Girardeau competed on the North squad. With the South team trailing in the contest, Jeff Limbaugh, who did not start the game, remembers the chant from the crowd. "Everybody in the crowd start hollerin, 'Scott Central, Scott Central.'" Gene Bess of Three Rivers, who was coaching the South team, gave the crowd its wish. For the final time, the fab five was reunited on the basketball court. The South squad rang up 96 points in its 13-point victory over the North. Led by Donnie McClinton's 36, the Scott Central starting five contributed 76 points to their team's total. The following year, McClinton would be playing for Bess at Three Rivers.

When the Scott Central class of 1980 graduated in the spring, all five Braves players went off to college and attempted to play basketball, at least briefly. Limbaugh, Jones and Timmons went to various junior colleges; Porter enrolled at Drury, a small school in Southwest Missouri, while McClinton started his college career in Poplar Bluff. Besides McClinton, who became a junior college All-American under Gene Bess and finished his career at Southeast Missouri State, the other Braves players never achieved a level of success in college as they did in high school. "Other than Donnie (McClinton), we were not superstars as we individually went to college," commented Limbaugh. "We were like ducks out of water. We didn't have our four buddies to run with."

There was later one other reunion of note. It happened between McClinton and Slater's Joe Kleine. The star center was not happy at Notre Dame and left after one season to go to Arkansas. While playing for the Razorbacks, Eddie Sutton's team scheduled a game against Southeast Missouri State. Former high school coach Ed Arnzen, who by this time was an assistant coach at SEMO, remembers walking into the gym in Fayetteville when the Arkansas center spotted his old high school rival. "Kleine takes a look at McClinton and says, "Oh no, you again!" For his part, Kleine, now retired from basketball and living in Little Rock, remembers what he told his teammates before the game. "I want this game bad." He also recalls their reaction. "They were looking at me like why do you want to beat Southeast Missouri State so bad? I said, 'just trust me.'" On this night, Kleine got his revenge of sorts, as Arkansas won the game.

Once he moved to Cape Girardeau to go to school at SEMO, Donnie McClinton never left. In the summer of 2004, he was living in a spacious two story home, married with two children. A new Cadillac Escalade was parked in the garage. The distance from Cape to Haywood City is less than thirty miles, but McClinton realizes he's traveled a long way since the days he got off the school bus to play pickup basketball games on a dirt court. He's never forgotten his humble beginnings. He still goes to church in his hometown. "I enjoy going back home. Never forget your roots," said McClinton. "A lot of people say bad things about Haywood City, but I still love Haywood City, and I would do anything to help Haywood City." The ties that bind not only extend to his hometown but to his high school alma mater as well. "Scott Central is like family," said McClinton who still enjoys watching and rooting for the Braves. "It's in my blood, it's in my heart, it's where I got my start."

After his last game in a Scott County Central uniform, McClinton had this to say about the match-up against Kleine. "He didn't intimidate me. I intimidated him." An older, wiser, and more mature McClinton would like to revise those remarks. "I was young when I made that statement. No, I did not intimidate him," he said with a smile. "That was just a young Donnie McClinton speaking there – just young and excited. I have nothing but good things to say about Joe."

Jeff Limbaugh remembers the last time he saw the 6'11" center. It happened back at the hotel the night Scott Central beat Slater for its thirty-second victory of the season against only one defeat. Limbaugh and a few other players were celebrating in a room with their coach. Kleine is walking down the hallway and hears the commotion. Limbaugh picks up the story from here. "We looked out the front of Ronnie's door and the door is just full of body. Joe Kleine was walking down the hallway and he had looked in and seen us in there. He ducked his big head and he walked in the room and he stood up. He said, 'Mr. Cookson.' Ronnie said, 'Yeah Joe what do you need?' He said, 'I just got one question to ask you sir.' He looked at Ronnie and he looked around the room at us and said, 'Who in the hell beat you all?'"

CHAPTER NINE
The Cookson Invitational
1985-1986

"This has kind of turned into the Ron Cookson Invitational. I hope he invites us back next year."

Wellsville coach Fred Norman

David Heeb will never forget his first memories of Scott County Central basketball. He was seven years old in 1986 when Ronnie Cookson's team had once again made it to the state finals. The opponent was Wellsville, a school in the town by the same name about 90 miles northwest of St. Louis. The championship game was in the fourth quarter. Heeb had to go to the bathroom. He relayed his request to his uncle sitting next to him. His uncle told him he would take him as soon as the game was over. Heeb would be waiting a long time.

At the beginning of the season Scott County Central found itself in a familiar position – defending state champs. In March of 1985, the Braves defeated Northeast Nodaway, giving Cookson his fifth state title. His fourth championship had come in 1983, three years after Donnie McClinton and crew destroyed Slater at the Hearnes Center. In the early 80's, the championship game was moved from Columbia to Springfield; Scott Central had moved back down into the 1A classification. In the winter of 1986, the Braves entered state tournament play with a record of 23-6. Never before had a Ronnie Cookson team made it so far with so many losses.

Heeb had made the journey to Springfield from his hometown of Morley to watch his cousin, Terry Bell, play for the Braves. More than eight thousand fans packed the Hammons Center on this night to see if Scott Central could stop Wellsville's Fred Johnson, the leading scorer in Missouri high school basketball history. Before the game, the Scott Central players watched in awe as Johnson warmed up. Dunking a basketball wasn't much of challenge for the Wellsville star. The guard and his 48-inch vertical leap preferred loosening up by trying to touch the *top* of the backboard, three feet higher than the ten foot tall basketball goal.

Johnson leapt into statewide and even the national spotlight earlier in the season when he set shattered the scoring record, also held by a Wellsville player. Bill Roundtree was the player Ronnie Cookson once described as, "the best sophomore I've ever seen." The Scott Central coach made the comments after his team defeated Wellsville in the 1980 semifinals. The 6'1" guard went on to score 3,243 points in his high school career before going on to play at the University of Missouri. His record only lasted four seasons. Fred Johnson started playing varsity ball as a freshman, one year after he began dunking basketballs.

Johnson and his family (not to be confused with Fred Johnson of Oran) can trace their roots to the St. Louis area. When Fred was a small boy, his mother, four brothers and five sisters moved to Martinsburg. They later moved a few miles down the road to Wellsville, a town of approximately 1,500 residents in east central Missouri. It was a life that many Scott Central athletes could identify with. "After basketball, there's nothing here," Johnson once said. "Mexico (Mo.) is only 26 miles away, and we'll go there to just hang out and bum around. But you can't do anything but play basketball in Wellsville."[286]

His home life also had a familiar echo. His basketball coach described his situation. "I don't think it's been all that easy for him," said Fred Norman. "He never could afford a car and he doesn't even have a driver's license. I've offered to take him to get it, but he doesn't want to put anyone out. I think even though he always has a smile on his face, sometimes it's not really there, you know what I mean?"[287]

One thing that brought a smile to everyone's face was watching Johnson play basketball. He started on the varsity as a freshman, one season after Roundtree graduated. He scored 26 points in his first game. Someone once asked him when he knew he would break the scoring record. "In my freshman year," he replied.[288] Johnson averaged 21 points as a freshman. He played basketball that season at 6'1" and 190 pounds. He continued to get bigger and better. He averaged 24 points as a sophomore and 30 as a junior.[289] By the time of his senior year, Johnson was 6'4" and weighed 220 pounds. Over the summer, he attended a basketball camp in Lexington, Kentucky. Deep in the heart of Bluegrass Country, he won the slam-dunk competition. "He can play all facets of the game," said his coach near the end of Johnson's last year. "Fred picks up eight or 10 points off steals and the same with offensive rebounds. He's developed other areas of his game. He can shoot, he can pass, he plays good defense."[290] Johnson was making an incredible 76% of his shots from the floor. No one could stop him or seemingly, the Wellsville Tigers.

After an early season loss to Fulton, the Tigers record stood at 3-1. They won their next 17 games in a row heading into a Friday night game against Bowling Green. Wellsville doubled the score of its opponent, 100-50. Fred Johnson scored 25 points that night and put himself into the record books. After four years and 110 games, he was the new scoring king of the Show-Me State. A Missouri Tigers game against Oklahoma State in Stillwater the following day prevented Roundtree from witnessing it. "Fred is very special to me," said the Missouri guard. "I'm glad it was broken by somebody I knew."

Now with a record of 21-1, Wellsville could focus on team goals the rest of the season. The first objective was to win their conference. After a blowout victory over Silex, Fred Norman's team had one regular season game left against the Clopton Hawks. The outcome of the contest would determine the conference championship. The two teams had met earlier in the year during a tournament. Wellsville won that game convincingly by 16 points. On this night, things wouldn't be so easy; Norman's club had scored 90 or more points in ten games that season. Clopton coach Dale Miller was determined to slow down the pace of the action. He succeeded. After the first quarter, Clopton led 14-10. With Johnson scoring nine points in the second quarter, Wellsville managed to take the lead at halftime, 23-21. The slow speed of the game, described as "an almost unbearable pace for the Tiger faithful" by the Wellsville newspaper, continued in the third quarter. [291] Despite playing an unfamiliar style, Wellsville managed to extend the lead to four points and led 35-31 heading into the final quarter. In the next eight minutes, the action came to a crawl. Wellsville, with the most prolific scorer in Missouri high school history, scored only two points. Clopton scored six points to tie the game and at one point held the ball and ran more than three minutes off the clock. Tied at 37, the game was going into overtime. Fireworks were about to begin.

With three minutes put onto the clock, the players lined up at half-court for the jump ball. There wasn't much doubt as to who would win the tip. Fred Johnson, with his four-foot vertical, delivered the ball to a teammate who quickly fed Wellsville player Keith Ganaway for a lay-up. The Tigers had a quick two -point lead. But a Clopton assistant quickly grabbed the arm of a referee as he was heading back down the court to point out that the players had lined up backwards on the tip-off. Ganaway had put the ball into the Clopton goal. The officials called timeout and they huddled with the coaches at the scorer's table. The Wellsville paper describes what happened next.

"To say that there was a heated discussion at the scorer's table, on the floor, in the stands, and anywhere else that was within earshot would be a mild understatement. Coach Norman indicated later that both referees were willing to start the overtime period again and replay the whole three minutes, as they felt responsible for lining the teams up wrong. However, Coach Dale Miller of Clopton apparently would have none of that, and when his point of view prevailed, in his gym, you could see the veins popping on Coach Norman's neck as he was being restrained by two of his players. The two points were transferred to the Clopton side of the board."[292]

It was now Clopton with a 39-37 lead. Then the referees whistled a Wellsville player for a technical foul. A free throw put Clopton up by three points. Wellsville put the ball in Fred Johnson's hands. He quickly scored to put the Clopton lead back at one, 40-39. As Clopton inbounded the basketball, one of their players was quickly tied up by the Wellsville defense. Jump ball. Wellsville had won the opening tip and scored, the same bucket that was ultimately awarded to Clopton. At the scorer's table, the possession arrow still pointed toward Wellsville. Another argument broke out among opposing coaches and referees. The officials decided to give the ball back to Clopton. In the last few minutes, an "unbearable pace" turned into a furious flurry of activity.

The Hawks turn the ball over. Wellsville misses. Clopton turns the ball over on a five-second violation. Wellsville misses again. A Clopton player misses a free throw. A teammate gets the rebound but steps out of bounds. Trailing by a single point, Wellsville has one last chance. The Tigers shoot the ball with five seconds left in the overtime. The shot misses but a Wellsville player gets the rebound and puts it up. But before the shot is released, the referee blows his whistle and calls a three-second violation – "the first one called all night," points out the Wellsville paper. On the inbounds play, a Clopton player is fouled. He misses the front end of a one-and-one. Wellsville gets the rebound but can't get off a shot. Clopton hangs on to win the game and the conference championship.

Wellsville coach Fred Norman was seething after the game. "There are an awful lot of people upset over this. It's shades of Glasgow all over again. We're protesting, but you know what happens with protests."[293] Norman filed his protest with 2:38 left to go in the overtime following the controversy over the opening tip. "Shades of Glasgow" was a reference to another controversial game played four years before.

In 1982, Bill Roundtree's senior year at Wellsville, the Tigers played Glasgow in the first round of the state tournament. Wellsville led 38-34 after three quarters. But an error by the official scorer changed the score to a 36-36 tie. Glasgow eventually won the game in overtime. Norman lodged his protest with just a minute to go in the fourth quarter. But the Missouri State High School Activities Association threw out the protest on technical grounds, saying it must be made at the time of the infraction. Norman wasn't taking no for an answer. The school hired a St. Louis attorney and planned to sue the MHSAA.[294] It also sought an injunction banning Glasgow from playing any additional games until a decision was reached. The court decided against Wellsville and Glasgow was allowed to continue tournament play. The Glasgow Yellowjackets finished third in the state that year.

Just as in 1982, state officials would take no action regarding the game against Clopton. After the contest, coach Norman made a prediction. "The bottom line is that we may not lose any more games after this."[295] A team in the Bootheel would ultimately have something to say about that. Finishing its schedule with a loss knocked Wellsville out of its number one ranking. The Tigers dropped to the number two spot in the final regular season poll. Undefeated Northeast Nodaway entered district tournament play in the number one position (what was called the regional tournament in the '70's was now known as the district tournament). Scott County Central, with six losses and all its starters gone from last year's team, was nowhere to be seen in the rankings.

Playing three games in the district tournament, Wellsville won its sixth title in seven years. During district play, the Tigers outscored the opposition by an average of 50 points. Wellsville moved on to the state tournament. Their first opponent was the Southern Boone Eagles. Meeting the Mid-Missouri team in Jefferson City, Fred Johnson forgot his uniform. It would be the only thing he forgot to do that night. Pumping in 18 field goals and shooting nine for 13 from the free throw line, Johnson scored 45 points and led his team to an 80-50 victory. "He is simply the best basketball player in 1A and he is right up there with the best in all four divisions, "commented Southern Boone coach Dave Gill after the game.[296]

Two nights later on the same court with 2,500 fans looking on, Wellsville defeated Sturgeon 78-52. Johnson scored 35 points but it was his teammates that impressed Sturgeon coach Dick Smith. "I don't want to take anything away from the other teams that are left, but if there's a better team in 1A ball, I don't know who they are. Everybody talks about Freddie Johnson, but they've got a lot of other good kids, too."[297]

Now with a record of 27-2, Wellsville had one game left before the final four in Springfield. The Tigers would get their shot at revenge against the Clopton Hawks. This time, Wellsville headed to the northeast part of the state to meet Clopton in Kirksville on the campus of what was then called Northeast Missouri State University (now Truman State). "We've been thinking about this game for two weeks," admitted coach Norman.[298]

In his eighth year at Wellsville, Alfred Lee (Fred) Norman had transformed the program. The year before he took over, the team's record was 2-18. His first year record of 12-13 was his only losing season. "For the first three years, I had to deal basically with outlaws; I had to be super-strict with the kids."[299]

Norman played his high school ball at Tipton, in west-central Missouri. He played college basketball in the state, first at Central Methodist in Fayette, and later at Westminster in Fulton. "I had 'white man's disease' really bad – I couldn't' get off the floor."[300]

After he became a coach, his parents were invited to address the crowd at one season ending sports banquet. They told the Wellsville audience that growing up, Norman and a friend used to dress up in fur coats and wrestle, pretending to be gorillas. Their son was also something of an Elvis imitator.[301] His flair for the dramatic would soon find its outlet on Missouri high school basketball courts.

He started his coaching career at Wellsville in the fall of 1978. He was closing in 200 career victories, had coached two Missouri state scoring champions and taken two teams to the final four. A victory over Clopton would give him and his team a chance at the one thing that had proved elusive, a state championship trophy.

Back in the gym at Kirksville on a Saturday night, Wellsville jumped out to 18-10 lead at the end of the first quarter and served notice early this night would be different. Clopton never controlled the pace of the game and never took the lead in the contest watched by an estimated 2,700 fans. Wellsville got its revenge in a 59-43 victory as Fred Johnson led all scorers with 21 points. The Tigers were headed to the final four in the opposite corner of Missouri – Springfield – and the campus of Southwest Missouri State.

High school hoops hysteria had officially come to Wellsville. "Don't bother calling any friends or relatives in Wellsville this Thursday or Friday," said the *Mexico Ledger*. "And if you drive through the small community of 1,546 southeast of Mexico on Highway 19, you'll think you've stumbled onto a ghost town."[302] In an editorial the following day, the newspaper captured the essence of small town basketball magic.

"Basketball is unique among high school sports team in small towns. When a school's team wins, it seduces the area and brightens the winter for the entire communities. (The Wellsville area) once again has been caught up in this marvelous whirlwind called March Madness."[303]

Semi-finals were scheduled for Thursday with the state championship game to be held on Saturday. Wellsville was pitted against number one ranked Northeast Nodaway while Scott County Central faced Lockwood in the other bracket. With number one playing number two, there were no doubt fans who went to the Hammons Center on Thursday night thinking the semi-final game was *the* state championship game. "They're big, they shoot well, they're fast and quick, they play good defense and good offense – other than that, they're not much," joked coach Norman about his upcoming opponent. While Northeast Nodaway had impressive size – their center stood 6'8" – Norman sounded confident in his team's ability to match-up. "Quick up there isn't necessarily quick down here and I think we've got a lot of things they haven't seen."[304]

What Northeast Nodaway and a large contingent of the crowd had never seen before was the Wellsville pre-game warm-up routine. It ended on this night, as it did every night, with a resounding dunk by Fred Johnson. The game began with the crowd expecting more athletic demonstrations from the impressive Wellsville forward. What they saw instead was a balanced attack. With Johnson held to eight points, his teammates picked up the slack in taking a 32-23 lead into the locker room at halftime. Johnson got going in the second half, scoring 13 points as he and his teammates extended their lead at one point to 19 points. The final score was 61-49. Northeast Nodaway coach Claude Samson was impressed. "It wasn't just Johnson. Their other kids hit from the outside more than we thought they would. We were just out horsed."[305]

The Wellsville Tigers had "out horsed" every single one of their opponents in the state tournament thus far. The 12-point victory over Northeast Nodaway was the closest game they had played since their overtime loss to Clopton. Wellsville would now have to wait to play on Saturday. They knew who their opponent would be. Scott County Central defeated Lockwood in the first semi-final game. Once again, the only thing that stood between a phenomenal talent and his team was Ronnie Cookson's club. Wellsville had been on their radar screens all season long.

* * *

At Scott Central, Braves players knew all about Fred Johnson. News of the exploits of the Wellsville guard had made its way to the Bootheel for months. His team was the top ranked school for most of the year while mentions of Johnson in the media included *USA Today, The Sporting News*, and *Sports Illustrated*. No one, not even the players themselves, had given much thought to winning a state championship in 1986. Everyone knew that Wellsville was going to walk off with the title.

Cooksons' team had lost all five starters from the 1985 squad that sprinted through the state playoffs by winning tournament games by an average of 24 points. That team featured 6'7" Doug Blissett and 6'4" Tim Ware. Neither player jumped center. That honor belonged to teammate David "Bullnose" Harris. Bullnose stood 5'8". "He could touch over the top of the square on the backboard," remembers Jay Cookson. The coach's son was a junior on the '85 team. Like everyone else who played a key role on the '86 squad, Cookson came off the bench the previous season. He described what it was like to play on a roster dominated with so much talent. "You were in that middle group of guys. The first team would go out and start beating somebody, get them down 20 or 30, you would go in and run it to 40, then it's time for the bomb squad (third string) to come in. We didn't get to play much."

Only one game separated the 1985 Braves from an undefeated season. The 6'7" Blissett was called for traveling while going up for a dunk against Lennies McFerren's Charleston Bluejays in the annual Christmas Tournament in Cape Girardeau. The bucket would have tied the game. Scott Central lost in the championship game by four points. As good as Cookson's '85 club was, it could have been even better if Lowell Hamilton didn't move. The 6'7" Hamilton played his college ball at the University in Illinois where he started for a 1989 team that made the NCAA Final Four. He attended Scott County Central in grade school before moving to Chicago.

The responsibility for carrying the team the following season first began to sink in immediately after the '85 championship game. In the locker room, the coach had separated the juniors and seniors. To the senior class, Ronnie Cookson had nothing but praise and congratulations for their hard work and efforts. As for the juniors, "He says I want to tell you boys something. If you want come back here next year, you better get home, get off that bus Monday and get to work," recalls his son. The burden of carrying on the Braves tradition was squarely on the shoulders of the class of '86. Jay Cookson still laughs at what his thoughts were on that day. "Is he talking to us? We're going to be 15-15 next year." The coach's lecture did get Jay and his teammates to start pondering the possibilities. "We were all looking at each other thinking, wow, he thinks we can come back up here. It kind of planted a seed in our head." Just moments after claiming his fifth state championship trophy, the coach's thoughts had once again turned to the next season.

For a team with little playing experience, it also lacked another critical component: leadership. "There was no leaders. I played probably more than everybody of the juniors," remembers Jay, who also admitted, "I wasn't no leader." Into this void stepped two players, Jeff Turner and

Stanley Blissett. While Turner played a great deal his senior season, Blissett rarely got into games. In fact, he almost didn't play at all that year. Blissett developed early and contributed greatly in his junior high and junior varsity days. By the time he was a senior, other players had passed him up. He had also taken a job at a restaurant in Sikeston. Returning to school in the fall of 1985, Blissett confessed to his fellow players he was seriously considering quitting. To his teammates, especially Turner and Cookson, alarm bells went off. They recognized that Blissett had a role to play, even if he never stepped foot on the court. A son went to his father with an urgent request. "We all went to dad and said, 'Hey, Stanley is going to quit. You gotta do something.'" Cookson met with the frustrated player and did something he had never done before. He told Blissett he could work as often as he needed to and come to practice when he could. There was one contingency; the entire team had to sign off on this arrangement. Cookson didn't want anyone on the team complaining if he was passed over on the bench when Blissett entered a game. Jay and his teammates quickly arranged a players-only meeting. The coach's son put the question in front of the entire squad. "If he gets put in front of anybody during a game, does anybody in this room have a problem with it? Everybody in the room said nope, if he goes in front of me, he goes in front of me. That's fine."

With team leadership established, the seed that their coach had planted began to take shape about halfway through the 1985-86 season. Jay remembers an area sportswriter attending practice one afternoon. The writer mentioned that he had recently seen Wellsville play. The players were full of questions about Fred Johnson and his talented team. "You've seen Fred Johnson play - you've really seen him play?" The writer assured Jay and his teammates that he had and also offered an opinion. "He said you guys could play with them. I said really - you think we can? He said, 'yeah, I think you can.'" While the players were still somewhat skeptical, "it did give us a little bit of confidence that maybe, if we make it that far we could make it pretty close." After their victory over Lockwood in the semi-finals, Scott Central would soon get the chance to find out how close they could come.

***

From the time he was a little boy until he graduated high school, Jay Cookson spent practically every waking moment with his father.

Each day, Jay would ride to school with his dad. Just as Arnold Ryan did, Cookson opened the gym each morning for his players to shoot baskets. After class ended in the afternoons Jay would hang around the gym and watch practice. He was seven years old when his father won his first state championship. The younger Cookson was often the target of player's practical jokes. "I can remember they'd lock me in the lockers." Watching that '76 team and his father's work habits on the practice court, he knew the sacrifices involved. Often, it would be eight or nine o'clock at night before father and son returned home. Ronnie Cookson was Jay's dad, but a father figure to dozens of Scott Central students over the years. As a child, the son had a difficult time understanding his father's role. "He paid more attention to other kids than he did me," remembers Jay. "I'd want to do something but he would take a kid to the doctor on a Saturday when I'd want to go fishing." Gradually, with age came maturity and slowly Jay came around. "It took me sometime to realize that those kids needed him. They depended on him. They didn't have a father."

Away from the game of basketball, it's his father's generosity that stands out in Jay's mind and others as well. "Ronnie always spent his own personal money," (on his players), remembers former assistant Ron Cook, who left Scott Central in the early 1980's to coach at Jackson. "It's the extra things you do that allow the kid to play ball." This willingness to help others wasn't isolated to his players and their families. "People would always say, your dad takes care of those ballplayers, whenever they needed a job, he'd let them work, he'd help them out," remembers his oldest son. "He sure did, and you didn't see half the stuff he did for kids that didn't play basketball." Jay tells the story of one poverty stricken family that used wood to heat their home in the winter months. Word got back to the coach that their chainsaw had broken. "Saturday morning rolled around, Dad and I got up that morning, cut wood, and filled the truck, backed up to their porch and threw wood on their porch. Dad give his mom forty or fifty dollars to buy groceries."

Jay and others recall the year the team was preparing to go to the state tournament and there were some questions as to whom the coach would include on the roster. One of the players on the varsity was a special education student who never played. Cookson could have taken more talented members of his junior varsity squad. He chose not to do so, instead taking the player who had been loyal to him, regardless of his contributions on the court. "It would be good for him to go up and see something like that, probably be the only time he ever gets to do something like that," Jay recalls his father saying. The player, who sat on the bench all year long, finally got his chance. "In the championship game, when the game was won, he (Cookson) put him in and he got to play in the state championship game and he got a medal," said Mike Marsh. *The Daily Standard* Sports Editor left the paper in the early 1980's to become a schoolteacher – at Scott County Central. "That kid, that's probably going to be the biggest thrill of his life. Ronnie understood that, and he gave him the chance. Ronnie is one of the most loyal people I've ever been around."

Of all the stories regarding his father, there's one that particularly stands out in Jay's mind. It was a winter night after practice. After giving rides home to several of the players, Ronnie and Jay were headed back to Morley. It was cold and dark, and they found themselves in the middle of a snowstorm. The Cooksons spotted two men attempting to change a flat tire along the side of the road. Ronnie slowed down to stop, much to the surprise of his son. "I say you're not stopping are you? He says, 'Yeah, I'm not leaving these people out here.'" Jay instantly sensed trouble, "rough, rough looking fellows." His father told him to stay in the truck. If anything happened to him, his father instructed, Jay was to leave as quickly as he could. When Ronnie got out, Jay slid over to the driver's seat and quickly locked the doors. Well before his sixteenth birthday, Jay began to practice using the clutch and shifting gears. "I can farm. I can drive anything," he thought. Ronnie walked up to the two men, changed their tire and returned to the truck without incident. Jay never forgot that night and what his dad did for the stranded travelers. "This is what made me look at him the rest of my life as a different person."

Until his last year in high school, the oldest Cookson son was never tall. The summer between his junior and senior year, he grew six inches. "I weighed 145 pounds and I was 6'4" and a half by the time basketball season was over my senior year." One of the taller players on the team and rail thin, the sudden growth spurt caused problems. "I grew so much so fast and I was so weak my legs would go numb out there on the court." Jay had desire for the game of basketball, but not necessarily the greatest talent. It proved frustrating for both coach and player. "He wanted me to be good, I wanted to be good, but my body wasn't good." Like the rest of his teammates, Jay didn't play that much his junior season. During his senior season, he started and played a lot in certain games, but found himself sitting on the bench for other contests. It's a challenge a coach faces when his offspring is on the team. "I think he was afraid people were going to think he's playing his son."

Like so many of the athletes at Scott Central, Jay and his friends developed a passion for the game of basketball. It's what they did all year long. "We didn't have no girlfriends in the summer," remembers Jay. "A typical Saturday night for us - we'd get five or six of us – and we might go to Sunset (the predominantly black neighborhood in Sikeston) and play basketball. Everyone else has their girlfriend and going out and we'd go to Sunset or we'd go anywhere and we'd play basketball. That was our Saturday night. We had three-wheelers. You'd have four people on your three-wheeler, a boom box, and a basketball and go to somebody's house and play basketball all day long. Everybody did that. We lived to play basketball and that was all that mattered to us."

Jay and his teammates entered state play with six losses in their first 29 games, unimpressive for Scott Central standards. Of the school's five championship seasons to that point, two of the teams lost three games. The other three teams -1976, 1980, 1985 – three of the most talented in Scott Central history – had lost only game apiece. None of that mattered once state tournament play rolled around. Entering the championship game against Wellsville, Scott Central had won their previous four games by an average of 27 points. Reaching the final four in Springfield with a semi-final game against Lockwood, the Braves ran into their opposition at the hotel before the game. "They were a bunch of big old football players. I remember seeing them at the hotel and all these guys have metals and patches all over their jackets. We have clothes in brown paper sacks," said Jay. Scott Central won the game by 28 points. After the game on the team bus, the players chanted, "We're number two! We're number two!"

Scott Central players knew they were expected to lose on Saturday to Wellsville. So did Ronnie Cookson. His preparation for the championship game departed from the usual. He didn't allow his players to watch any game film of their upcoming opponent. He also didn't want his team to watch Wellsville play their semi-final game. After just a few minutes, everyone departed for a team meal. On the bus ride to the restaurant was when the "number two" chants broke out. While ignorance of the opponent may have been bliss, alone it wouldn't be enough to defeat Wellsville. When the two teams met at the Hammons Center on March 15, 1986, the Braves needed a dose of something only Ronnie Cookson could provide. The full-time coach and part-time psychologist had just the right prescription.

***

In the opposing locker room, Wellsville coach Fred Norman sounded just as confident as he had before his team's victory in the semi-finals against Northeast Nodaway. "This isn't last year's Scott County Central team, "said Norman, in reference to the 1985 1A state champs. "They have weaknesses we'll have to attack. We'll have to handle their press, of course, but if they full-court press us too much, they won't be able to pack it in on Freddie Johnson. You look at them as a whole, and I think we've got their size, we're just as quick and we've got lot more muscle," he added. A lot more muscle indeed. In addition to 6'4", 220 lb. Fred Johnson, the team's other forward, Keith Ganaway, stood the same height and was pushing 240 pounds. The two bookends looked more like NFL linebackers than high school basketball players. Scott Central would counter with two inside players, senior forward Richard Sims and sophomore center Terry Blissett, weighing no more than 175 pounds each.

When Cookson's players took the floor that night, they finally got to see the Wellsville team they had heard so much about. Everyone was especially curious and a little awed by Johnson, a player that had been in the news for months. Wellsville was already on the floor when the Braves made their appearance from the locker room. But instead of starting their warm-up routine, they stood and gawked. "Half of us just ran to half court and just stopped and started looking down at the other end to see what he did," recalls Jay Cookson. "You're in a 1A school and you look down there and this guy is almost touching the top of the backboard." Inspired by their gravity-defying opponent, the Scott Central players decided to put on a pre-game show of their own. "We got down at our end and we thought, heck, we can get up too," said Jay. "Me and Ricky (Sims) we were dropping the ball in pretty good, we were dunking it." That is, until an official put an end to the exhibition. "The referee came up to us and said, 'what in the world are you boys doing?' He said, 'you know how many people are watching me here? Stay off the rim boys. You're going to get me in trouble.' We were up against the world when we went against him (Johnson)."

Once the game began, it probably did seem like the entire planet was against the Braves. After trading buckets early on, the contest was tied at four when Wellsville went on a run. Before the Braves scored again on a free throw, Wellsville reeled off 13 straight points. Jay remembers lining up for the free throw that broke the Scott Central scoring drought. "I'm looking at the score, it's 17-4," said a son who was also conscious of his father's legacy. "My dad has never been beat in the state tournament - ever." Teammate Ricky Sims offered Jay an analysis of the early action. "He said, 'Man, we're getting the hell beat out of us.'" A free throw and a late bucket cut the lead to ten points, 17-7. Still, Scott Central looked overmatched and overwhelmed – exactly the same way many of their opponents looked over the years encountering the Braves withering press and fast break. But being down by ten points was only part of their problem. The end of the quarter meant the players had to march off the court and face their coach, a far more intimidating prospect. "We all look at each other," recounts Jay. "We're like man – I ain't walking over there first cause he's gonna kill the first person he can grab. He's going to make an example out of somebody."

The coach recognized his team wasn't as talented or as strong as their opponents. The only way Scott Central could hope to compete was if his team somehow had a mental edge. Just when his players expected him to spew venom, he offered them a boost of confidence. "We walked over there and Dad says, 'See boys, I told you that press would hurt them.' He said you got them right where we want them'. At first, Jay and his teammates were puzzled by their coach's assessment of the first quarter. "We're all looking at each other like man what game is he watching. What do you mean the press is getting to them? Have you seen the score up there?" Only in hindsight can a son appreciate his father's comments. "Sometimes something would happen and you would think, oh that wouldn't be that big a deal. That was some kind of little mistake. He might punch you, slap you, spit on you, pinch you, poke you; just abuse you. But then sometimes, you mess up really bad and you think he's going to kill me and that's when he pats you on the back. That was kind of a pat on the back – let's go boys, let's go. By God we came back."

The comeback that had started at the end of the first quarter continued in the second. By halftime, Scott Central had cut the lead to six points, 28-22. Wellsville shot 55 percent from the floor while the Braves hit only 39 percent of their shots in the first half. The Tigers had given Cookson's team their best shot and couldn't shake them. Scott Central was now confident, inspired and more relaxed on the court after a jittery and sometimes sloppy beginning. But what makes a great game is how it ends, not how it begins. For the more than eight thousand fans packed into the Hammons Center that night, they would see a great ending...and then another...and then another....and still one more. Fans on each side would find it titillating, frustrating, maddening, exhilarating. Someone on that court would eventually walk off state champions and somewhere in the crowd seven year old David Heeb would eventually get to go to the bathroom.

***

When second half action tipped off, Scott Central scored first, cutting the lead to four points. On Wellsville's first possession, a charging foul gave Fred Johnson his second foul of the game, while teammate Keith Ganaway also picked up a foul on the next time his team had the ball. The fouls would eventually take their toll. In the interim, Wellsville used its size to its advantage. A Johnson bucket later pushed the lead back to seven points, but just when it looked like Wellsville would again dominate their opponent, Scott Central fought back. A nine-two Braves run, capped off by a Jeff Turner basket, tied the score at 34. Turner was fouled on the play and headed to the free throw line for a chance to put Cookson's team in the lead. Before he could do so, Fred Norman wanted a timeout. With 4:23 left in the third quarter, it was all even. Everything that had happened before was just a warm-up. The real game had begun.

Back on the court after the timeout, Turner hit his free throw, giving Scott Central their first lead of the game. Back and forth it went for the final four minutes of the period. On nine different occasions, the lead changed hands. Brian Boeckelman put Wellsville up by one point, 42-41, just before the quarter ended. His coach later found out the senior forward played his last game with a broken bone in his hand.[306] Two other things gave Fred Norman something to worry about. Ganaway had picked up his fourth foul while Scott Central had outscored his team by nine points since the end of the first quarter.

In the fourth quarter all but two of Wellsville's points would be scored by either Johnson or Ganaway. A Johnson bucket with a little over five minutes left stretched the lead to five points. Cookson called timeout. On two different occasions, Scott Central cut the lead back to three, but Wellsville answered each time. With 2:25 to go, Wellsville led by six points, 58-52. In the next to last season of Missouri high school basketball without a three-point shot, Cookson's team had a lot of ground to make up if they were to win the school's sixth state championship. A pair of unlikely heroes would soon emerge.

A Ricky Sims bucket cut the lead to four points. Two possessions later, a Scott Central player missed a shot but Sims was there for the rebound and the put back. The Scott Central senior had eleven rebounds on the day, six on the offensive boards. Wellsville led 58-56. Back at the other end, the Braves fouled Fred Johnson. The scoring champion sank both free throws to push the lead back to four. A minute was left in the game. The Braves didn't waste any time. Quickly getting the ball down court, guard Terry Bell hit a running jumper to trim the lead to two points. The Braves applied full-court pressure, but Wellsville managed to break the press. With the lead and the ball at their end of the court, Wellsville tried to run out the clock. They couldn't do it. The Scott Central pressure forced a turnover and a foul. Sophomore center Terry Blissett was headed to the free throw line for a one-and-one opportunity. If he made both, the game would be tied with 12 seconds left. But he missed the first shot and Wellsville's Johnson grabbed the rebound. With time running out and the ball in the hands of their best player, Wellsville fans and probably just about everyone else in the Hammons Center thought the game was over. Fred Norman said later, "I thought we had it won five different times."[307] Surely, this was one of the five. From underneath the goal, Johnson started dribbling up the side near the Scott Central bench. A double team stopped his dribble. Maybe the abrupt stop threw him off balance. Perhaps there was a slick spot on the court. With the ball and the game in his hands, Johnson fell. The referee blew his whistle. Johnson was called for traveling. Scott Central had one last chance to tie the game.

Wellsville called timeout. There were 10 seconds left. Norman's team undoubtedly talked about which Scott Central players were most likely to take the last shot. The Wellsville coach had learned a lot about the Scott Central program and the Cookson style after losing to the Braves in the 1980 semi-finals. "This won't be like my first year down there," Norman had said even before the final four began. "Scott County Central gave me the education of my life."[308]

Over in the Scott Central huddle, Cookson was preparing to unleash an unusual lesson plan. The one player Wellsville didn't count on was Stanley Blissett. The 5'8" senior guard was on the court as time wound down. He was only on the team because his fellow players desperately wanted him there and because his coach came up with a compromise that pleased everyone. Wellsville didn't challenge the inbound pass to him. Blissett quickly turned and fired a 15-foot jumper toward the goal. Blissett, who almost quit at the beginning of the season because he had a job, saved his teammates at the end of the season with his shot. The ball went in. Scott Central had tied the score at sixty. A last second desperation shot by Wellsville missed. The teams were headed to overtime.

With three minutes back on the clock and both teams at center court, a jump ball would launch the overtime session. With the teams anxious to start, it took the referees three tries before play could resume. On the third attempt Johnson tipped the ball to a teammate. Wellsville had the first chance to take the lead. The two teams traded buckets before another Stanley Blissett bucket put the Braves up 64-62. It was Scott Central's largest lead of the night. Wellsville knotted the score and later forced a turnover when Scott Central's Brian Coffee had the ball stolen from him. With 29 seconds left in overtime, Wellsville had the ball and a chance for the final shot. A timeout sent both teams to the bench. Jay Cookson remembers what happens next.

"Here comes Brian (Coffee) and Brian is just bawling. This is a marine drill sergeant later in life." Upset about the turnover, Coffee thought his play had given the game to Wellsville. On the Scott Central bench, Ronnie Cookson wasn't about to concede defeat. "Dad comes up and tells Brian, 'I want to tell you what, you better stop that. We got a long way to go. This game isn't over yet." The coach was right. There was a long way to go.

Ganaway missed a shot for Wellsville and although Scott Central got the rebound, the Braves didn't have the ball for long. Wellsville forced a jump ball and the possession arrow pointed to them. Forced to foul, Scott Central sent Johnson to the line with nine seconds to go in overtime. Just before he took his free throws, Cookson called timeout to give him some additional time to think about it. It didn't help the Braves. When play resumed, Johnson made both attempts. Wellsville led 66-64. During the timeout before Johnson shot, Cookson had drawn up the team's last second strategy. He later revealed the plan. "Terry Bell was supposed to go coast to coast."[309] The junior guard was ready. "If you were at the end of the game, you got one chance to score, you want Bell to have it in his hands," said Jay Cookson.

After the second Johnson free-throw, a Scott Central player inbounded the ball to Bell. With nine seconds on the clock and down by two points, the guard knew his mission. Get the ball quickly down the court and take the shot that would tie the game. As he made his way up the left side the court, he encountered a Wellsville double-team. Using a reverse dribble, he sidestepped the pressure and crossed half court in the middle of the floor. He spotted an open teammate on the right wing. It was Jerry Porter. The freshman was the last of five Porter brothers to play for Cookson at Scott Central: Otto, Johnny, Melvin, Calvin and now Jerry. The freshman had spent almost the entire year playing on the junior varsity team. But for some reason, Cookson decided in the biggest game of the year, to put his freshman on the floor and into the spotlight. Jay Cookson remembers sitting on the bench earlier in the game when his dad made the move. The coach got up and started walking. "I thought where in the world is he going? Just started looking down at the end of the bench. Jerry is the last guy sitting there, the freshman, doesn't even have a warm-up shirt like ours. He's sitting down there probably looking at the water bottles or something. He goes down and grabs Jerry and puts him in. When he goes by, everybody's going, what's he doing putting him in? Next thing you know Jerry is tearing everybody up on the court." When Porter first entered the game near the end of the first quarter, he helped spark the rally that cut into Wellsville's 13-point lead.

Now with the ball in his hands and just a few seconds left, the freshman didn't hesitate. He took one step toward the goal and let the shot fly toward the basket. Porter's shot went in as the first overtime ended. Scott Central had been spared again: first by a senior reserve and now by a junior varsity star. Tied at 66, the second overtime would soon begin. Sitting in the stands that night at the Hammons Center was Otto Porter. As the first one in his family to play for Cookson, was he surprised at all when Jerry took the shot? "No. We were never afraid to take that shot. We always had the green light to do (that) because Cookson pretty much knew that we knew the game and we pretty much did whatever it took."

Once action resumed, neither side showed signs of letting up. Two points for Wellsville was answered by a Terry Bell bucket. Another Wellsville basket was followed by another Ricky Sims rebound and tip in. When Fred Johnson made a shot to put Wellsville up by two points, Bell came back with a jumper from the free throw line to tie the score at 72. Less than 30 seconds remained on the clock. As dramatic as the end of regulation and the first overtime had been, the finale to the second overtime would be the most stunning. With 12 seconds to go, Terry Blissett fouled Johnson. The fifth foul of the night sent the sophomore center to the sidelines. Just as he had done near the end of the first overtime, Johnson stood at the free throw line with the chance to put his team back on top. The all-time Missouri high school scoring champ had scored 35 points in the game. The total wouldn't change. He missed the front end of a one-and-one opportunity and Scott Central had the ball. The Braves quickly raced to the other end. As Stanley Blissett drove toward the goal to make a lay-up, a referee's whistle blew. A foul was called. It was on Fred Johnson. It was his fifth foul of the game. Johnson's high school career was over. As the scoring champion walked off the court, everyone in the gym, including the Scott Central bench, stood up and applauded. Jay Cookson recalls the overflow crowd that night. "I remember the Fire Marshall locking the doors, not letting people in. You could go out but they locked the doors coming in. I can remember looking around the top – it was ten deep around the walking areas. You just couldn't fit another person in that place." The standing ovation the fans gave Johnson that night was loud, long, and well deserved. The Wellsville player ended his career with 3,552 points over four years.

Now it was Scott Central's turn at the free throw line. Stanley Blissett had two shots. His first one was short. His second attempt went into the cylinder and kicked back out. Scott Central's Ricky Sims, as he had done all night, was there to grab the rebound. He put up the shot.

It was blocked right back into his hands by Keith Ganaway. He took a second shot. Ganaway blocked it again. But once again a whistle blew. The referee called a foul on Ganaway, his fifth and final foul. Now only two seconds remained. Sims had two free throws to give Scott Central the lead and the game. He missed both of them. As the buzzer sounded with the score tied at 72, the contest was headed into its third overtime. Both teams could claim a moral victory of sorts. Wellsville had only survived because Scott Central missed four consecutive free throws. But on the Braves sidelines, the players and the coach knew that Wellsville's two big forwards were out of the game. "When we missed those four free throws, I didn't think it was my night," coach Cookson later admitted. "But I felt good knowing that both Johnson and Ganaway had fouled out."[310] Son Jay was more confident. He believed the game changed as soon as Johnson left the floor. "When he fouled out the Wellsville bus driver could have gone and started it up cause there was no way we were going to lose that game. It was over." The third and final overtime would prove him right.

Scott Central scored nine of the first eleven points of the third overtime. When a Wellsville bucket sliced the lead to five points, 81-76, only 30 seconds remained. A Braves free throw pushed the lead up to six and when Wellsville missed their final shot, a shot at the buzzer by Scott Central made the final score 84-76. Appropriately, Terry Bell scored the final Scott Central bucket. The Braves junior guard led his team in scoring on the night with 17 points. Through four quarters and three overtime periods, Bell never left the court.

The Braves sixth state championship tied a Missouri high school record. It was Scott Central's sixth title in the last eleven seasons, all under coach Ronnie Cookson. As the final buzzer sounded, the Braves bench burst into celebration with the players putting their coach on their shoulders. Refusing to quit after trailing by 13 points early in the game, his team had pulled off the biggest upset of his career. "You couldn't expect any more from a game," said Cookson. "This is the toughest game we've ever had up here (in the finals)."[311] Incredibly, the smaller Scott Central team out-rebounded Wellsville 48-32.

In the post-game ceremony, the Wellsville team walked to the middle of the Hammons Center to accept their second place ribbons. When a state official put one around the neck of coach Fred Norman, the medal attached to it fell to the ground. For the first time all night, the Wellsville coach had a smile on his face. In his third trip to the final four, Norman had once again come away empty. "We really thought we could do it this year," he said afterwards. "There's a certain amount of luck involved in this game, no doubt about it, but how many opportunities are you going to get?"[312] It turned out that Norman would get no more opportunities at Wellsville. He left the school at the end of the year to take a job at Waynesville, a larger school in the middle of the state.

Norman's best player, Fred Johnson, had played his final high school game but his connection to the Cookson Clan wasn't finished. The next year, he and Jay were teammates at Three Rivers in Poplar Bluff, playing basketball for coach Gene Bess. In his sophomore season, Johnson received second-team All-American honors. He finished his basketball college career with two years at Southwest Missouri State under coach Charlie Spoonhour.

Jay Cookson, now married and living in Morley in the house next to his parents, still can't believe what happened that night back in 1986. Every now and then, he'll pop a tape of the action into his VCR and try to figure how Scott Central ever won. "That game was a miracle. It was nothing short of a miracle us winning that basketball game."

As one might imagine, the game surfaced as a topic of conversation when Cookson and Johnson were teammates in Poplar Bluff. During weekends in college, Jay would bring Fred back to Morley for basketball at the Scott Central gym. He also took time to needle his teammate about the miracle in Springfield. He remembers the first time he brought him to the Cookson house. "I brought him home and I said Fred, you go up there in the trophy room if you want to see your trophy, I won't charge you for it," Jay said with a smile.

One other thing should be noted about that season and that game and it speaks volumes about the approach by both Carroll and Ronnie. The brothers always found a way to beat a star player in a big ballgame. In 1975, it was Lawrence Butler of Glasgow; in 1980, Joe Kleine of Slater; in 1986, Wellsville's Fred Johnson. Kleine and Johnson scored the identical amount in their championship games – 35 points – but the Scott Central teams walked off with the crown. All three of them, Butler, Kleine and Johnson, averaged right around 30 points per game. All three went on to play Division 1 college basketball. But when they came up against a Cookson team, their weakness, or that of their team, was exploited. Advance got Butler into foul trouble and the Glasgow star lost his effectiveness, only scoring 13 points. Against Slater, Scott Central let Kleine have his points but shutdown his teammates. In the match-up against Wellsville, Johnson dominated until his fifth foul sent him and seconds later teammate Keith Ganaway to the sidelines. "(Against) Wellsville, we knew we had to get to the bench," remembers Jay. "It just took us three overtimes to get there."

Three overtimes and one Scott County Central championship later, young David Heeb finally got relief. The performance that night by cousin Terry Bell and his teammates had turned the seven year old into a die-hard fan. "I probably didn't miss ten games over the next ten years," remembers Heeb, who would go on to play for the Braves in high school. Those next ten years would see more of the same: talented teams, dominating performances and championship caliber play. The next decade would also bring something else; swan songs for both Ronnie and Carroll Cookson. The curtain was set to close on an amazing era of Bootheel ball.

CHAPTER TEN
The Straw That Stirred The Drink
1987-2004

"That's the thing that people don't understand about Ronnie Cookson, is that for 25 years, he was the straw that stirred the drink in the entire Scott County Central community."

High school basketball coach and former Scott County Central player
David Heeb

In the winter of 2004, David Heeb's Bell City Cubs had the goal of finishing their season at the Hearnes Center in Columbia. In the first round of state tournament play in Sikeston, Heeb could look down at the other bench and see his past. He was hoping it was also a glimpse into his future. At the end of the game, the first person he embraced was Ronnie Cookson. It wasn't that long ago that Heeb was afraid to speak to the former Scott Central coach.

Heeb grew up in Morley. His father is from Chaffee. David's great-great grandfather owned land around the turn of the 20th century that became part of the new town. Heeb Street in Chaffee is named for him.

In Morley, his first basketball coach was Larry Mosley, brother-in-law to Otto Porter and the rest of his talented basketball-playing brethren. Three years later, starting junior high at Scott Central was when he first got introduced to Cookson. "What an experience that was," remembers Heeb. "The first two years I played for him, I never spoke to him. Never. I was scared to death of him." Things began to thaw his freshman season. David, like dozens of other Scott Central athletes, frequently got rides home after practice from his coach. Cookson's youngest son Brad is a year older than David. They would often stay after practice and shoot baskets. It didn't take long for Heeb to realize there was another side to Cookson away from the game. "I guess I kind of warmed up to him."

Developing into a basketball fan during the triple overtime game against Wellsville, Heeb watched a basketball dynasty growing up. On the playground or in pick-up games, he modeled himself after the high school heroes. "I would be in the driveway – 'I'm Jerry Porter, I'm Terry Blissett.'" Heeb remembers. "I just looked up to those guys. I just loved basketball. I can quote you the years that they won the state tournament and I can tell you who the starters were on that team and this team. I was just a gym rat and I just loved it." As the Scott Central success grew on the basketball court, so did its reputation with others. "The thing that I remember more than anything is maybe we would be at a camp somewhere or we'd be playing ball with friends from other schools, somebody would go, 'He's from Scott Central' and everybody would go, 'Oh, I bet he's good.'"

Heeb understood a big reason why those Scott Central teams were successful was because of their coach. Cookson always knew how to handle his players. "He understood the psychology of dealing with individuals better than any coach that I've ever been around or any coach that I've ever worked with," said Heeb. "I think he understood that you can't treat everybody the same way. You can discipline everybody the same. But you can't yell at everybody, you can't put your arm around everybody. You put your arm around this guy; he may try to take advantage of it. You give an inch - he'll take a mile. The next guy, if you yell at him, he may go into a shell."

The pupil began to absorb the lessons of the teacher. While in high school, Heeb first began to entertain thoughts of a coaching career. "I started coaching when I was a senior in high school. I coached a little league baseball team in the spring. I was 17. Two of the players on that team were Dominatrix Johnson and Randy Conn."

Almost a decade later, Johnson and Conn would again be on a club with Heeb as their coach. Their team was the Bell City Cubs. In the first round of state tournament play, their opponent was Scott County Central. Sitting on the Braves bench as an assistant was Ronnie Cookson. He had left his head coaching position nine years earlier. In between the improbable victory against Wellsville and his final game in the winter of 1995, Fred Norman's statement had come true. The 1A state tournament had become the Ronnie Cookson Invitational. The Scott Central coach wrapped up his career while rewriting the history books.

***

After the winter of 1986, Cookson and his Scott Central teams had won six state championships. Over their next seven years, they would double that total, winning six titles in seven years. From 1985 through 1991, the Braves won every single 1A state championship. From 1983 through 1994, Scott Central claimed the title in all but three seasons; a quarterfinal loss to Springfield Catholic in 1984 by two points in overtime, a 1992 defeat to Van Buren by a single point, and a 1994 loss to Lockwood, 64-60, in the title game. In all three years, the team that defeated Scott Central ended up winning the championship. In other words, all that separated Cookson from possibly winning 12 consecutive titles were three losses by a combined total of seven points.

Wellsville and Scott Central met in a rematch in the 1987 title game. This one didn't take any overtimes. The Braves led by as many as twenty points in the second half and won the game by sixteen. The following year, junior Jerry Porter, the last of the Porter brothers to play for Cookson, joined the last of the Timmons brothers to play for the legendary coach. Marcus Timmons started on the varsity squad beginning his freshman season. Their first season together produced a first for their coach: an undefeated season. The 34-0 Braves won the state title game by 25 points in 1988; the same year the three-point play was introduced into Missouri high school basketball. Jerry Porter capped an incredible high school career by playing in his fourth and final state championship game the next season. The Braves defeated Clopton 63-53 in 1989, one of the narrowest margins of any title game in Cookson's career. It also marked the fourth and final time that Cookson would match-up against coach Dale Miller. No other coach met Scott Central in the final four more often than Miller and his Clopton Hawks.

Miller, the son of a southern Missouri timber worker, began his high school coaching career at Clopton in the 1975-76 school year. He retired from coaching in the spring of 1991. To put it another way, he had the unfortunate timing to begin coaching the year of Cookson's first state championship. He left the year the Braves grabbed the trophy for the 11th time. Miller's Clopton team first met Scott County Central at the quarterfinals in Flat River in 1979, one day after the Braves narrowly defeated Chaffee in the heat deprived Bloomfield gym. Scott Central won the game by 33 points en route to their second state title. The second time Clopton would encounter Scott Central was at the championship game in 1983. Miller watched from the sidelines as Anthony "Moon" Timmons, the older brother of Marcus and Dean and younger brother of Mayfield, poured in a state championship record 47 points as the Braves defeated the Hawks 89-71. Two years later, Cookson and Miller matched up in the 1985 semi-finals. Scott Central won the game by 26 points. Their third final four contest and the last of the four match-ups occurred in the 1989 championship game. A smile came to the coach's face when he thought about his games against Cookson. "You never could believe what he told you because he was a con artist," remembers Miller. "When you got ready to play him, three players had the flu and they probably wouldn't show up that night. I knew that when I was talking to him. I didn't pay any attention to that. He was one of a kind."

Losing to Cookson four times overall and twice in the finals, Miller always appreciated how his counterpart treated the opponent. "He was almost apologetic a time or two after beating us, realizing that it's a tough game to lose – the state championship," recalls the coach. "Even in the 79 year when they drilled us, he'd say something that would make you feel better about your ball team."

In his 16-year coaching career, Miller won more than three hundred games. His teams finished second in state three times and twice finished third. A highly successful coach in his own right, Miller believes no one compares to the man who led the Scott Central program for twenty-five years. "Not in high school basketball in the state of Missouri. I don't think there's anything close to it."

The Clopton school district is located near the Mississippi River town of Clarksville in northeastern Missouri. While making clear it was *not his opinion*, Miller did offer insight to how other coaches and schools from around the state viewed the beacon of success located in the southeast corner of the Show-Me State. "The fact that Bootheel basketball, (people were) poor, that's all they do (play basketball). If you go into the Bootheel, I guess they acknowledge that as the state of Missouri, but a different place."

The coach and his team from that "different place" were in the process of adding their own chapter to the Missouri high school basketball history books. With success came increased scrutiny. Whispers of recruiting charges began to circulate against the Scott Central program. It just didn't seem possible to certain people that the

Bootheel school with a student population under 200 could be such a dominant force in high school basketball. Even friends and supporters professed amazement at the enduring success of the Braves program. "I had several talks with him about how in the world do your teams get that well oiled?" remembers Miller. "I said I just don't see how you can be that good and (have) that much talent. I know that you play lots and lots of basketball, but we play lots and lots of basketball."

Acknowledging the subject in a 1991 interview, Cookson offered perhaps his strongest opinions ever on the topic. In the middle of his seventh consecutive state title run, the Scott Central coach told the *Kansas City Star,* "Some coaches have tried to get us put on probation. We've been accused of recruiting, things like practicing too much. We stick by the rules. Because we win, everybody thinks we've got to be doing something illegal. But we're always trying to get better." To his critics, Cookson also offered this. "It's the lazy coaches who don't do anything for their kids who don't get better."[313]

Former coach Ed Arnzen could sympathize with Cookson on this subject. As someone who coached at a parochial school, he often heard rumors that Notre Dame recruited players. He flatly denies the charges and defends his friend as well. "I was always accused of recruiting and I never did. I did not recruit. I doubt that Ronnie did, to be honest. But you'd always hear that from other people."

One of those people who heard the accusations over the years was former Oran player Fred Johnson. He arrived at Scott Central in the early 1980's to coach the girls program. "I thought Ronnie had all these tricks, broke all these rules," recalls Johnson who quickly discovered there was a big difference between rumor and reality. "I was disappointed when I went down there. I told him where's all these tricks? He didn't have any tricks. It was just practice."

Carroll Cookson's programs weren't immune from recruiting rumors either. Former Advance player Richie Walker played for both Carroll and Ronnie. He defends the action of both coaches. "If somebody came to them and said coach, we're gonna move into the town, is there a place a stay? You bet he (Carroll) would look and Ronnie would look. But as far as people saying, he paid them off or they're paying their rent, that's bull. That's not right. They wouldn't do it. But as long as it conformed to the rules and the rules set by the state, you bet. They'd do it in a minute – doesn't hurt to have an extra ace in your playing cards."

This much does seem true. High school students and their families sometimes move to different school districts. If the student in question also happens to play basketball, that's even better from a coach's perspective. According to former coach Miller, even Ronnie Cookson has admitted his program has been the beneficiary of students moving into the Scott Central school district over the years. "I remember one time – he said, 'Dale, you know, it's just different down where we're from.' He said eight or 10 of us coaches are together and all of a sudden you look around and one team in the area has 12 players and they all can't start – they move somewhere else."

None of the rumors over the years was ever substantiated by state officials. Two additional points can be made in Cookson's defense. Scott Central supporters will point out that as many potential players moved out of the school district as moved in. Secondly, the two most prominent basketball families during the Cookson era, Porter and Timmons, had long established area ties.

***

While Jerry Porter finished his high school career in 1989, the last Timmons brother to play for Cookson had two more seasons left. Marcus Timmons would also become the first Cookson athlete to play Division 1 college basketball. While in high school, he became the only player in Missouri history to start in four consecutive state championship games. Jerry Porter played in four but came off the bench against Wellsville. The 6'7" Timmons received Mr. Show-Me Basketball honors in recognition as being the best player in the state his senior year. During his four seasons, Scott Central went 130-3 and a perfect 4-0 in title games. Two of the losses during his high school career came in the Christmas Tournament in Cape Girardeau. His sophomore season, Jackson, a 4A school in Cape Girardeau County, snapped Scott Central's 53 game winning streak with a one-point victory in overtime in the championship game.[314] A year later, Lennies McFerren's Charleston team defeated Ronnie Cookson's crew by a two points en route to an undefeated season and a 3A state championship. That Charleston team was led by Lamont Frazier, a nephew to Ricky. Beginning his college career at the University of Missouri in the fall of 1990, Frazier would eventually start for a Norm Stewart team that went through an undefeated Big 8 season and made it the final eight of the NCAA tournament.

Timmons was almost his teammate. Late in his junior season, Marcus indicated that he was leaning toward going to Columbia and playing basketball at Mizzou. His coach indicated the official selection process would be over before Timmons started play his senior year. "Marcus is planning on signing early (in November) so everybody can get off him and he can work on his studies," said Cookson.[315]

When the early signing period rolled around in the fall, Timmons did commit. It wasn't with Missouri however but instead with Southern Illinois University in Carbondale. Shortly before the fall signing period began, Norm Stewart's team went on NCAA probation. Timmons opted to play his college basketball closer to home in Carbondale, about 70 miles away.

During his four years at SIU, Timmon's teams won more than 90 games and made one NIT and three NCAA tournament appearances. Coach Rich Herrin tapped a vein of small town talent in Southern Illinois, Southeast Missouri, and surrounding areas.

Herrin has done it in large measure with local – and rural – talent. Seventeen scholarship players during his tenure have come from within a 100-mile radius of Carbondale. Many from the tiniest towns. Among this season's starters:

- *(Chris) Carr is from Pilot Knob, Mo. (population 783)*
- *(Paul) Lusk is from New Baden, Ill (2,602)*
- *Forward Marcus Timmons is from Haywood City, Mo. (263)*
- *Guard Shane Hawkins is from Pinckneyville, Ill. (3,372)*

Throw in top reserve (Scott) Burzynski from Valier, Ill., (population 708) and the Salukis frequently field a quintet whose combined population is 7,728 according to the 1990 U.S Bureau of Census.[316]

Winning more than 220 games in his high school and college careers, Timmons hated losing. "If our team loses, I go punish myself," he once told the *St. Louis Post-Dispatch*. "I go run, and run till I start hurting – I start cramping up. That's my punishment."[317]

"There's nobody in America that's won that many games in eight years," said SIU coach Herrin. "He can do it all. He's a great rebounder. He's a great passer. He can put it on the floor. He can guard people. He's a very unselfish player."[318] After finishing his college career in the spring of 1995, Timmons made his way to Australia, where as of 2004, he was still active in professional basketball.

Back in high school, while Timmons nearly joined Lamont Frazier at Missouri, a Scott Central teammate came close to joining Marcus at SIU. Guard Mark Mosley also signed to play basketball with Salukis. Failing to meet eligibility requirements, he went to Moberly Junior College. Two years later, he became Cookson's second athlete to play Division 1 college basketball. Mosley played his final two seasons at Alcorn State. But around Scott Central, he's known for something else. "There was a Porter or a son of a Porter on every state championship Scott Central ever had except for 93. Mark Mosley's mom is Otto Porter's sister," said Jay Cookson.

***

It was Mosley and Timmon's junior year in 1990 that fans at the Hammons Center in Springfield were spotted wearing "Welcome to the Cookson Invitational" sweatshirts. The coach wanted no part of it. "I have nothing to do with it," Cookson insisted. "This isn't the Ronnie Cookson invitational, it's the state tournament. What I have is a fine bunch of kids to work with. It's had nothing to do with Ronnie Cookson."[319]

The Braves went 32-1 that season and won the state championship game by twenty-six points. After the season, Cookson thought about leaving Scott Central. He was a finalist for the head coaching position at Poplar Bluff. "I just didn't feel like I could move," the coach said years later. "Money wise – the money wasn't any better." In the late 1970's, the coach had considered taking over the women's team at Southeast Missouri State. The reigns of that program were later taken over by Ed Arnzen. "With the success he had, Ronnie should have been in college somewhere," said former Puxico player Gene Wilfong. "But you can't coach in college unless you start in college. You just can't get there."

There was perhaps another reason why Cookson never left. "Dad don't like change," said son Jay. "At all," seconded his brother Brad.

The victory in the 1990 championship game was the 500th of Cookson's coaching career. To both sons, the passion and purpose that their father brought to the game of basketball each day began to wane.

Cookson always insisted his players set goals for themselves. He had a few for himself as well. "He said, 'I had a goal. I wanted to win a state championship or 500 hundred games,'" remembers Jay. At the age of 45, after twenty seasons as a head coach, he had accomplished both. Near the end of his career, both sons began to notice the game of basketball wasn't the same.

To oldest son Jay, the 1986 game against Wellsville was a watershed moment for the coach. He believes the competitive fires in his father started to dim after that season. The off court activities where Cookson would get the whole team involved started to disappear. Growing up, he recalls Saturday mornings during deer season. "The whole ball team went with him," said Jay. "The ball team showed up at the house at 5:30 in the morning, and everybody went deer hunting. Everything dad did, 15 kids went." According to Jay, all that began to stop after the triple overtime game. "After about '86, he quit all that stuff. I think he thought he proved to the world, by God, if I can win with this group of kids, what else can you do? Everything else was just gravy."

Brad Cookson, nine grades behind Jay, played for father's last team. Both sons sat on the bench next to their father growing up, watching basketball, and learning the coach's distinctive style. They learned a few tricks along the way as well, including how to handle their father's legendary paddle. "You had a technique that you learned," said Brad. His older brother explained. "Catch the paddle is what we called it. Whenever you'd bend over and he would swing, you would kind of jump," said Jay. "You got hit so much, you got good at it." Added Brad, "It was no big deal."

Brad saw his father change in the early nineties. The volume of the coach's voice from the sidelines began to turn down. "My senior year, he hardly didn't ever yell," said Brad. Jay recalls watching his father during the 1994 state championship game. "Dad didn't work the refs, he didn't work the kids. You're just sitting there watching him going, what are you doing? All you got to do is do your thing and you're going to win." Scott Central lost the game to Lockwood, marking the only time a Cookson team made it the finals without winning. In 13 appearances in the final four of the state tournament, Cookson's teams went 25-1.

By the winter of 1995, the coach's lost passion for basketball was abundantly obvious. "You knew something was wrong when he cancelled basketball practice to go deer hunting a few times my senior year," remembers Brad. "That would have never happened before." Late in the season, Cookson submitted the following letter to the Scott County Central administration and school board:

This letter is being written to advise you that I will be retiring at the end of the 1995-1996 school year.

I have enjoyed working and coaching at Scott Central for the past 25 years. I would like to thank all of you for the support and cooperation you have given me. I have really enjoyed working with the kids.

I am submitting this resignation in advance of my 1996 retirement date in order to make the task of finding a replacement run smoothly.

I am willing to work next year as an assistant coach or to have an assistant coach who will take over in the 1996-1997 school year.

In order to keep my present salary which will greatly determine any retirement amount, I will be willing to accept extra duties and help out anywhere necessary in the school system.

Sincerely,

Coach Ronnie Cookson

A new coach was brought in for the next season. Cookson stayed on to help him out, but his coaching career was over. His reign at the helm of the Scott Central program represented one for the ages in terms of return on investment. After twenty five years, 634 wins, twelve state championships, and untold influence on hundreds of athletes, the teacher, coach, and athletic director retired at a salary of $35,000 a year.

During his final season of 1995, Cookson's team won its district and qualified for state tournament play. Appropriately, his team's first round win over Cooter set a tournament record for most points. The 123-76 victory propelled Scott Central to sectional play against South Iron. Cookson ended his career as he started it. His 1971 team lost to South Iron in the state tournament with John Matchell scoring 40 points. In 1995, South Iron defeated Cookson's team with Matt Matchell on the team and father John in the stands. Afterwards, he shook hands with both of them. "You can't believe how much I thought about that."[320]

In a quarter-century of coaching, Cookson's clubs qualified for state tournament play on 18 different occasions. Of the six years they didn't win the championship, the team they lost to ended up winning the title four times. The only two times in Cookson's career where that didn't happen was against South Iron in 1971 and again in 1995.

Cookson's club ended the year with a 23-7 record. One of the games in his final season was against Twin Rivers. Down on the opposing bench, Ronnie saw a familiar face, that of his brother. Carroll Cookson had bounced around at several schools after departing Advance in the late 1970's. He worked briefly in the private sector, coached at Puxico one season, returned to Advance for a short period and then took a series of coaching and administrative jobs around Southeast Missouri. According to his brother, Carroll was always in search of a better opportunity. "One day I was with him and he had three contracts in his pocket to coach at different schools. He was always looking for something," remembers Ronnie.

In the spring of 1993, Carroll was ready to retire. That's when he received a phone call from Forrest Jackson, the former superintendent at Kelly High School, and the uncle of former Chaffee players Wade and Doug Sanders. Jackson had gone on to become superintendent of Twin Rivers, a school in Butler County southeast of Poplar Bluff. One of Carroll's coaching stints had been at the school in the 1980's. Twin Rivers wanted him to come back. Cookson accepted and started work at the school in the fall of 1993. It's his second season at Twin Rivers that Carroll will always treasure.

The 1994-95 Twin Rivers Royals went through their regular season undefeated. They were the state's number one ranked team in 2A. Entering the district championship game, Carroll's team faced a daunting task. Their opponent was the Portageville Bulldogs, coached by Jim Bidewell. His teams had won the state tournament four consecutive seasons. The four-year run by Portageville came near the end of a remarkable quarter century period for Bootheel ball. Starting in 1972 with Carroll's Advance Hornets, teams from the six contiguous Bootheel counties of Scott, Stoddard, Mississippi, New Madrid, Dunklin, and Pemiscot won thirty-two state basketball championships over a twenty-five season span.[321]

The Portageville streak ended in the winter of 1995. Cookson's team won the game 69-61 and advanced to the first round of state play. Portageville coach Bidewell was impressed. "You don't beat one man when you play them. You get them outside and they'll take it inside. You stop them inside and they'll hit a three. They are a team."[322] Bidewell predicted Twin Rivers would beat their next opponent, Cape Notre Dame. He was right. On the same night brother Ronnie's career came to an end against South Iron, Twin Rivers defeated Notre Dame 59-55. Cookson's team was on its way to Flat River and the campus of Mineral Area Junior College for the quarterfinal round. They were one game away from the final four.

Their opponent would be Cardinal Ritter from St. Louis. By talent, tradition, and bloodlines, Cardinal Ritter was a formidable opponent. The Lions run to the state title had ended the previous season in the same arena in the quarterfinals. Ritter entered that contest as the state's number one ranked team and were led by future Georgetown star Jahidi White. They were upset by Portageville in double overtime 60-58 as Jim Bidewell's team went on to the last of its four consecutive titles.

With Jahidi White off to the Big East conference, Cardinal Ritter still had plenty of firepower. Junior Chris Carrawell would soon be playing basketball at Duke while teammate Loren Woods would start his career at ACC rival Wake Forest before transferring to Arizona. A teammate to the 6'7" Carrawell and the 7'1" Woods was Richard Austin. His brother was Earl Austin Jr., a standout at Ritter during the eighties. His uncle was Wes Unseld, the former University of Louisville star who went on to an NBA career with the Washington Bullets. Twin Rivers had no comparable marquee talent. Their tallest starter was listed at 6'4" (but was probably two inches shorter).[323] No one for the Royals would be playing Division 1 basketball that fall. What they lacked in ability, they made up for with guts and guile. If it was possible for an undefeated number one ranked team to be an underdog, this game was it. "We think it will be a war," said Cardinal Ritter coach Preston Thomas.[324] The Cookson brand of Bootheel basketball had one last shot at being a giant killer.

The game was on a Saturday night. Former Advance player Richie Walker made the drive up to Flat River with a group of Carroll's former players. "We took up a van and we took up about 12 of the coach's past players," said Walker. It's a game he will always remember. "That was the greatest high school basketball game I ever saw in my life."

It didn't start out that way. "I think Twin Rivers can play with Ritter, if they aren't intimidated," Portageville coach Bidewell predicted. "That's very important when you play Ritter."[325] Early on, Twin Rivers looked intimidated. A Loren Woods basket and four points by Chris Carrawell, the last two coming on a thundering dunk shot after a Twin Rivers turnover, had Ritter up 6-0. The Lions maintained their six-point advantage midway through the first quarter. But up 9-3 with less than four minutes to go, the Ritter offense went ice cold. They failed to score a single point the rest of the period while the Royals answered with six points, the last four coming on two buckets by center Jeremy Jackson. After eight minutes, it was tied at nine.

After a three-point shot put Twin Rivers in the lead for the first time in the game early in the second quarter, it was the Royals' turn for the offense to malfunction. After leading 12-11, Twin Rivers was outscored by Cardinal Ritter 19-8 the rest of the first half. Cookson's team went into the locker room down by 10 points, 30-20.

Opening the second half with the basketball, Ritter looked content to stall and take some time off the clock. After several passes near mid-court, Ritter worked the ball inside. But a charging foul gave possession back to Twin Rivers. Neither team could find its stride. In a quarter marked by several missed shots, turnovers, and fouls, Twin Rivers barely made a dent in the Ritter lead. With eight minutes to go in the game, Cookson's team trailed 40-31.

In the final quarter with less than five minutes to go, Twin Rivers made their move. Guard Richard Simmers made a three-point shot from NBA range to slice the lead to four points. The Royals applied full court pressure. Ritter subsequently turned the ball over and Twin Rivers quickly converted with a lay-up. The lead was down to two 46-44. The teams traded buckets over the next minute of action when Ritter once again tried to take some time off the clock. Up 50-48, the Lions couldn't hang onto the ball. Another turnover sent it back to Twin Rivers. They promptly worked the ball inside to center Jeremy Jackson. He attempted a shot over the 7'1" Woods. The future number one NBA draft pick blocked it. Getting his own rebound, Jackson went right back up. This time he made it. The game was tied at 50, and Cookson's crew sent a clear signal that any early symptoms of intimidation had clearly worn off. Jackson led Twin Rivers in scoring on the night with 22 points in a contest marked for its physical play. "We travel around the country and no game has been that rough," noted Cardinal Ritter coach Thomas. "I thought (Jackson) was Dick Butkus with some Air Jordans on."[326]

Once again, pressure by the Twin Rivers defense forced a turnover. Royals player Jason Cates found himself with the ball and one defender left to beat. He drove the lane, pulled up, and shot an 8-foot jumper. The only two points Cates made on the night came at a crucial time. It put Twin Rivers back on top for the first time since early in the second quarter. The Royals had the lead 52-50. Carroll Cookson was two minutes from his first final four since the 1975 Advance Hornets.

Cardinal Ritter scored on its next possession. The game was tied. A Matt Stahl baseline shot put Twin Rivers back in the lead. A Loren Woods bucket tied it once more. With just under a minute to go, it was 54-54. Twin Rivers would try to play for the last shot. Dribbling and passing near mid-court, the Royals played pitch and catch with the ball as time ticked off the clock. Carroll Cookson had no desire to stop the action and set up a play. It wasn't his style. "People might ask why didn't you call timeout? Well, the point is, I've watched too many games lost on in inbound play. I'd try to get my guys set up by standing up and telling them. They're supposed to know who is supposed to take that shot."

Twin Rivers forward Matt Stahl, who had scored the last bucket for the Royals, seemed to indicate he had designs on taking the final shot. Standing on the right side near the Twin Rivers bench, he began to make his move toward the bucket with less than 15 seconds left in the game. Chris Carrawell was the defender. He dominated the stat sheet for Cardinal Ritter, leading the team in scoring, rebounds, assists and blocked shots. He was the reason TCU coach Billy Tubbs was in the stands that night. He also led his team in steals. The future Duke All-American was about to get the biggest one of his high school career. Just as Stahl began to attempt a crossover dribble, Carrawell stole the ball. He raced to the other end of the floor and put up a shot. With three seconds left, Ritter had the lead 56-54. Twin Rivers had one last chance.

The inbound pass landed at half-court in the hands of Richard Simmers. Driving down the left side, he took just a few dribbles. Close to the place he earlier made a three-point shot, Simmers sent it skyward toward the bucket. The ball hit the front rim just as the final horn sounded. It bounced up and hit the backboard. It headed downward, not to the goal, but toward the floor. Several Twin Rivers players immediately collapsed on the court. For the first time all year, they felt the sting of defeat.

The game had ended and Cardinal Ritter was moving on to Columbia, where they would claim the state title. Cookson's Twin Rivers team was heading home. The coach had addressed high school athletes hundreds of times after games. He always found something to say, win or lose. But this time was different. He needed help and knew exactly who could provide it. Carroll Cookson's last request as a high school basketball coach was to his floor leader on his first state championship team. Cookson sought out Richie Walker. He had a favor to ask. Could the former Advance guard say something to his players? The emotional loss, the team's only one of the year, had drained the coach. He told Walker there was nothing he could say to them; they played their hearts out and still came up short. Now he wanted the glue of his '72 team to put the right touch to the end of the '95 season. Walker didn't know exactly what to say either, but he was not about to disappoint his former coach. He walked into the locker room, still thinking of the right words. Years later he recounted what happened next. His voice still choked with the emotion felt on that day. "I said, 'Guys, I want to thank you – because I just watched the greatest basketball game in my life. You're not going to the state championship and that makes me sad.'" With those words, Walker left the room. Carroll Cookson retired. The curtain closed on the greatest coaching tandem of brothers in Missouri high school basketball history.

***

Steve Cookson, Carroll's son, knew the transition to retirement would be difficult for his father and his uncle. The game of basketball had been a way of life for both of them for decades. Watching a high school basketball game from the bleachers wouldn't be easy. "It was several years before Ronnie went to a game," said his nephew.

At Scott Central, the warning signs that a transition to new coach may prove difficult were flashing even before Cookson left. His son recalls days at school when the coach wasn't around. "I know when dad would be gone to coaches' clinics, that place was just a madhouse.

People didn't go to class, people were fighting over basketballs, people were throwing basketballs at one another," said Jay. The breakdown in discipline extended beyond the basketball court. "I mean the whole school just turned into a madhouse. I thought when he leaves, it's going to be like this all the time."

David Heeb was a junior on Cookson's last team in 1995. He agrees with Jay's assessment. "That's the thing that people don't understand about Ronnie Cookson is that for 25 years, he was the straw that stirred the drink in the entire Scott County Central community. He kept discipline and order. He made everybody's job at that school easier because he had the pulse of the kids of that school."

During Heeb's senior year, Cookson stayed on as an assistant to the new coach. For players used to hanging on Cookson's every word, it was difficult to adjust. "He may say something and just out of habit you would listen to him more than you would the other guy. Not that the other guy wasn't a good coach. I mean – you've been trained on Cookson so many years."

Just as Jim Keeling discovered following Carroll Cookson at Advance in 1979, succeeding a legend is a difficult task. The first coach didn't last long at Scott Central. Neither did the second. In the first eight years following Cookson's departure, the basketball team didn't win a district tournament. Fewer players began going out for the sport. Fewer fans attended the games. "When Dad left, the gym emptied," said Jay.

Nothing demonstrates the dramatic change in fortunes more than one story that has circulated over the years in Scott Central circles. While the tale may be more legend than truth, it suggests something more than a coach was lost when Cookson departed. The story concerns one of his successors. During basketball season one day after practice, a player asked the coach for a ride home. The coach told him he would do it, but he expected gas money in return. The sense of commitment, the feelings of loyalty, the camaraderie and friendship that a coach developed with his players had all begun to crumble once Cookson left.

Another symbol of the stunning turnabout came at the Christmas Tournament in 2000. Scott Central lost to Chaffee. It marked the first time the Braves had lost a game to their conference rival since 1974. While the Chaffee basketball team always struggled to remain competitive, the school's marquee program had taken a striking turn for the worse. A former football coach had seen the view from the summit and then saw it all slip away.

***

As Mick Wessel walked into the Amick-Burnett funeral home in Chaffee on the night of June 28, 2004, his mind raced backwards to more than two decades before. He thought about a football game that always had meaning to him, but now had taken on a whole new level of importance. The game took place in 1983. The two players on his mind were running back Gary McLard and tight end Chris Payne.

In many ways, it seemed improbable that the two would be linked. Their backgrounds, personalities and talents could not have been more opposite. McLard, focused, intense, and blazing fast, lived in a foster home before being adopted by a Chaffee couple. Payne, son of the school's superintendent was laid back, rarely serious, and anything but speedy. What the tight end did possess was an ability to get open in the secondary and soft hands that almost never failed him. While the 6'1" Payne was taller and slower, McLard was stocky, muscular and physically mature beyond his years. He grew a full beard his sophomore season and opposing teams accused him of being older than his middle teenage years would suggest.

Their opposite styles produced similar results. In the fall of 1983, both players were honored with all-state status. One of the big reasons for the recognition was their performance in a game against Adrian, a town roughly sixty miles south of Kansas City. On a Saturday afternoon under bright skies on a muddy field, their efforts helped land the team in the game that its coaches and the town always dreamed of: the state championship.

The 1983 Chaffee Red Devils football team had an inauspicious debut. It lost two of its first three games. A victory over Grandview evened the record at 2-2. After that contest, an opposing team didn't score against Chaffee over the next five games. Terry Glenzy's defense proceeded to shutout opponents for 23 consecutive quarters. The streak was finally snapped in the final regular season game against St. Vincent's of Perryville, but Chaffee won the game 8-6 in large part to McLard's 193 rushing yards. The Red Devils finished the regular season at 8-2 and for the first time in four seasons had made its way to the playoffs. An opening round victory, an 18-0 shutout in front of the home crowd at

Mark Whitaker Field sent the Red Devils west to Adrian. The winner of the game would be headed to the Show-Me Bowl at Busch Stadium with a state championship trophy on the line.

Traveling some 350 miles and playing on a rain soaked field, Chaffee struggled for most the game. After an Adrian field goal with about nine minutes to go in the fourth quarter, Chaffee trailed 10-0. Adrian kicked off and Gary McLard was waiting. Standing on the 15-yard line, the ball bounced before it ever got to him. Teammate Eric Glastetter yelled at McLard to fall on it. Gary had other ideas. "Just go!" he said. McLard picked up the ball and started running. By the time he stopped, he was 85 yards down the field in the Adrian end zone. An extra point made the score 10-7. "That's the first kickoff or punt return for a touchdown we've had since I became head coach," Wessel said afterwards. [327]

After the kickoff, Adrian had the ball and clung to a three-point lead. On a third down play, their quarterback fumbled. Chaffee recovered on the Adrian 43-yard line. Making their way down field to just outside the 10-yard line, McLard received the handoff on three consecutive downs. The Red Devils were running out of plays and out of time. With fourth down and three yards to go, Chaffee called timeout with less than a minute left. "The big debate was whether to go for the field goal (and the tie) or go for it all," said Wessel. "The field down there was pretty messed up and it was a tough angle."[328]

Wessel made the call to go for it. Knowing Adrian would be keying on McLard's every move, Chaffee made the decision to use him as a decoy. On the snap, quarterback Kevin Uhrhan moved to his right and acted like he was going to hand it off. The play-action fake worked perfectly. Streaking to the other end of the end zone was a wide-open Chris Payne. Uhrhan turned back to his left and lofted the ball in the air. When it came down in Payne's hands, Red Devils fans erupted. The tight end's touchdown catch meant Chaffee had the lead for the first time all day. The extra point made the score 14-10. After the kickoff, Uhrhan intercepted an Adrian pass on the second play from the line of scrimmage. Chaffee ran out the clock and ran off the field knowing they were they headed to Busch Stadium.

Acting as informal assistant coach that season was former Red Devils player Tony Dalton. Five years after playing his last game at Mark Whitaker Field in the semi-finals of the state playoffs against Cass-

Midway, the all-state lineman had come home. Dalton spent four seasons playing football at Ole Miss. Wessel remembers watching his talented lineman run onto the field his freshman year in college. "Probably one of the biggest thrills as a coach is to see one of your kids playing in a major college football game. I'll never forget him running onto the field at Memphis State." For the first three seasons of Dalton's college career, he played on the defensive line. His senior season, he switched to offensive tackle. Wessel remembers what Ole Miss assistant coach Romeo Crennel told him about Dalton. "He said if Tony would have come in at Ole Miss as an offensive lineman, he would have been a number one draft pick." Crennel knows something about evaluating NFL Talent. In the fall of 2004, he was returning to his position as defensive coordinator of the defending Super Bowl champion New England Patriots.

After college, Dalton signed on as a free agent with the Denver Broncos. During training camp, he made up his mind the NFL lifestyle was not for him. "I remember him calling and saying, 'I'm coming home,'" remarked Wessel. "He said I'm not a holier than thou person but I don't want to live my lifestyle like this (with) drugs and alcohol." Dalton packed his bags and headed for Southeast Missouri. He tutored the young offensive and defensive lineman for the Red Devils. Now Dalton and the Chaffee team were headed to St. Louis to play in the state championship game, a contest that Tony and the rest of the class of 1979 thought they were destined to play in.

The championship game was scheduled for 9:00 a.m. on a Saturday morning. Chaffee's opponent was Norborne, a town some 60 miles east of Kansas City. The early morning schedule meant wake-up calls at 5:00 a.m. and a breakfast of cereal and dry toast. Playing in Busch Stadium in the state championship game, tight end Chris Payne walked onto the field before the game singing:

"There she was just a walking
Down the street singin'
Do wah diddy diddy dum diddy do
Snapping her fingers
And a shuffling her feet singin'
Do wah diddy diddy dum diddy do"

The Manfred Mann tune was made popular by one of his favorite movies, "Stripes." Payne and his teammates would battle many things that day: an early morning schedule, adjusting to Astroturf, and an opponent that had allowed only 58 points during the regular season. But any fears of being overly nervous were quickly dismissed by Payne's melodious antics.

Once the game kicked off, Chaffee again found itself trailing. A Norborne touchdown was later countered by a McLard end zone run. However, the Red Devils went for two points on the conversion and failed. Chaffee trailed by one point.

With less than two minutes to go in the game, Norborne had the ball and a 7-6 lead. Electing to play it conservatively, their offense ran three straight running plays. On fourth down, they decided to punt. Lining up to boot it away, the Norborne special teams unit forgot to block linebacker Eric Glastetter. Blitzing in from the left side, he blocked the punt attempt and a teammate recovered. Chaffee had the ball on the Norborne 32-yard line, 1:35 on the clock and no timeouts. On second down, Uhrhan called a pass play. Designed for the quarterback to drop straight back, a Norborne lineman penetrated the backfield and forced Uhrhan to scramble. He started running to his right. The defense pursued him. He kept running. And looking. And hoping. Nearing out of bounds, he saw someone wide open down the field waving his arms. It was Gary McLard. Uhrhan, soon to be a pitcher at the University of Missouri, let it fly. McLard caught the ball with his back to the end zone. Turning toward the goal, he ran over the last of the Norborne defenders and into the end zone. There were 49 seconds left on the clock. Identical to the game against Adrian, Chaffee staged a late and dramatic fourth quarter comeback and led for the first time all day. The extra point made the score 13-7. Another last second desperation pass ended with another Uhrhan interception. Game over. For the first time in school history, Chaffee was a football champion.

While players rejoiced on the field, Red Devils fans went wild in the stands, and two Chaffee alums celebrated in a coach's box above Busch Stadium. Tony Dalton and Sikeston coach Charlie Vickery spent the morning manning headphones and mapping strategy high above the turf. Five years after the bitter playoff loss in the fall of 1978, Chaffee claimed its first football title in coach Mick Wessel's sixth season as head coach.

No one knew it at the time but Chris Payne only had a little more than three years left to live after walking off the field that morning. Early in his college career, he noticed he had trouble sleeping because of pain in his body. Eventually, he went a doctor to have it examined. He checked into the Chaffee Hospital for tests. Local doctors sent him on to M.D. Anderson in Houston, Texas. Payne was dying from cancer. The end came in December of 1986. Home from college over the Christmas break, a few of his high school friends flew down to see him. Shortly before the visit, his condition rapidly deteriorated. When they saw him for the last time, Chris was unconscious. Tubes were jammed in his arms and up his nose. The body of the former all-state tight end had shriveled almost beyond recognition. It was now only a matter of time. The final heartbreaking reunion came only a few days before the final news. His friends, now back in Southeast Missouri, found out one night Chris had died. The message was delivered in the place where they had spent so many days growing up, at Houck Field House in Cape Girardeau during the Christmas Tournament. Chris Payne was twenty years old.

Nearly seventeen years later, coach Mick Wessel saw another one of his former players for the last time. More than two decades after Gary McLard celebrated a game winning catch in the end zone at Busch Stadium, Wessel looked down to see his running back and a football by his side. The thirty-seven year-old McLard was lying in a casket at the funeral home in downtown Chaffee. Driving out of town in the early morning hours just a few days before, he had lost control of his car while going over a viaduct. The car flipped over, ejecting its driver. McLard broke his neck and was killed instantly. His body was discovered a few hours later.

On the night of McLard's funeral, the family had asked Wessel to speak at the service. The experience had been an emotional one from its beginning. When the former football coach walked in during an earlier visitation period, a photo of McLard was on display. It was a picture of him from high school wearing his football uniform. Later that same night, during the funeral service, was when Wessel saw the body of McLard with a football inside the casket. Standing up to speak, the coach inevitably thought of the sport that had united him with the player, the game that linked McLard and Payne, and the fate that both had now met. "Those plays are still visible in my mind. I can just close my eyes and still see those two kids, two super kids," said Wessel. "That's a tough cookie to swallow." The two players who scored touchdowns in the game that made the state championship possible were the first two players from the team to die; combined they only lived fifty-seven years.

What McLard and Payne and the rest of their teammates had accomplished was more than win some football games. Their performances had rallied a community. "I had one fan lean over to me and say if you die now and went to heaven you'd be disappointed," said Booster Club President Bill Hagan after the miracle rally at Busch Stadium, "because you'd already been there."[329] By one estimate, 1,500 Chaffee fans, or about half the town, witnessed the game. Many will always remember the sign that someone posted on the way out of Chaffee that weekend. It read, "Will the last one out of town please turn out the lights?"

The Chaffee football team had a few more winning seasons in the '80's, but never made it to the playoffs again. The Red Devils last winning team was 1990. The next season, Chaffee won three games, then two the following year. Single victory seasons soon became common with many years the team not winning a game at all. Wessel left the coaching ranks and retired from teaching by the middle of the decade. He could see the downfall unfolding not long after the championship season. "I remember the amount of time kids put in the weight room and then it just started slipping there in the mid-eighties." Even more important than the attitude of the players, Wessel believes, was the lackadaisical approach exhibited by their parents. "I can remember a parent telling me they didn't understand why their kid had to be at every football practice." After Wessel departed, the program continued to deteriorate. A lack of dedication was accompanied by a lack of discipline. One afternoon during practice, a coach yelled at a player. The player shot back, "You know what your problem is coach? You just need to get laid." With the team struggling year after year, people in Chaffee even began discussing what would have been at one time unthinkable in a town that once lived for football Friday nights. Maybe it was time to abandon the sport and shutdown the program completely.

***

Generational lament is common. Older generations always think they had it harder, that today's kids aren't as disciplined or as focused, that things were somehow better "back in the day," regardless of when that day occurred. Arnold Ryan's players used that line of thinking when they defended their coach's behavior and accomplishments after leaving Puxico. "The type of kids changed. It went from the Accepting Generation to the Questioning Generation," former Puxico player Frank Hoggard told writer Matt Chaney. "Kids came to have things we didn't have in high school, like cars and television. He had to mellow and put up with a lot."[330] The same things are said today about Ronnie Cookson. "It's a whole different era. Ronnie knows that. That's why Ronnie got out," said Jeff Limbaugh, part of the Scott Central class of 1980. "Ronnie knows because it was slowly fading. All it was going to do was drive him to his grave really because he was not going to be able to control it, because of the way the kids acted and reacted. It kept getting worse and worse and worse. There's a bunch of variables involved: Nintendo video games, sports cars, computers, everything. We didn't have it. We had a key to the gym, our tennis shoes and a basketball."

Today's generation of athletes *is* different (it always is). But different doesn't always mean worse. The quickness, agility and jumping ability of today's athlete are readily apparent to anyone who watches the games. Terry Wills grew up playing basketball in Advance for Ronnie and Carroll Cookson. "Everybody says, they're not as good as we were – that's not true. They can step out there about half court and they can shoot and they can jump out of the gym, they're quick. So far as people going they're not as good as I was – no – they're better."

One other thing is obvious when comparing today's generation to athletes of yesterday. They're bigger and more muscular. Weightlifting has changed athletes and the way the game of basketball is played. Limbaugh joked about the weight-training regimen during his days at Scott Central. "We had some weights one time out on the gym floor and a couple of us stumbled over them and hurt ourselves so we took them and put them away." Those days are long gone. David Heeb admits that when given a choice between more shooting or more weight training, he'll choose the weights. "We lift through season. We lift on game days because if you don't, you're going to get passed up," said the Bell City coach. "In today's high school game, the stronger team wins most of the time. You're better off spending time in the weight room than you are shooting a basketball, the way they let you play now."

One of the biggest hurdles when dealing with the younger generation is always the culture that surrounds them. In an age of multi-million dollar shoe contracts, high school players going directly to the NBA, and nightly highlight reels on ESPN showering attention on superstars, the individual is celebrated and worshiped. A team game is difficult to teach in an age when even the U.S. military uses the recruiting slogan, "An Army of One." Former Scott Central player Melvin Porter is one who has noticed the transformation. "Everything (used to be) about winning. It wasn't about me. That's where these kids are now. It's about me."

***

When Porter got out of college, he ran into one of his former high school teachers. Knowing the recent graduate was looking for work, the teacher asked him what was more important – doing what he wanted to do or making money? Porter knew the answer immediately. "I said making money. I am broke." He took a job with Procter and Gamble at their plant north of Cape Girardeau. For the next several years, life unfolded exactly as Porter wanted. He was a married man, raising a family, with a steady income. "Sure enough, for the first ten or twelve years life was about making money." But as he and his wife raised their five boys, his priorities began to change. In the summertime, Porter would coach his sons in organized basketball leagues. When his third son was in the fifth grade, Melvin coached an all-star team from Cape that played in a tournament in Columbia. After the first day of action, Porter's team received the second place seed. The number one ranked team had beaten Porter's club earlier in the day. The two teams would most likely meet in a rematch the next day for the tournament championship. He started inquiring about his opponent. "I got to asking one of the other coaches up there if he had ever heard of the St. Louis Jets," said Porter who remembers the reply. "Oh yeah, they're awesome. They haven't been beat in two or three years."

The second day unfolded as the tournaments seeds predicted. Porter's team from Cape Girardeau faced the St. Louis Jets in the championship game. The coach decided a change in tactics was necessary if the outcome was to be different from the previous day. "We're not going to guard anybody except their two great players," he told his team. "One of them scored 25 points against us and the other one scored 30. I said we're gonna double up on those two players and we're not going to guard anybody else. If the other three kids beat us, they beat us." The strategy paid off. "We ended up winning the championship up there and it was just a blast. It was so much fun."

Driving home from Columbia was when Porter broke the news to his wife. "In the next year or two, I will be coaching somewhere," he told her. When the coaching position at Scott County Central opened up in the spring of 2002, he placed a call. "When the job came open and I called Ronnie (Cookson) and said I'm 100% interested." Cookson, sitting on the school board at Scott Central and knowing Porter had a good job, had one question. "He said. 'Are you crazy?' Yeah, I guess you may call it that, but I'm gonna coach if I get the chance."

He got his chance. "They interviewed me and offered me the job and I said I'm going to take it." There was one final issue – the matter of salary. "After the interview, they said, you hadn't asked about what we pay. I said I know it won't be very much, but I want to coach," said Porter. "I'll be doing what I love, working with kids and seeing these kids develop. I think that's a greater reward than money. I really believe that." Even so, the low salary was still a shock for the 15-year Procter and Gamble veteran. "When they told me, my mouth just dropped. I couldn't believe it." He started coaching at his high school alma mater in the fall of 2002.

Porter quickly realized how things had changed since the days his team raced to back-to-back state championships in 1979 and 1980. Gone are the days of unsupervised practice. "There's been a couple of times that I may leave, tell the kids that I'm going to pick up somebody or something. I'll get back and the principal will say, 'you can't be doing that. It's a liability,'" said Porter. "It's just kind of shocking. So now, when I leave the gym, everybody has to leave the gym."

He also noticed how the style of play has changed from an earlier run and gun era. "The kids here that I've been coaching, they would rather come down and setup and run a set play instead of getting the ball out and running it." Porter picked up on a trend that others have commented on; the organization man has become the organization kid. If it's not set by an appointment, scheduled by an adult, or sanctioned by an official league, it simply doesn't happen. Impromptu and spontaneity have been lost. "These kids, the majority of them, when basketball season is over, they don't pick up another basketball until the beginning of the season next year."

Early in his second season, Porter admitted he was struggling. His brother-in-law, Larry Mosley, had gotten sick, and the burden of coaching teams from the grade school to the high school had all fallen on Porter's shoulders. His high school team was 5-9 and had lost six games in a row. He went into his former coach. "I could use some help," Porter told Cookson. "A lot of times, it's just having that person there to talk to, to get his opinion, it just goes so far." Cookson became his assistant in January. He sat on the bench with Porter at games, attended practice sessions, and gave his former all-state player advice. "He told me once you do something, do it, stick with it, and however it ends up, it ends up. As time goes, as you get more and more experience, you'll figure it out."

After Cookson got involved, Scott Central won 11 of its next 14 games. The Braves won their district title. Their opponent in the first round of state play was Bell City. Melvin Porter, in his second season at Scott Central, looked down at the other bench and hoped to see a glimpse of his future. David Heeb won a state title in his second year at Bell City. Now in his fourth season, Heeb was after his second. On the night of March 9, 2004, the two men and their teams met. The winner was three games away from realizing his dream.

***

Probably most of the players and many of the fans didn't know it that night, but Bootheel history and its basketball legacy were on display at the sold out Sikeston gym. David Heeb's grandfather from Chaffee sat in the stands. He drove down to the game with lifelong Scott County resident Bob Kielhofner. Kielhofner's parents sold the family hardware store in Chaffee to Harlan Whitaker in 1952. Whitaker's Hardware is still in business, one of the few merchants in downtown Chaffee to survive the economic swings of the past few decades. Ronnie Whitaker, Harlan's son and current owner, sat just a few rows behind Kielhofner and Heeb. Underneath the goal at one end, Steve Cookson watched the game between Bell City and Scott Central. Cookson, the former Advance star, the son of Carroll and nephew of Ronnie, drove up from Naylor, where he was the school's superintendent. Across from the Scott Central bench, another former Advance star took in the action. Terry Wills, who played his junior high ball for Ronnie and was a junior the year Carroll won his first state title, had gone on to teach at Scott County Central. Keeping one eye on the crowd and the other one on the court, Fred

Johnson floated around the gym. The former Oran star player, who did his student teaching at Scott Central and would drive to Haywood City to get Otto Porter for games of pickup basketball, worked at Sikeston High School and used to coach the Bulldogs basketball team. Brad Cookson, Ronnie's youngest son, showed up that night as well. He was impressed by the size of the crowd. "There was more Scott Central people there than I had seen since '91."

The connections didn't stop there. Out on the court, guard Dominatrix Johnson started for Bell City. While the senior season ended his high school basketball career in a Cubs uniform, it began in the orange and black of Scott Central. He switched schools after his freshman season. David Heeb had known Johnson for years, first coaching him in baseball nearly a decade ago. "He was all-star baseball player as a kid," said Heeb. "I actually thought he could be a better baseball player because he's a left-handed pitcher. Those are hard to find."

The Johnson family ties are deep in the Scott Central community. Both his parents attended the school and played basketball for the Braves. Melvin Johnson, Dom's father, was an all-state performer in 1981. That Scott Central team lost in the first round of the state tournament that year and former assistant coach Ron Cook thinks he knows why. "We probably could have won had Melvin Johnson not sprained his ankle." Johnson had sprained the ankle in the district championship and did not play the next game. The Braves lost to North Pemiscot, the team that went on to claim a state championship.

More than two decades later, when Melvin and his family relocated to Bell City, Braves fans howled in protest and claimed Dom had been recruited. Nothing was ever proven. Heeb defended the decision by the Johnsons. "You just have to know the family. If they would have just moved one kid, I could have seen what everybody was fussing about. When their whole family picks up and moves," said the Bell City coach, "you know you're doing the right thing. They moved for the right reasons."

The acrimony reached a point where Melvin Johnson found it necessary to clarify his actions. He called an area sportswriter to tell his side of the story and explain the family's decision. It had nothing to do with athletics, he told Marty Mishow of the *Southeast Missourian*, and everything to do with academics. His son was struggling in the classroom, and he thought a move to Bell City would give his child a boost. He also told Mishow no one from Bell City approached him regarding the possible transfer of Dom and said the move was an unpopular one in his household. "I caught flak from my whole family. No one wanted to move except me," Melvin explained. "The reason I wanted to tell somebody this is I just want people to leave him alone."[331]

Left alone on a basketball court, the 6'0" guard was a difference maker in the Bell City lineup. Johnson started for the basketball team his sophomore season. The Cubs promptly won the state title. Now a senior, he was a big reason why Heeb's team entered the game against Scott Central with a 25-4 record. The lefthander was quick, could pass and handle the ball, and possessed a nice shooting touch. With former Scott Central player Johnson on the court and Scott Central graduate David Heeb on the sidelines, Bell City played the type of basketball Braves fans could appreciate. "We're going to run at you, we're going to keep it simple, we're going to go to the boards. On defense, we're going to pressure you," said Heeb who added that 90% of the Bell City style comes from Cookson's influence. "I would say the only big difference from what they did and what we do is that we play a lot more man to man. He was a lot more zone and zone press."

Heeb took the job at Bell City right out of college. Early in his career, night after night, he would show up at Ronnie Cookson's house and talk basketball with his mentor. Living next door, Jay Cookson would see Heeb's vehicle parked in the driveway. "Dave would come over and they would stay up to midnight five nights in a row."

During Bell City's state championship run in Heeb's second season, the retired Cookson played a role. After Bell City won the district title, Cookson asked Heeb if he needed any help scouting upcoming opponents. Heeb quickly accepted the offer. "We went and scouted my next game together against Delta C-7. We drove down and scouted the game together. On the way home, he told me what he thought," remembers the coach. "Then when we played that game Monday night in Sikeston he drove all the way over to Poplar Bluff and scouted the next game for me and called me at midnight that night and told me this is what you need to do. He was absolutely right again. He really helped me a lot."

If Heeb needed any additional confirmation that his choice of mentor was the right one, it came one summer during a coaching clinic. One of the lecturers at the clinic was Charlie Spoonhour. The college basketball coach began telling the attendees about a certain coach and a particular program. Heeb could only smile. The coach was Ronnie Cookson and the program was Scott County Central.

The program that Cookson dominated for a quarter century had finally made another appearance at the state tournament. It took nine years and three coaches, but the Braves were back. Their journey didn't last long. Led by Dominatrix Johnson's 23 points, Bell City pulled away in the final quarter to defeat Scott Central 59-54. Heeb called it a "bittersweet" victory. "I love those kids on the other side so much," he said. "It's like having to go fight one of your family members. There's just no nice way to do it."[332]

After the game, both coaches talked about the impact Cookson has had on them. In the Bell City locker room, the celebration was low-key. "That's the Ronnie Cookson influence. He told us, 'Act like you've been there before,'" Heeb said.[333]

Porter knew he couldn't have made it this far without the assistance of his former coach. "I just appreciate his help. He has so much knowledge about the game. Anybody that would ever turn that knowledge down is just crazy."[334]

With Scott Central's season over, Cookson once again offered his assistance to the Bell City coach. Heeb was familiar with their opponent in the quarterfinals and told Cookson the biggest help he could give him was to provide a scouting report on his own team. "I asked him what did you do to us? What was your strategy? He kind of gave me some insight into my own team that helped me tell my own kids this is how everybody else might play us," said Heeb. "To get it from him, that's the best book out there, the book that Cookson has got on you."

Playing defending state champion Verona in the quarterfinals, Johnson scored 28 points and Bell City won by 27. "I thought our depth hurt them a lot," Heeb said after the game. "Our conditioning hurt them a lot. I thought they wore down."[335] Heeb's team was on its way to the Hearnes Center and the final four. With a new arena opening on the campus of the University of Missouri in the fall of 2004, these would be the last basketball games played on its court. The Missouri Tigers had already closed out their home schedule.

Bell City's depth was again a factor in the semi-final game against

Bevier. Heeb's team used 10 different players on their way to a convincing 30 point victory. Commenting on Bell City's deep bench, opposing coach Randy Julius said, "It's not just hard, it's a little demoralizing." Johnson again led Bell City in scoring with 22 points. But he saved his best for last.

In the state championship game against St. Elizabeth, the senior guard poured in 40 points as Bell City won the game 74-62. It was the seventh time that season that Johnson had topped the 40-point mark. Less than a week later, the all-state player who averaged almost 30 points his final season announced his college choice. Like so many other Bootheel basketball stars over the years, Johnson would begin his career at Three Rivers, playing junior college ball for Gene Bess.

Closing out high school basketball at the arena in Columbia, David Heeb's team delivered Cookson Clan connections in spades. Heeb, who played on Ronnie Cookson's last team, coached the final game at the Hearnes Center with a star player, Dominatrix Johnson, who began his career at Scott Central. Johnson's father, Melvin, was a junior for the Braves in 1980 when Cookson's team defeated Joe Kleine and Slater by 42 points on the Hearnes Center floor. And when the Hearnes Center opened, Carroll Cookson's Advance Hornets took part in the first high school game played on the court when they defeated Mound City in the semi-finals in 1973. A Cookson team opened it and a Cookson protégé closed it down.

After four years of coaching, Heeb had two state championships. It took both Carroll and Ronnie nine years to get that many. In the four years before he arrived at Bell City, the team went 35-62.[336] He accomplished the turnaround with a coaching style and philosophy that can trace its roots to Arnold Ryan's Puxico teams of the 1950's and perfected by two brothers and Puxico natives starting in the 1960's. That lineage and Heeb's success don't go unnoticed by the Cookson Clan. "He's keeping what dad did alive," said Jay Cookson.

What Jay's dad has accomplished will be difficult for Heeb or any young high school coach in Missouri to match. Twelve state championships during an eighteen year period and a career winning percentage of almost 83% are the benchmarks and 36 players that went on to perform in the collegiate ranks are his lasting legacy. "Ronnie Cookson was destiny's man," said former Advance Superintendent Bill Bradshaw, now retired and living in Cape Girardeau. "He was at the right school, at the right time, with the right philosophy. Everything worked out perfect for him. I'm not saying he couldn't have done the same thing at Cape Central or at Sikeston. I'm just saying he was the right everything. As far as basketball is concerned, he's a legend. I don't think anybody could duplicate the success he's had."

Steve Cookson agrees. "I really feel coaches like Arnold Ryan, my dad, Ronnie, Lennies McFerren, those type of coaches that were just totally consumed and were very passionate during the game, I think that today's society would not allow them to be successful as what they were." Cookson is a former high school coach himself who has since moved into administration. Like others, he believes changes in societal attitudes are the biggest impediments to the all consuming approach as practiced by his father and uncle. "There's just a different mind set today, it's a totally different world. They were only able to get by with it in their last years because of their reputation and what they brought with them from the past. I can't envision that anymore." He then laid out his reasons. "Parents are much less trusting and more involved with the coaching and their kids. More accusatory, more litigious, students and parents are both more spoiled today." He cited one more vital factor. "Probably what made them successful back in those times was there was something more important than you getting your way - that was the team."

Even with all that, Steve knows there will always be the temptation for both his father, now retired and living and Puxico, and Ronnie, still living in Morley, to return to the game of the basketball. He is both pragmatic and philosophical in his advice. "I counsel them both to just stay away. Go watch a game if you want to," said Cookson. "(But) it's not the same as the way you all could do and can remember and it never will be again.

"When it's all said and done, you do what you're doing, you record it, remember it, move on. None of us knows what lays ahead for us – we hope it's good things."

EPILOGUE

In late December 2004, an earthquake off the coast of Southeast Asia triggered a tsunami of almost incomprehensible proportion. The 9.0 magnitude quake sparked enormous and deadly tidal waves responsible for killing more than 100,000 people with the body count escalating on a daily basis. As aid poured in from around the world, people in this country began asking the inevitable question: could it happen here? Writing on the op-ed pages of *The New York Times*, Dennis Smith shattered a myth and served up a history lesson.

> **"Americans believe that earthquakes are a West Coast problem. But the largest earthquake ever in the United States we know of, probably at least as large as the one that destroyed most of San Francisco in 1906, occurred in the area of the Mississippi Valley in 1811. Boats were thrown over in the river and people drowned. Whole islands simply disappeared. This earthquake, and its aftershocks a year later, were so destructive that Congress passed the first federal relief act in 1815 to support the farmers whose previously healthy and farmable land was turned to swamp, sand and mud."[337]**

The 1811 and 1812 earthquakes, centered in the Missouri Bootheel along the New Madrid Fault, could serve as a metaphor for the career of one of the nation's most successful high school coaches from the same part of the country. Both featured record setting performances, a long lasting legacy, and are little known today outside the region. But for those who appreciate geologic history or know the coach will not soon forget the events of the former or the contributions of the latter.

***

One year after he gave up his head coaching duties, Ronnie Cookson retired from teaching at Scott Central. He took a job at an agricultural company in Grant City, along Highway 61 between Morley and Sikeston. His boss was one of his former players, Jeff Limbaugh, the point guard for his 1979 and 1980 state champion teams. The two men frequently talk basketball, and when they do, invariably the topic of Ronnie's best club is debated. The coach, understandably, hedges when discussing which team was the greatest. To do so would make one state championship team happy, but leave eleven other squads wondering why their coach found them wanting. Limbaugh has no such reservations.

"When we got nothing to do, we usually talk basketball," admitted Limbaugh. He talked about two teams that are most often compared to the one he played on. "I seen Marcus Timmons and them play a bunch. They was salty," he said, referring to the Braves teams in the late 1980's and early 1990's. He also mentioned Cookson's first state championship team from 1976. "We used to play them every day. At least three of them were there every day. So I know how good Otto Porter and Ricky Thomas was. They was salty." But the saltiest of all, Limbaugh believes, was the 1980 Scott Central Braves. "We just got done beating a team with a seven footer by forty points. Marcus and them would have hard a time beating us if we could have put us both in our prime. Otto and them would have had a hard time beating us. Even as we progressed – our junior year, their team had a hard time beating us (playing over Christmas break) as we practiced with them every day."

Talk to almost anyone who saw Cookson's teams play over the years, and those three eras of Braves basketball are the ones mentioned most. Many outsiders share Limbaugh's opinion. Joe Bradshaw played against Scott Central first at Chaffee and then at Advance. Now a schoolteacher at Cape Central, the 1980 edition of Ronnie Cookson's club will always standout to him. "I happen to think that Scott County basketball team is the best basketball team I've ever seen," commented Bradshaw. "That doesn't mean now, on television, you'll see teams in various places because of their size or whatever, but that team never shot anything but a lay-up. They had marvelous passing skills, marvelous ball handling skills. They weren't very deep but they run up and down the court. They knew each other so unbelievably well. You had two floor leaders out there in Limbaugh and Melvin Porter."

Mike Marsh has followed the exploits of Braves basketball since the late 1970's, first as a sports reporter and then as a teacher at Scott County Central. He saw every Cookson championship team play except the first one. He shares Bradshaw's and Limbaugh's opinion. "That was the best team I've ever seen. You would see a guy get a rebound, kick the ball out over to another guy for a lay-up and the other team wouldn't even know what hit them," Marsh said in reference to the team that went 32-1. "I heard that bunch over at Puxico back in the 50's was like that."

As the son of Carroll and the nephew to Ronnie, Steve Cookson has played and seen a lot of high school basketball over the years. The 1980 Braves made a vivid impression. "They were just phenomenal," said Cookson, who played on a state championship team for his father in 1975. "They knew where each other were. They pressed, they could just overwhelm other teams."

As one might expect, Braves players from other eras beg to disagree. To Otto Porter, the first state championship team was the best state championship team. "The other guys, they can say their state championship was good, it was nice, but the school's first - it was the best. No doubt about it."

In the summer of 2004, Porter was preparing to move from Cape Girardeau to Morley. He has a son in grade school the same age as one of Melvin's boys. Otto wants his son to play basketball the same place he did. While it will be a few years before these players begin to make their mark, another one of Melvin's sons is already playing varsity basketball. The next generation of Porters has arrived at Scott County Central.

***

Fifteen miles to the north in Scott County, Wade Sanders thoughts have also turned to the next generation of basketball players. More than two decades after graduating high school, he decided to switch careers. He went back to college. Like Melvin Porter, he made the decision that he wanted to coach high school basketball. He'll have his degree in the spring of 2005. Wherever he ends up, Sanders wants to stay awhile. "I'd like to have winning seasons, but I'd like to stay somewhere and build up a program and a reputation for myself as a good, fair coach rather than win at all costs."

Sanders knows he'll be a lot older than a lot of coaches getting their start. He thinks that will work to his advantage. "Part of the problem that some of these young coaches have is that they want to be buddies with their kids, you know. It will be easier for me because I'll be 45 years old, and I'm not going to be your buddy to a 17 year old. I'll treat you with respect and you'll treat me with respect or you're not going to play."

The words respect and discipline pop up frequently when Sanders talks about coaching. His philosophy sounds like one which players under Ronnie Cookson would recognize. "Rule number one, if you get a foul, you're going to keep your mouth shut and you're going to lift that right hand."

Sanders played his last high school game in 1980. Long after the knee injury cut short any plans of playing in college he still is recognized for his all-state basketball talent. One Friday night, at the football field in Chaffee, he sat in the stands before game. One of the referees walked over to where he was sitting. He introduced himself and said he wanted to thank Wade for all the great basketball memories he provided. The official was Ron Whittier, one of the referees that day in the Bloomfield gym in 1979 when Chaffee came up just short against Scott Central in the first round of the state tournament.

***

Cookson's team went on to the win the state title that season. It was the coach's and the school's second basketball championship. Ten more would follow to make an even dozen, a Missouri high school record. By the early 1990's, he was not only a recognized face in the Bootheel, but known by basketball fans and coaches across the state. While he always ready to supply the media with a quote, he wasn't always necessarily comfortable in the spotlight. An amateur sociologist and his two sons provide the insight.

Writing in the *Atlantic Monthly* a few years ago, David Brooks attempted to explain the difference between "Blue" and "Red" America, the colors synonymous with Gore and Bush voters in the close and controversial presidential election of 2000.[338] Brooks spent time in a Washington D.C. suburb (Gore Blue) and a small Pennsylvania town (Bush Red). Brooks concluded the difference between the two camps wasn't primarily money, morality or level of education, but rather the sense of self. Gore voters saw themselves as exceptional, above-average, wanting to stand out from the crowd. Contrastingly, Bush voters wanted nothing more than to fit in; normal and average were considered compliments. Someone who desired to standout was someone who couldn't be trusted. Life for Gore voters revolved around work and career aspirations. Life for Bush voters focused on family and the community. Ronnie Cookson is comfortable in Red America. That's not a political judgment (I don't know what his politics are), but instead a statement about his conduct.

The idea of not wanting to show-off or standout came to mind after Jay and Brad Cookson related a story about their father. Three and a half hours of conversation with the two brothers can give one tremendous insight into the behavior and personality of a father and coach. The revealing incident took place during a state tournament in the early 1990's at the Hearnes Center in Columbia. Jay was watching a basketball game with his dad. State officials had roped off special reserved seating for coaches close to the floor. It was opportunity for the coaching fraternity to mix and mingle, to see and be seen. Ronnie Cookson wanted no part of it. Instead he and Jay walked to the very top of the Hearnes building, away from the other coaches, away from the noise, away from everything. Father and son watched the game alone. When I asked why he did this, both Jay and Brad mentioned the same thing: embarrassment

"I think he was embarrassed because he was good," said Jay. Humility always served Cookson and his teams well. "We don't think we're better than anyone else down here and that's because we're just country," Cookson once told a reporter. "We know that everyone puts their britches on one leg at a time and that's something we have to realize."[339] Cookson transmitted those humble attitudes to his players. "Now even more, I don't like hotdogs," said Mike Marsh. "(Cookson's teams) did not hot dog, they did not trash talk, they just kicked your tail."

According to son Brad, there's another source of embarrassment for the coach. "I think he was embarrassed because he really didn't know the X's and O's. North Carolina is running this kind of offense and UNLV is doing this – he would have no clue as to what you're talking about." The X's and O's of the game, a particular type of play on offense or a certain style of defense, are almost never mentioned by Cookson when discussing his success. There is one word, however, that is always mentioned. "Cookson says work was the key to 1-A title."[340] The headline appeared after Scott Central's first state championship in 1976. Nearly two decades and another eleven titles later, the coach was preaching much the same message. "There's a fine line that separates winning and losing and I'm not sure why I've had the success in a lot of things I've had. I just believe that hard work will lead to success," he said in 1994.[341] At the time he made that statement, Cookson was farming 350 acres, operating a domestic rabbit farm, selling seed corn and de-tasseling corn in the summer in addition to his duties as teacher, coach and athletic director. "I just like to challenge myself."[342]

One example of work ethic trumping strategy involves the vaunted Scott Central press. Everyone knew that it was devastatingly effective, but no one could exactly describe it, including the coach. "He was invited to come to coaching clinics everywhere. He'll tell you about it and laugh about it to this day," remembers Jeff Limbaugh. "'What was the press Mr. Cookson?' they would ask, 300 coaches in an auditorium. And he couldn't tell them. We never practiced it. All it was," said Limbaugh, "was a press."

Cookson never had to articulate the press to his players. That's because day after day, week after week, year after year, they practiced it for hours in the gym. It became habit. Habit became instinct. "We're creatures of repetition," said Richie Walker who played on Ronnie Cookson's first seventh grade team in Advance. "If you want two people to dance, they practice so that they don't have to think about what they are doing. Basketball is a game in the same fashion. You practice it so that when you're out there – you're not thinking about it, you're doing it. If you have to physically think about it, then you're not doing it. You get that way through practicing, through repetition. That's the only way."

Hard work and long practices were the only ways that Cookson knew. As the victories and the titles mounted, he talked of how he relished the pressure. But after his career was over, he admitted that was the one thing he didn't miss at all.[343] "I don't miss the pressure," he said. "I tried to be perfect."

That drive for perfection resulted in a basketball utopia in the unlikeliest of places, a tiny rural school district in the Bootheel of Missouri, surrounded by some of the deepest pockets of poverty anywhere in America. But Cookson and his teams never focused on the obstacles, only on the achievements. It was an atmosphere his players appreciated long after departing Scott County Central. After graduating in 1987,

Terry Bell continued playing basketball. But ultimately, he walked away from the college game. One of his teammates remembers asking him why he left. "He said it wasn't any fun because you're not playing for that pride anymore, for your school, for your community," said Jay Cookson. "We were a family."

APPENDICES

Appendix 1 – Cookson's Career Record

Cookson and Scott County Central
1971-1995

*Year	Wins	Losses
1971	21	8
1972	17	9
1973	20	8
1974	10	15
1975	23	6
*1976	32	1
1977	10	15
1978	20	7
*1979	30	3
*1980	32	1
1981	24	4
1982	16	8
*1983	30	3
1984	29	2
*1985	33	1
*1986	28	6
*1987	28	5
*1988	34	0
*1989	31	2
*1990	32	1
*1991	33	0
1992	24	6
*1993	27	6
1994	27	7
1995	23	7
Totals	634	131

*Indicates State Championship Season

*Based on Newspaper Accounts, Scott Central Records, and the book
"From the Beginning…The History of Missouri High School
Basketball Championships."*

Appendix 2 – Scott County Central's Run to the Titles

1976

Round	Opponent	Score	
Sectional	Delta	79	57
Quarterfinals	Wright City	80	54
Semifinals	Drexel	91	48
Finals	Glasgow	82	71

(Hearnes Center - Columbia)
Record – 32-1

1979

Round	Opponent	Score	
Sectional	Chaffee	71	68
Quarterfinals	Clopton	102	69
Semifinals	Harrisburg	92	60
Finals	Sparta	75	51

(Hearnes Center - Columbia)
Record – 30-3

1980

Round	Opponent	Score	
Sectional	North Pemiscot	97	74
Quarterfinals	Bismarck	85	44
Semifinals	Wellsville	86	63
Finals	Slater	94	52

(Hearnes Center - Columbia)
Record – 32-1

1983

Round	Opponent	Score	
Sectional	Emminence	66	40
Quarterfinals	Sparta	78	59
Semifinals	Walnut Grove	49	47
Finals	Clopton	89	71

(Hammons Center - Springfield)
Record – 30-3

1985

Round	Opponent	Score	
Sectional	Van Buren	67	46
Quarterfinals	Purdy	95	59
Semifinals	Clopton	74	49
Finals	Northeast Nodaway	73	58

(Hammons Center - Springfield)
Record – 33-1

1986*

Round	Opponent	Score	
Regional	Delta C-7	69	40
Sectional	South Iron	90	71
Quarterfinals	Wheaton	84	54
Semifinals	Lockwood	74	44
Finals	Wellsville	84	76 (3 OT)

(Hammons Center - Springfield)
Record – 28-6
*State playoffs expanded from 16 to 32 teams

1987

Round	Opponent	Score	
Regional	North Pemiscot	74	54
Sectional	Van Buren	61	58
Quarterfinals	Sparta	81	69
Semifinals	King City	89	43
Finals	Wellsville	85	69

(Hammons Center - Springfield)
Record – 28-5

1988

Round	Opponent	Score	
Regional	North Pemiscot	71	31
Sectional	Ellington	83	54
Quarterfinals	Clever	78	66
Semifinals	Harrisburg	87	52
Finals	Walnut Grove	78	53

(Hammons Center - Springfield)
Record – 34-0
*Three point play introduced in Missouri high school basketball

1989

Round	Opponent	Score	
Regional	Delta C-7	78	49
Sectional	Meadow Heights	85	36
Quarterfinals	Clever	63	58 OT
Semifinals	Greenfield	72	33
Finals	Clopton	63	53

(Hammons Center - Springfield)
Record – 31-2

1990

Round	Opponent	Score	
Regional	North Pemiscot	77	50
Sectional	Winona	99	63
Quarterfinals	Clever	65	36
Semifinals	Pattonsburg	100	42
Finals	New Franklin	71	45

(Hammons Center - Springfield)
Record – 32-1

1991

Round	Opponent	Score	
Regional	North Pemiscot	80	33
Sectional	Ellington	56	50
Quarterfinals	Macks Creek	100	73
Semifinals	New Bloomfield	92	49
Finals	Greenwood	56	48

(Hammons Center - Springfield)
Record – 33-0

1993

Round	Opponent	Score	
Regional	Gideon	58	57
Sectional	Van Buren	66	38
Quarterfinals	Macks Creek	63	61
Semifinals	Tarkio	86	63
Finals	Green City	72	51

(Hearnes Center - Columbia)
Record – 27-6

All state championships are 1A titles
with the exception of 1980 - 2A.

Avg. Points Scored* – 78.5
Avg. Margin of Victory – 24.4

Other State Tournament Appearances
1971 – Sectionals
1981 – Sectionals
1984 – Quarterfinals
1992 – Sectionals
1994 – Second Place
1995 – Sectionals

Appendix 3 – 1980 Scott County Central Braves (32-1) Missouri State Champions

Game Number	Team	Scott Central	Opponent	Setting
1	Matthews	95	42	Oran Tournament
2	Oran	101	78	Oran Tournament
3	Bell City	99	63	Oran Tournament
4	Puxico	93	61	Regular Season
5	Delta	94	46	Regular Season
6	Oak Ridge	96	52	Regular Season
7	Advance	109	84	Regular Season
8	Oak Ridge	94	41	Christmas Tournament
9	Kelly	98	71	Christmas Tournament
10	Clearwater	72	63	Christmas Tournament
11	Cape Central	66	62	Christmas Tournament
12	Notre Dame	99	67	Regular Season
13	Illmo-Scott City	106	57	Regular Season
14	Lilbourn	95	74	Regular Season
15	Oran	102	72	Conference Tournament
16	Illmo-Scott City	97	53	Conference Tournament
17	Kelly	104	67	Conference Tournament
18	East Prairie	100	62	Regular Season
19	Chaffee	86	57	Regular Season
20	Oran	99	58	Regular Season
21	Kelly	89	65	Regular Season
22	Bell City	59	61	Regular Season
23	Bloomfield	94	51	Regular Season
24	Parma	92	35	Regular Season
25	Richland	89	61	Regular Season
26	University High	88	48	Regular Season
27	Richland	126	46	Regional Tournament
28	Puxico	86	52	Regional Tournament
29	Chaffee	65	51	Regional Tournament
30	North Pemiscot	97	74	State Tournament
31	Bismarck	85	44	State Tournament
32	Wellsville	86	63	State Tournament
33	Slater	94	52	State Tournament

	1951 and 52 Puxico Indians	1979 and 80 Scott Central Braves
Claim to Fame	Back to back state championships under legendary coach Arnold Ryan. Considered best team in state regardless of size of school.	Back to back state championships under legendary coach Ronnie Cookson. Considered best team in state regardless of size of school (1980).
Style of Play	Fast break, full court press. "Run-shoot-run"	Fast break, full court press. "Shoot, holler and foller"
Two Year Record	79-2	62-4
Average Points	84.1	89.6
Breaking the Century Mark	19 times	12 times
Average Margin	40.1	25.9
Cookson Clan Connection	Players Leon and Carroll Cookson	Coach Ronnie Cookson
Going out in style	Defeated Shelbyville with future University of Missouri Star Norm Stewart by 48 points in 1952.	Defeated Slater with future University of Arkansas Star Joe Kleine by 42 points in 1980.

Appendix 4 – Interviews *(sorted by date)*

Name	Date	Location
Ronnie Cookson	Feb 15 2003	Morley, MO
Ron Cook	April 18 2003	Chaffee, MO
Ronnie Cookson	July 11 2003	Branson, MO
Carroll Cookson	July 11 2003	Branson, MO
Jeff Limbaugh	October 24 2003	Grant City, MO
Carroll Cookson	February 4, 2004	Puxico, MO
Richie Walker	February 5, 2004	Morley, MO
Steve Cookson	February 10, 2004	Naylor, MO
Nick Lanpher	February 11, 2004	Benton, MO
Bill Bradshaw	February 12, 2004	Cape Girardeau, MO
Ed Arnzen	February 19, 2004	Cape Girardeau, MO
Wade Sanders	February 19,2004	Chaffee, MO
Gene Wilfong	February 21, 2004	Murfreesboro, TN
Denny Alcorn	February 25, 2004	Morley, MO
Mike Jensen	February 26, 2004	Sikeston, MO
Melvin Porter	March 3, 2004	Morley, MO
Terry Wills	March 4, 2004	Cape Girardeau, MO
Leon Cookson	March 5, 2004	Arnold, MO
Bob Kielhofner	March 11, 2004	Kelso, MO
Don Heeb	March 15, 2004	St. Louis, MO
Mike Marsh	March 17, 2004	Morley, MO
Melvin Porter	March 17, 2004	Morley, MO
Monty Montgomery	March 20, 2004	Chaffee, MO
Jim Fowler	March 20, 2004	Chaffee, MO
Steven Whitaker	March 20, 2004	Chaffee, MO
Nick Walls	March 22, 2004	St. Louis, MO
Joe Bradshaw	March 31, 2004	Cape Girardeau, MO
David Heeb	April 6, 2004	Bell City, MO
Jim Davis	April 7, 2004	Puxico, MO
Lennies McFerren	April 8, 2004	Sikeston, MO
Jay Cookson	April 20, 2004	Morley, MO
Brad Cookson	April 20, 2004	Morley, MO
Richard Pyland	April 27, 2004	Sikeston, MO
Charlie Vickery	April 27, 2004	Sikeston, MO
Fred Johnson	April 27, 2004	Sikeston, MO
Otto Porter	April 28, 2004	Morley, MO
Pete Townsend	April 28, 2004	Jackson, MO
Brad Fowler	May 3, 2004	Cameron, MO *(via telephone)*
Chris Abernathy	May 5, 2004	Columbia, MO
Dale Miller	May 5, 2004	Clarksville, MO
Donnie McClinton	May 10, 2004	Cape Girardeau, MO
Terry Glenzy	May 12, 2004	Chaffee, MO
Gerald Pilz	May 21, 2004	Rolla, MO
Troy Walls	May 24, 2004	Cherokee Village, AR *(via telephone)*
Mitch Wilkins	May 25, 2004	Troy, MO
Leonard Bishop	May 25, 2004	Dallas, TX *(via telephone)*
John Merk	May 26, 2004	Fayette, MO
Doug Sanders	June 13, 2004	Arlington, Texas
Mick Wessel	July 20, 2004	Whitewater, MO
Joe Kleine	July 22, 2004	Little Rock, AR *(via telephone)*

ENDNOTES

[1] St. Louis Post-Dispatch, February 23, 1979
[2] Chaffee Signal, February 28, 1979
[3] Morris, Roger. Partners in Power. Henry Holt and Company, Inc. 1996
[4] St. Petersburg Times. October 3, 1999
[5] The New Yorker. February 11, 1991
[6] Ibid
[7] St. Louis Post-Dispatch. August 26, 1990
[8] Knox, Ray and Stewart, David. The Earthquake America Forgot. Gutenberg-Richter Publications. 1995
[9] United States Geological Survey
[10] The New Yorker. February 11, 1991
[11] Ibid
[12] St. Louis Post-Dispatch. September 17, 1989
[13] St. Louis Post-Dispatch. October 20, 1989
[14] St. Louis Post-Dispatch. July 25, 1990
[15] The six Bootheel counties are (from north to south): Scott, Stoddard, Mississippi, New Madrid, Dunklin and Pemiscot
[16] St. Louis Post-Dispatch. October 30, 1990
[17] St. Louis Post-Dispatch. October 19th, 1990
[18] St. Louis Post-Dispatch. October 21, 1990
[19] St. Louis Post-Dispatch. November 16, 1990
[20] Southeast Missourian, December 2, 1990
[21] Washington Post. December 2, 1990
[22] St. Louis Post-Dispatch. December 12, 1990
[23] St. Louis Post-Dispatch. December 9, 1990
[24] St. Louis Post-Dispatch. December 6, 1990
[25] www.thecaperock.com
[26] Penick, Jr. James Lal. The New Madrid Earthquakes. Revised

Edition. University of Missouri Press. 1981
[27] Center For Earthquake Studies. Southeast Missouri State University
[28] Stepenoff, Bonnie. Thad Snow, A Life of Social Reform in the Missouri Bootheel. University of Missouri Press. 2003
[29] Goodspeed's History of Southeast Missouri. Goodspeed Publishing Company. 1888

[30] Ibid.
[31] Powell, Betty F. History of Mississippi County. 1975
[32] Goodspeed's History of Southeast Missouri.
[33] Ibid
[34] Douglas, Robert Sidney. History of Southeast Missouri. Lewis Publishing Company. 1912.
[35] Ibid
[36] Ibid
[37] The Little River Drainage District of Southeast Missouri
[38] Ibid
[39] Southeast Missourian, November 11, 2001
[40] The New Georgia Encyclopedia
[41] Sikeston Standard. December 8, 1922
[42] Ibid
[43] Southeast Missourian, January 23. 1923
[44] Southeast Missourian, January 3, 1923
[45] Southeast Missourian, January 19, 1923
[46] Southeast Missourian, January 5, 1923
[47] Southeast Missourian, January 23, 1923
[48] Sikeston Standard, December 8, 1922
[49] Scott County Historical Society. History and Families. Turner Publishing. 2003
[50] Snow, Thad. From Missouri.
[51] Ibid
[52] Reuber, Helen. As I Remember It. Self-Published.
[53] Ibid
[54] Ibid
[55] "Show Us the Money." Forbes Magazine, October 9, 2000. While the article in the Forbes 400 2000 edition does not mention Sikeston, it does reference several other communities that have all boasted of having

"more millionaires per-capita" than any other town at one time in their history. These communities have a lot in common with Sikeston. All of them trace their wealth to a twenty-five year period around 1905 with a natural resource boom as the source.

[56] Sikeston Standard, December 23, 1941

[57] Sikeston Standard, January 9, 1942

[58] Capeci Jr., Dominic J. The Lynching of Cleo Wright. University of Kentucky Press.

[59] Ibid.

[60] Ibid

[61] Ibid

[62] FBI Report, February 16, 1942

[63] FBI Report

[64] Ibid

[65] St. Louis Post-Dispatch January 26, 1942

[66] FBI Report

[67] Ibid

[68] FBI report, February 17, 1942

[69] Mike Jensen Interview

[70] St. Louis Post-Dispatch, January 28, 1942

[71] New York Times. January 27, 1942

[72] New York Times, February 7th, 1942

[73] Enterprise-Courier. February 12, 1942

[74] Sikeston Standard, January 27, 1942. One of the many fascinating aspects of the case is that Blanton was the father of the Scott County Prosecuting Attorney. See Dominic Capeci's "A Lynching of Cleo Wright," for a full exploration of this relationship. Bootheel author Thad Snow described C.L.Blanton's columns this way; "Spicy, irresponsible, and ungrammatical, and often vulgar or slanderous." He also added, "Everybody read it and looked forward to it."

[75] Capeci Jr., Dominic J. The Lynching of Cleo Wright.

[76] FBI Report

[77] Sikeston Standard, March 13, 1942

[78] Sikeston Standard, July 31, 1942

[79] New York Times, May 30, 1999

[80] Chaffee Signal, March 8, 1951

[81] The Frisco map most likely dates the town from the time railroad

tracks came through it; thus the reference to "three years old" in 1905.

[82] Handbook of Texas Online. The Texas State Historical Association.
[83] Chaffee Historical Society
[84] Western Historical Manuscript Collection – Columbia. History of the St. Louis-San Francisco (Frisco) Railway Company.
[85] Ibid
[86] Ibid
[87] Porter, Patsy Finley. The History of Chaffee. Southeast Missouri State Teacher's College term paper.
[88] Southeast Missourian, July 1, 1925
[89] Gordon, Sarah H. Passage To Union. How the Railroads Transformed American Life, 1829-1929. Ivan R. Dee, Inc. 1996
[90] Daily Republican (Cape Girardeau) December 27, 1917
[91] Chaffee Signal, November 13, 1914
[92] A mogul is defined as a heavy locomotive for freight traffic, having three pairs of connected driving wheels and a two-wheeled truck.
[93] The first official state championship in high school basketball didn't take place until 1927
[94] Chaffee Signal, September 15, 1921
[95] The 1922 Shopmen's Strike. International Brotherhood of Boilermakers, Iron Ship Builders, Blacksmiths, Forgers and Helpers. Copyright 2002.
[96] History of the Baltimore and Ohio Railroad. John F. Stover. Purdue University Press. 1987
[97] Sikeston Standard. July 4th, 1922.
[98] St. Louis Post-Dispatch. July 6th, 1922.
[99] St. Louis Globe-Democrat. July 6th, 1922
[100] St. Louis Post-Dispatch. July 24th, 1992
[101] St. Louis Post-Dispatch. July 9th, 1922
[102] St. Louis Post-Dispatch. July 10th, 1922
[103] St. Louis Globe-Democrat. July 12th, 1922
[104] St. Louis Globe-Democrat, July 6, 1022
[105] Chaffee Signal, July 20th, 1022
[106] St. Louis Globe-Democrat, July 7th, 1922
[107] Chaffee Signal, July 20th, 1922
[108] Ibid
[109] Sikeston Standard, November 7, 1922

[110] Porter, Patsy Finley. The History of Chaffee. Southeast Missouri State Teacher's College term paper.

[111] Chaffee Historical Society

[112] Chaffee Signal, July 17th, 1925

[113] The bank was originally called the German-American Bank. In 1914, right around the outbreak of World War I, the bank's name changed to the Chaffee Trust Company. Three years later, it became the Security Savings Bank.

[114] Chaffee Signal, October 31, 1929. The dateline for the story is October 25th. What is considered "Black Tuesday" on Wall Street came four days later.

[115] Western Historical Manuscript Collection - Columbia

[116] Chaffee Signal, May 8, 1924

[117] Patsy Finley Porter letter

[118] Ibid

[119] Chaffee Signal, December 17, 1942; September 2, 1943

[120] Chaffee Signal, February 3, 1944

[121] Chaffee Signal, July 13, 1950

[122] Chaffee Signal, April 8, 1987. Capshaw served from 1967 to 1971 and then from 1975 to 1987.

[123] Sikeston Standard. July 11, 1922. In addition to Chaffee, the Klan claimed organizations or in the process of forming groups in Cape Girardeau, Morehouse, Caruthersville, Hayti, Steele, Jackson and Kennett.

[124] Sikeston Standard. October 27th, 1922.

[125] Sikeston Standard. November 3rd, 1922

[126] Chaffee Signal, September 18, 1924

[127] Ibid

[128] An all-black school was never established in Chaffee

[129] Chaffee Historical Society; Chaffee Signal

[130] Chaffee Signal, September 3, 1925

[131] Chaffee Signal, February 3, 1944

[132] Chaffee Signal, November 3, 1938

[133] Highway 55 became Highway 77 after Interstate 55 came through Southeast Missouri.

[134] KFVS Television in Cape Girardeau went on the air on October 3,

1954
[135] Chaney, Matt, My Name is Mr. Ryan. Four Walls Publishing. 1994
[136] Southeast Missourian, March 15, 1951
[137] Chaney, My Name is Mr. Ryan
[138] Puxico 1883-1983. Published by the Puxico Centennial Planning Committee
[139] Forister, Robert H. History of Stoddard County. Stoddard County Historical Society
[140] Puxico 1883-1983
[141] Ibid
[142] Chaney, My Name is Mr. Ryan
[143] St. Louis Post-Dispatch, September 9, 1950
[144] St. Louis Post-Dispatch, March 5, 1991. Cincinnati led the nation in scoring that season with a 77-point average.
[145] Puxico 1883-1983. Published by the Puxico Centennial Planning Committee
[146] St. Louis Post-Dispatch March 5, 1991
[147] Ibid
[148] Chaney, My Name is Mr. Ryan
[149] Ibid
[150] Ibid
[151] The sub-regionals and state playoff competition were both one and out. In the sweet sixteen format of the 1950's, the regional winner and runner-up advanced to state play
[152] Southeast Missourian, March 6, 1951
[153] Southeast Missourian, March 7, 1951
[154] Southeast Missourian, March 8, 1951
[155] Southeast Missourian, March 9, 1951
[156] St. Louis Globe-Democrat, May 24, 1985
[157] Southeast Missourian, March 16, 1952
[158] Piggott Banner, November 23, 1951
[159] Ibid
[160] Ibid
[161] Southeast Missourian, March 13, 1952
[162] St. Louis Post-Dispatch, March 14, 1952
[163] St. Louis Post-Dispatch, March 15, 1952
[164] Stewart, Norm. Stormin' Back. Missouri Basketball Coach Norm

Stewart's Battles On and Off the Court. Sagamore Publishing. 1991

[165] Southeast Missourian, March 14, 1952

[166] Southeast Missourian, March 14, 1952

[167] St. Louis Post-Dispatch, March 17, 1952

[168] Chaney, My Name is Mr. Ryan.

[169] Puxico had other Division 1 players as well. After high school, Puxico starting guard Elmer Fortner would join Leon Cookson at a Mississippi Junior College. They both transferred to Memphis State after their freshman season. While Cookson left school to go into the army, Fortner played with Win Wilfong and Forest Arnold on the 1956 team that finished second in the NIT. Later, Win Wilfong's brother Gene and Forest Arnold's brother Orby would also play basketball at Memphis State.

[170] Southeast Missourian, November 7, 1999

[171] St. Louis Post-Dispatch, December 22, 1988

[172] Southeast Missourian, December 25, 1988

[173] Ibid

[174] Poplar Bluff Daily American Republic February 18, 1958

[175] Standard-Democrat, May 15, 1994

[176] Pyland followed Carroll and Ronnie to the College of the Ozarks

[177] It is now called the University of the Ozarks

[178] Arkansas Democrat-Gazette, December 31, 2001

[179] Ibid

[180] St. Louis Post-Dispatch, December 22, 1988

[181] Advance Advocate, April 13, 1966

[182] Ibid

[183] The Daily Standard, February 29, 1972

[184] Ibid

[185] The Daily Standard, May 20, 1970

[186] Columbia Missourian, March 5, 1972

[187] The Daily Standard, January 25, 1973

[188] The Daily Standard, March 1, 1973

[189] The Daily Standard, March 3, 1973

[190] Southeast Missourian. November 7, 1999

[191] Columbia Daily Tribune, March 9, 1974

[192] The nomenclature used to describe Missouri high school basketball post-season play has changed over the years. Regional action is the

equivalent of today's district play.

[193] The Daily Standard, March 11, 1975

[194] Columbia Missourian, March 15, 1975

[195] Columbia Missourian, March 16, 1975

[196] Ibid

[197] Southeast Missourian, June 6, 2002

[198] Ibid

[199] The Daily Standard, January 25, 1971. The state tournament had three tiers in the early 1970's; S, M and L.

[200] The Daily Standard, March 1, 1971.

[201] Ibid

[202] St. Louis Post-Dispatch, December 22, 1988

[203] The Daily Standard, March 2, 1971

[204] St. Louis Post-Dispatch, December 22, 1988

[205] St. Louis Globe-Democrat, March 10, 1975

[206] The Daily Standard, January 17, 1975

[207] Bulletin-Journal, December 14, 1975

[208] The Daily Standard, March 15, 1976

[209] Southeast Missourian, December 28, 1975

[210] Southeast Missourian, January 5, 1980

[211] The Daily Standard, March 10, 1976

[212] The Daily Standard, March 11, 1976

[213] Ibid

[214] The Daily Standard, March 14, 1976

[215] Ibid

[216] Columbia Missourian, March 13, 1976

[217] SEMO played at the time in the since disbanded MIAA conference.

[218] The Daily Standard, March 15, 1976

[219] Sanders family tree information courtesy of Francis Sanders

[220] Millard Fillmore became President in 1850 when Zachary Taylor died in office. Fillmore Sanders was born two years later.

[221] The Signal, August 2, 1956

[222] Glenzy and Heeb are among several Chaffee High School athletes who played for Bob Goodwin and later coached football in the area. They include Ryland "Dutch" Meyr (Cape Central), Gary Lynch (Cape Central), Ed Hanna (DeSoto) and Gary Glenzy (Pinkneyville, IL).

Heeb, Glenzy, Meyr and Hanna all played college football at Southeast Missouri State for Coach Kenny Knox.

[223] The Red Devils won state championships in baseball in 1975 and 1977, later adding a third title in 1983. The class of 1977 had two division one baseball players. Lindy Duncan would go on to become an all Big 8 shortstop at the University of Missouri. Scott Wachter would play college baseball at Southern Illinois University and later the University of Arkansas.

[224] Southeast Missourian, September 15th, 1974

[225] All State Linebacker Brian Glastetter led the Red Devil defense that season. . "He was one of the top five dominant players that I've ever coached and I've coached some good ones," remembers Vickery.

[226] The position at Cape Central opened when "Dutch" Meyr resigned after coaching one season. Meyr led the Cape Central Tigers to a 9-2 season in the fall of 1977, ultimately losing in the playoffs to Hazelwood Central. He also coached the Tigers briefly in the 1960's. Meyr was a captain on the 1956 undefeated Chaffee team.

[227] According to Vickery, Sapp is "really considered one of the premier, if not the premier coach in Southeast Missouri."

[228] Sapp was still in college at Cape Girardeau his first year. He would ride the train down to Chaffee every day.

[229] Chaney, Matt. Legend in Missouri. 1997. Four Walls Publishing

[230] St. Louis Post-Dispatch, December 22, 1988

[231] Newspaper accounts and Notre Dame Yearbooks

[232] Bulletin-Journal, January 27, 1979

[233] The two towns later consolidated and dropped the Illmo

[234] Interview with Brad Fowler

[235] Interview with Bill Bradshaw

[236] Ibid

[237] Southeast Missourian, February 26, 1962

[238] Southeast Missourian, February 26, 1962

[239] Bulletin Journal, February 24, 1979

[240] There was no three point shot in Missouri High School basketball at the time.

[241] Daily Standard, February 25, 1979

[242] Newsweek, April 28, 1975

[243] Ibid

[244] Chaffee Signal, February 28, 1979

[245] St. Louis Post-Dispatch, February 26, 1979

[246] Ibid

[247] Southeast Missourian, February 28, 1979

[248] Bulletin Journal, March 1, 1979

[249] Of three written game accounts of that day, two have Chaffee in the lead when they took the shot (Daily Standard and Bulletin-Journal) while a third column (Southeast Missourian) places the Red Devils behind by one point. The Southeast Missourian account makes more sense. With the lead, the ball, and no time clock, there would have been no need to take a shot.

[250] Columbia Daily Tribune, March 3, 1979

[251] Columbia Daily Tribune, March 4, 1979

[252] Ibid

[253] Combs, James Leon. Bradleyville Basketball. The Hicks From The Sticks. Beaver Creek Publishing, 1999

[254] McFerren remembers playing against all-black schools from Caruthersville, Hayti and O'Bannon High School in the mid 1960's, more than a decade after the Brown vs. Board of Education decision.

[255] Frazier played one year at St. Louis then transferred to the University of Missouri where he played for three seasons.

[256] Southeast Missourian, December 30, 1979

[257] Charleston lost to Clearwater and finished fourth in the tournament. In a rematch with Cape Central in January, Charleston won.

[258] Ibid

[259] Ibid

[260] Gladwell, Malcolm. The Tipping Point. How Little Things Can Make a Big Difference. Little Brown and Company. 2000

[261] Southeast Missourian, March 2, 1980

[262] Southeast Missourian, January 20, 1980

[263] The Daily Standard, December 30, 1979

[264] Southeast Missourian, March 16, 1980

[265] Southeast Missourian, December 20, 1979

[266] Southeast Missourian, January 5, 1980

[267] The Daily Standard, February 12, 1980

[268] Interview with Donnie McClinton

[269] Southeast Missourian, March 4, 1980

[270] Southeast Missourian, March 6, 1980

[271] Columbia Daily Tribune, March 6, 1980

[272] Ibid

[273] Columbia Daily Tribune, March 8, 1980

[274] The Daily Standard, March 9, 1980

[275] Columbia Daily Tribune, March 8, 1980

[276] Ibid

[277] Slater News-Rustler, December 6, 1979

[278] The Democrat News (Marshall, MO), November 30, 1979

[279] Columbia Daily Tribune, March 8, 1980

[280] The Daily Standard, March 10, 1980

[281] Ibid

[282] Southeast Missourian, March 10, 1980

[283] Columbia Daily Tribune, March 10, 1980

[284] Ibid

[285] Ibid

[286] St. Louis Post-Dispatch, February 12, 1986

[287] Ibid

[288] Mexico Ledger, February 15, 1986

[289] St. Louis Post-Dispatch, February 12, 1986

[290] Mexico Ledger, February 15, 1986

[291] Wellsville Optic-News, February 26, 1986

[292] Ibid

[293] Mexico Ledger, February 22, 1986

[294] Columbia Daily Tribune, March 6, 1982

[295] Ibid

[296] Mexico Ledger, March 4, 1986

[297] Mexico Ledger, March 6, 1986

[298] Mexico Ledger, March 10, 1986

[299] Mexico Ledger, March 15, 1986

[300] Ibid

[301] Wellsville Optic-News, April 9, 1986

[302] Mexico Ledger, March 11, 1986

[303] March Ledger, March 12, 1986

[304] Ibid

[305] Mexico Ledger, March 14, 1986

[306] Mexico Ledger, March 17, 1986

[307] Ibid

[308] Mexico Ledger, March 12, 1986

[309] Southeast Missourian, March 17, 1986

[310] Ibid

[311] Ibid

[312] Mexico Ledger, March 17, 1986

[313] Kansas City Star, February 24, 1991

[314] The 53 game winning streak wasn't the longest of Cookson's career. His team also had a 63 game winning streak snapped by Jackson in the Christmas Tournament of 1991. The streak was one victory short of the state record set by Bradleyville and Glasgow.

[315] Springfield News Leader, March 10, 1990

[316] St. Louis Post-Dispatch, March 8, 1995

[317] St. Louis Post-Dispatch, March 4, 1995

[318] Ibid

[319] Springfield News Leader, March 10, 1990

[320] Standard-Democrat (Sikeston) March 9, 1995

[321] Bootheel state champions 1972-1996 (number of years): Advance (2), Charleston (9), Lilbourn (2), Malden (1), New Madrid County Central (1), Portageville (4), Scott County Central (12), North Pemiscot (1)

[322] Poplar Bluff Daily American Republic, March 6, 1995

[323] Ibid

[324] Poplar Bluff Daily American Republic, March 10,1995

[325] Ibid

[326] St. Louis Post-Dispatch March 12, 1995

[327] Southeast Missourian, November 20, 1983

[328] Ibid

[329] Southeast Missourian, November 28, 1983

[330] Chaney, Matt. My Name is Mr. Ryan

[331] Southeast Missourian, February 16, 2003

[332] Poplar Bluff Daily American Republic March 10, 2004

[333] Ibid

[334] Ibid

[335] Southeast Missourian, March 14, 2004

[336] Southeast Missourian, March 19, 2004

[337] The New York Times, December 28, 2004

[338] The Atlantic Monthly, December 2001

[339] Cape Girardeau News Guardian, March 11, 1990

[340] The Daily Standard, March 15, 1976

[341] Sikeston Standard-Democrat, May 15, 1994

[342] Ibid

[343] Southeast Missourian, February 4, 2001